In Restraint
of Trade

In Restraint of Trade

The Business Campaign Against Competition, 1918–1938

Butler Shaffer

Lewisburg
Bucknell University Press
London: Associated University Presses

Associated University Presses
440 Forsgate Drive
Cranbury, NJ 08512

Associated University Presses
16 Barter Street
London WC1A 2AH, England

Associated University Presses
P.O. Box 338, Port Credit
Mississauga, Ontario
Canada L5G 4L8

The paper used in this publication meets the requirements
of the American National Standard for Permanence of Paper
for Printed Library Materials Z39.48-1984.

Library of Congress Cataloging-in-Publication Data

Shaffer, Butler D.
    In restraint of trade : the business campaign against competition, 1918–1938 / Butler Shaffer
        p.   cm.
    Includes bibliographical references and index.
    ISBN 0-8387-5325-6 (alk. paper)
    1. Industrial policy—United States—History—20th century.
    2. Competition—United States—History—20th century.
    3. Competition—United States—Case studies. 4. Trade regulation-
    -United States—History—20th century. 5. Business and politics-
    -United States—History—20th century. 6. Businessmen—United
    States—Attitudes. 7. United States—Economic
    Conditions—1918–1945. I. Title
    HD3616.U46S43 1997
    338.973'009'041—dc 20   96-14519
                                                              CIP

SECOND PRINTING 1999
PRINTED IN THE UNITED STATES OF AMERICA

To the memory
and the investigative spirit
of John T. Flynn

Contents

Acknowledgments

I wish to acknowledge my gratitude to a number of persons whose assistance was helpful in the bringing of this book to publication.

First, I would like to thank Robert Love who, knowing of my interest in this subject matter, first encouraged me to write this book more years ago than I care to remember. Shortly thereafter, I received valuable assistance from the late F. A. Harper and Kenneth Templeton, who helped me to focus the scope of this inquiry.

I must also acknowledge the help provided by Mills F. Edgerton, Jr., of Bucknell University Press, as well as Julien Yoseloff and the editors of Associated University Presses. I further wish to express my gratitude to Janet Knoedler for her critical review and analysis of my work. Her perspective and constructive suggestions helped greatly to improve the original manuscript. I also wish to thank my daughters—Heidi, Gretchen, and Bretigne—for their invaluable assistance in helping to produce the graphics contained in this book. I also want to acknowledge the help of Jeannie Nicholson and Martha Fink.

Acknowledgment must also be made to the *Southwestern University Law Review*, which published portions of my research as separate articles in volumes 10 and 20 of the law review. I wish also to acknowledge the following permissions to reprint copyrighted materials contained in this book:

"Business and Government," by John T. Flynn. Copyright © 1928 by *Harper's Magazine*. All rights reserved. Reproduced from the March issue by special permission.

The Logic of Collective Action, by Mancur Olson. Reprinted by permission of the publishers from *The Logic of Collective Action: Public Goods and the Theory of Groups*, by Mancur Olson. Cambridge, Mass.: Harvard University Press, Copyright © 1965, 1971 by the President and Fellows of Harvard College.

The Epic of American Industry, by James Walker, 1949. Permission granted by HarperCollins Publishers.

"Toward Stability," an editorial appearing in *Business Week*, 10 May 1933, at page 32. Permission granted by *Business Week*.

ACKNOWLEDGMENTS

An article appearing in volume 131 of *The Iron Age*, 25 May 1933, at page 835. Permission granted by Chilton Company, Capital Cities/ABC, Inc.

"A Current Appraisal of the National Recovery Administration," by Dudley Cates, in volume 172 of *The Annals of the American Academy of Political and Social Science*, March 1934, at pages 132–34. Reprinted by permission of Sage Publications, Inc.

Two articles, appearing in volume 26 of *The Oil and Gas Journal*, 2 February 1928, at page 36, and 12 April 1928, at page 36. Permission granted by *Oil and Gas Journal*.

In Restraint
of Trade

Introduction

> [T]he forces which count toward a readjustment of institutions in any modern industrial community are chiefly economic forces; or more specifically, these forces take the form of pecuniary pressure. Such a readjustment as is here contemplated is substantially a change in men's views as to what is good and right, and the means through which a change is wrought in men's apprehension of what is good and right is in large part the pressure of pecuniary exigencies.
>
> —Thorstein Veblen

Until relatively recent times, the symbiotic relationship existing between economic and political institutions has only been vaguely comprehended. It has been popular to view these two major sectors of American society as having a generally antagonistic relationship, with political institutions serving as a countervailing force to economic influence. This view is reflected in the traditional conception of economic history that suggests the American business system had, during the late nineteenth and early twentieth centuries, maintained an existence largely independent of, and indifferent to, the interests of the American public. The business community in this era is seen by many as ruthless and hegemonic, exercising nearly unlimited corporate power that threatened the very foundations of a free and competitive economic system. Those who hold to this view insist that the interests of the public required the imposition of political controls to regulate such matters as trade practices, pricing policies, and the size and entry of business firms in the market. It supports a consensus that government regulation of economic activity represents a national policy commitment to elevating the "ethical plane" of competition in order that market influences may more freely serve some vaguely defined "general welfare." One business scholar has reflected this attitude well:

> It is not always safe to leave business to its own devices; experience has shown that its freedom will sometimes be abused. . . . Competitors have been harassed

13

by malicious and predatory tactics, handicapped by discrimination, excluded from markets and sources of supply, and subjected to intimidation, coercion, and physical violence. Consumers have been victimized by short weights and measures, by adulteration, and by misrepresentation of quality and price; they have been forced to contribute to the profits of monopoly.

. . . [T]he nation's resources have been dissipated through extravagant methods of exploitation. These abuses have not characterized all business at all times, but they have occurred with sufficient frequency to justify the imposition of controls. Regulation is clearly required, not only to protect the investor, the worker, the consumer, and the community at large against the unscrupulous businessman, but also to protect the honest businessman against his dishonest competitor.[1]

This impression of the purposes and effects of the regulatory process is reinforced by a common historical view of the 1920s as the declining years of laissez-faire capitalism, in which "big business" had its last profligate fling before being brought under the discipline of rational, politically supervised economic planning. Indeed, the so-called Great Depression that ended this decade is generally perceived as one of the high-water marks of corporate dissipation and irresponsibility, ushering in the uncomfortable aftereffects of the 1930s. The New Deal is, to this day, regarded as a major turning point in government and business relationships, and represents to many the inevitable consequences of undisciplined market power. The National Industrial Recovery Act, the Agricultural Adjustment Act, the National Labor Relations Act, and the Fair Labor Standards Act, as well as the operation of intraindustrial agencies such as the Federal Communications Commission, the Securities Exchange Commission, the Civil Aeronautics Board, and the Federal Power Commission, are commonly depicted by historians as having imposed competitive discipline and socially responsible behavior upon a recalcitrant business community.

Paralleling this view of history, however, is a recognition that government regulation has generally served to further the very economic interests being regulated. The economist—and later United States senator—Paul Douglas was not the first to become aware of this fact when, in 1935, he observed with some bewilderment, "Public regulation has proved most ineffective. Instead of the regulatory commissions controlling the private utilities, the utilities have largely controlled the regulatory commissions."[2] Nor was he the last to perceive the truth of that proposition. Indeed, in the intervening years, research has revealed the dominant influence of commercial and industrial interests in shaping and directing government regulatory policies in order to advance such business interests.[3] While there is a debate as to whether businessmen had advocated the *establishment* of political agencies in order to structure the marketplace for their benefit or had only *captured* such agencies after they had been created, few would question the idea that the regulatory processes of government have been actively and purposefully employed by business interests in order to gain advantages denied them in the marketplace.

Though recognizing the existence of a legitimate debate on the question of the origins of regulatory legislation, one of the underlying premises of this book is that most political intervention into economic activity has been fostered by business leaders and trade associations desirous of restraining or eliminating those trade practices of their competitors that most threatened existing market positions or price structures. As historian Gabriel Kolko and others have observed, competition was very intense among business firms in the early twentieth century. Firms with established market positions wanted to reduce the impact of such competition and employed voluntary methods (such as mergers, pooling, trade association "codes of ethics," and other agreements) in efforts to stabilize competitive relationships. When such voluntary means failed due to lack of effective enforcement, influential corporate leaders, having found a condition of unrestrained competition and decision-making unacceptable to their interests, helped promote the enactment of legal restraints upon trade practices. As Kolko has written:

> The dominant fact of American political life at the beginning of this century was that big business led the struggle for the federal regulation of the economy. If economic rationalization could not be attained by mergers and voluntary economic methods, a growing number of important businessmen reasoned, perhaps political means might succeed.[4]

Or, as an earlier scholar, Myron Watkins, noted: "From the time of President Theodore Roosevelt's second administration there had been an insistent movement among certain industrial leaders for either a legislative or administrative definition of an exact standard of competitive conduct."[5]

It is the purpose of this book to inquire into the attitudes of business leaders toward competition during the years 1918–38 and to see how those attitudes became translated into proposals for controlling competition through political machinery under the direction of trade associations. This particular twenty-year period has been selected because of the fundamental metamorphosis taking place within the business community itself and the importance of this era in the history of government regulation of economic activity. During these years, men of commerce and industry began forging, through the trade associations, a consensus as to the proper scope and intensity of competitive behavior. This twenty-year period brackets American business experiences with two major industry dominated government regulatory systems: the War Industries Board (WIB) and the National Recovery Administration (NRA). Under these two systems, businessmen increasingly exhibited a disposition for a collectivized authority over one another, with trade associations serving as government-backed enforcement agencies. Perhaps the historian Robert Wiebe has best summarized the attitudes toward government-business relationships with which business leaders emerged from World War I. Recognizing that "[o]nly the government could ensure the stability and continuity essential to their welfare," men of commerce and industry did not focus upon a "neutralization of the government." On the contrary, "They wanted a powerful government, but one whose authority stood at their disposal; a strong, responsive government through which they could manage their own affairs in their own way."[6]

The attraction of so many business leaders to systems of government-enforced trade practice standards reflected a continuing institutionalization of economic life. The systemwide benefits of maintaining openness in competition—with no legal restrictions on freedom of entry into the marketplace or on the terms and conditions for which parties could contract with one another—were being rejected by business organizations more concerned with the survival of individual firms and industries. As a consequence, business leaders expressed an increasing desire for the maintenance of conditions of equilibrium that would help preserve the positions of existing firms. Free and unrestrained competition demanded a continuing resiliency in responding to market changes. The innovation in products, services, and business methods that made economic life creative and vibrant came to be seen as a threat to the survival of firms unable or unwilling to respond. Concerns for *security* and *stability* began to take priority over *autonomy* and *spontaneity* in the thinking of most business leaders.

There were a number of factors that helped to influence efforts on behalf of government-enforced equilibrium policies. To begin with, there were significant organizational and technological changes that occurred within the business system, both prior to and following World War I, to which businessmen had to respond. One analyst of the business scene, Carl F. Taeusch, declared that the factor that did the most to stimulate the growth of trade associations was "the advent of trade—or industrial—as opposed to individual competition."[7] Taeusch noted that starting with the early 1900s and continuing through the 1920s, American business underwent quite radical changes in the development of major new industries and new methods of manufacture and product distribution. The combination of these factors had a major impact not only upon the firms within the industries that were undergoing such changes but also upon businesses indirectly related to such industries. The principal new industries included those producing automobiles, airplanes, electrical power, and products powered by electricity (including radio, motion pictures, the phonograph, and consumer appliances). There was also a total revamping of the petroleum industry—which, prior to the automobile and electricity, had existed primarily as a source of lighting—accompanied by a realignment of the relative market positions of petroleum, electricity, and coal as fuel and power sources.

The revolutionary changes in distribution methods included the development of chain stores, direct selling by manufacturers, vertically integrated retailing organizations, and the growth of new consumer credit practices. The new manufacturing methods embraced many industries and resulted in a restructuring of business organizations to take advantage of new efficiencies brought about by such new production methods. The combination of these factors led to the growth of *product* (or "industrial") competition. Some of the consequences to industries of such radical changes are given by Taeusch:

> The use of structural steel and cement in the building industry has confronted the lumber interests with a problem of self-preservation; changes in food habits and the more aggressive tactics of new food businesses have faced the older staple-goods concerns with the problem of rapidly declining sales; style changes ruthlessly affect the use of textile goods. . . .[8]

Taeusch's explanation found support in the analysis offered by economist Joseph Schumpeter. Addressing himself to the "process of Creative Destruction," through which established firms are challenged and often replaced by new sources of competition, Schumpeter concluded that *price* competition is not the most significant factor to which firms have to respond. In his view, "it is not that kind of competition which counts but the competition from the new commodity, the new technology, the new source of supply, the new type of organization. . . . competition which commands a decisive cost or quality advantage and which strikes not at the margins of the profits and the outputs of the existing firms but at their foundations and their very lives." Citing retailing as an example, Schumpeter declared that the competition that was most critical arose "not from additional shops of the same type, but from the department store, the chain store, the mail-order house and the supermarket. . . ."[9] Whatever its relative significance vis-à-vis price competition, there is no doubt that the processes emphasized by Schumpeter served as the progenitor of economic advancements that revolutionized American life: the replacement of the horse by the automobile and of the kerosene lamp by the electric light; the opening up of worldwide systems of communication, transportation, and distribution; and the introduction of the consumer to an increased variety of services and products.

In such a volatile climate, change became one of the few constants upon which businessmen could rely. Economic survival often depended upon innovative resiliency; firms with higher unit costs and prices had to either become more efficient or drop out of the race. Instability and turnover were continuing threats with which firms had to contend. The severity of the competitive struggle was best reflected in the automobile industry: of the 181 firms manufacturing cars at some time during the years 1903 to 1926, 83 remained in business as of 1922, while 20 managed to survive through 1938.[10] In addition to the technological and organizational sources of change, trade policies proved disquieting. So intense was the pace of competition that many firms turned, with increasing frequency, to aggressive sales practices and lowered prices in order to gain some comparative advantage. The consequence, of course, was to further heighten the intensity of trade rivalry. Businessmen seeking nothing more than the most pragmatic route to survival in such a competitive and evolving environment became pariahs to industry colleagues.

Such aggressive trade practices provided the climate in which American business found itself as it entered World War I. Paradoxically, men of commerce and industry found, in the wartime management of the WIB, a temporary respite from what many regarded as the killing pace of commercial warfare. The economic cease-fire imposed by a centrally directed alliance of government and business afforded businessmen the opportunity of experiencing a less-menacing trade atmosphere. When peace was restored to the rest of the world, however, competitive aggression returned to the marketplace. Businessmen, recalling the managed harmony of the war years, confronted the intensely competitive 1920s with hopes of realizing a more durable and predictable setting in which to conduct business. Firms that viewed the processes of change as threats to their positions began organizing resistance. Speaking to this phenomenon, economist Walter Adams observed that such firms "quickly and instinctively understood that storm shelters had to be built to protect themselves against this destructive force."[11]

Businessmen confronted not only the kinds of changes observed by Taeusch and Schumpeter but a political environment within which antibusiness sentiments were widespread.[12] As Wiebe has observed, political hostility toward large industrial combinations, and a good deal of confusion over Supreme Court cases that sought to distinguish "reasonable" and "unreasonable" restraints of trade, left the business community in a somewhat unsettled frame of mind.[13] These "tensions from political uncertainty and economic instability"[14] generated a transformation in the thinking of business leaders. Politics and ideology became employed in the efforts of businessmen "to protect their positions of leadership in America's twentieth-century society in transition."[15] The result was a more conciliatory attitude towards government; for purely pragmatic reasons business leaders attempted to absorb reform movements and use them to their advantages.

A very broad range of social and economic conditions existed during the years 1918–38: a war, an era of seemingly endless prosperity, the Great Depression, and the New Deal with its promises of a politically engineered recovery. Continuing throughout this period, however, was an organizational transformation that had begun long before World War I: the "collectivization" of human society. The principle of "collective organization," postulating the superior interests of the *group* over those of its *individual members,* was emerging within the business system as well as within other sectors of society. Because "collectivism" reflects conservative, status quo sentiments, its underlying premises were consistent with business efforts to resist change. Industries organized themselves through the machinery of the trade associations and began the task of altering the attitudes, belief systems, and practices that represented the old order. Business decision-making that emphasized the well-being of the *individual firm* was to be eschewed in favor of attitudes that stressed the *collective* interests of the *industry* itself. Individual profit-maximizing was to be de-emphasized when confronted by the "greater interests of the group"; independence and self-centeredness were to be put aside in favor of a more "cooperative" form of "friendly competition."

Nothing so threatened the interests of this emerging industrial order as the free play of market forces at work in an environment of legally unrestrained competition. Nothing so preoccupied industry-oriented business leaders in the post–World War I years as the effort to structure this environment so as to keep the conduct of trade within limits that posed no threat to their collective interests. Throughout the years 1918–38, there was a consistent effort by many business officials and trade associations to develop a spirit of "business cooperation" through which, it was hoped, severe competitive pressures could be restrained. As we shall discover, many business leaders tried to establish systems of business relationships that would mitigate aggressive competitive practices and reduce the threat of economic loss to firms unable to withstand such competition. One finds industry leaders and trade groups railing constantly against the "price cutter," the "cutthroat" competitor, and the entrepreneurial interloper who dared to "invade the territory" of an established competitor. Such efforts invariably began with voluntary methods of "self-restraint." When voluntary approaches failed to produce the desired stability, many businessmen—mindful of the advantages experienced under the WIB—sought to effectuate this spirit of "cooperation" through politically backed programs designed to fashion a greater degree of centralized business decision-making. Characterizing their proposals as "industrial self-regulation," business spokesmen and trade associations worked to secure for themselves a diluted competitive environment that would not be threatening to their interests. Such political efforts to control trade practices led, ultimately, to the enactment of the National Industrial Recovery Act, a piece of legislation put to death in 1935 by the U.S. Supreme Court. We shall examine both the contributions and responses of businessmen to this recovery program and will consider the post-NRA period in order to determine whether its existence had significantly affected the policy recommendations of business leaders for controlling trade practices.

After a more general development, in the first four chapters, of business responses to competition, we shall examine a number of specific industries. In chapters 5 through 7, we shall look at such industries as steel, petroleum, coal, textile manufacturing, and retailing in order to obtain a more detailed understanding of competitive conditions and business responses to those conditions. These particular industries were selected for a number of reasons: (1) they were all considered major industries throughout the period encompassed by this book and were among the principal industries undergoing the substantial changes discussed by Taeusch and Schumpeter; (2) representing such diverse fields as capital goods manufacturing, natural resource development, consumer goods manufacturing, and retailing, they provide a fair cross section of American commerce and industry; (3) not having had a "public utility" status imposed upon them, these industries were, for the most part, open to entry by would-be competitors and had pricing practices determined by *market* rather than *political* influences; and, (4) because competition was particularly intense within these industries during this period, some of the most spirited and vocal efforts to tranquilize competitive inclinations came from these sectors of the economy. An examination of other industries reveals similar tendencies and influences at work, and it is believed that the industries selected for specific study herein offer a fairly representative picture of the development of business attitudes toward competition and regulation during the twenty years following the end of World War I.

1

Making the World
Safe from Competition

The evolution of society is substantially a process of mental adaptation on the part of individuals under the stress of circumstances which will no longer tolerate habits of thought formed under and conforming to a different set of circumstances in the past.
—Thorstein Veblen

THE WAR INDUSTRIES BOARD EXPERIENCE

In order to put business responses to competitive practices during the postwar years in proper perspective, one must begin with the WIB. The war itself served as a catalyst for the emergence of corporate institutionalism. As the historian William Leuchtenburg has stated:

The war confirmed the triumph of large-scale industrial organization. . . . [It] speeded both popular acceptance and acceptance in the business world of the virtues of large-scale, amalgamated, oligopolistic industries. . . . In 1916 America still thought to a great degree in terms of nineteenth-century values of decentralization, competition, equality, agrarian supremacy, and the primacy of the small town. By 1920 the triumph of the twentieth century—centralized, industrialized, secularized, urbanized—while by no means complete, could clearly be foreseen.[1]

The historian Robert Wiebe has observed that "the mobilization of 1917 and 1918 illuminated the degree to which an emerging bureaucratic system had actually ordered American society."[2]

With the trade associations helping to supply the coordination, the WIB politicized the bulk of the economic life of this country during World War I. This agency played the central role in the most elaborate and pervasive exercise of government regulation of economic activity undertaken within the United States up to that time. Aided by a myriad of other agencies and

21

subagencies, the WIB afforded the business community the unprecedented opportunity to experience business-directed government planning as a tool for the central direction of American industry. For some eighteen months, the American business system had a front row seat from which to observe and assess the apparatus for industry-wide control of commercial practices. The value of such an experience to many within the business community cannot be overstated. One must, therefore, begin any inquiry into postwar business attitudes with at least a brief description of the agency that had provided businessmen with some practical experience in controlling competitive behavior.[3]

In furtherance of the war effort, the WIB centralized the economic life of America into a highly structured bureaucracy under the effective direction and control of leading business interests. Matters relating to the production, pricing, and allocation of strategic goods and services were handled *not* by the impersonal forces of the marketplace, but by the quite personal direction of businessmen armed with governmental authority. American industry had, in short, become "mobilized" in the most literal, military sense of the word. Depending upon how one viewed the practice, American businesses found themselves subject to political "coordination" or "regimentation" in furtherance of collective goals. The historian Arthur Schlesinger Jr. has provided an accurate summary:

> For a moment Washington became the unchallenged economic capital of the nation. Through the War Industries Board, the government mobilized industrial production. Through the War Food Administration, it sought to control the production and consumption of food. Through the Capital Issues Committee, it tried to regulate private investment. Through the War Finance Corporation, it directed and financed industrial expansion. It took over the railroads and the telephone and telegraph system. It set up independent public corporations in diverse fields from the United States Housing Corporation to the Shipping Board Emergency Fleet Corporation, from the Sugar Equalization Board to the Spruce Production Corporation.[4]

Another historian, Frederick Lewis Allen, more succinctly characterized the WIB as an agency with "almost dictatorial power to decide to what uses the industrial machinery of the country might be applied."[5]

With the backing of the United States Chamber of Commerce, the Council of National Defense created the WIB in July 1917. It charged it to

> act as a clearing house for the war industry needs of the Government, determine the most effective ways of meeting them and the best means and methods of increasing production, including the creation or extension of industries demanded by the emergency, the sequence and relative urgency of the needs of the different Government services, and consider price factors, and in the first

instance the industrial and labor aspects of the problems involved and the general questions affecting the purchase of commodities.[6]

On 4 March 1918, pursuant to a directive from President Wilson, the WIB was reorganized as an agency separate and apart from the Council of National Defense; it now operated under direct responsibility to the president. The WIB was, then, the creature of implied wartime executive authority, not of any legislative enactment.

Under the virtual autocracy of its chairman, Bernard M. Baruch—a man whose role had been described by one colleague as "the supreme interpreter of the national good"—the WIB undertook the task of establishing priorities and setting the prices for, as well as allocating the use of, major resources. Grosvenor B. Clarkson, who had been director of the Council of National Defense, wrote that the WIB "directed both production and distribution; it said what should be produced and where, and it said who should have the product."[7] It fixed prices at which government agencies would purchase specific commodities. While those associated with the WIB spoke of prices being "negotiated" with given firms, the "negotiations" were undertaken in an atmosphere in which the board retained the ultimate power of commandeering the commodity.

The day-to-day operations of the WIB were conducted in what were referred to as "commodity sections." Decisions regarding priorities and prices for given products and resources were coordinated through some fifty-seven separate sections, each charged with the responsibility for a particular commodity. Even though the commodity section personnel represented the government, they were, as the historian Robert Cuff has observed, generally drawn from the very industries governed by each section.[8] Clarkson characterizes such persons as "[b]usiness men wholly consecrated to Government service, but full of understanding of the problems of industry."[9] While less polite analysis might raise the question of the conflicts of interest inherent in the staffing of government agencies by personnel from industries that are supervised by such agencies, it can at least be agreed that the basic decision-making functions of the WIB were in the hands of persons whose backgrounds and, presumably, postwar careers were tied to the business system. The commodity sections had their counterparts in what were known as "War Service Committees." Comprised of men representing the industries governed by the commodity sections, and operating under the general auspices of the United States Chamber of Commerce, the War Service Committees were designed, much like trade associations, to represent their industries in the decision-making processes of the WIB, further assuring business domination of this wartime system.

In essence, the commodity sections centralized the basic functioning of the American business system in a business-controlled agency of the federal government; the agency enjoyed an exercise of power from which there was, for all practical purposes, no right of appeal. Through these sections, the business community experienced the benefits of industry-wide regimentation. In Clarkson's words, the sections "were the substance of the stuff of which requirements, price-fixing, priority, and all the subsidiaries of those three were made. . . . They were more than the mobilization of industry. They were industry mobilized and drilled, responsive, keen, and fully staffed. They were industry militant and in serried ranks."[10] The commodity sections were designed to rationalize and coordinate both the demand and supply functions for their respective commodities, thus circumventing normal market pricing and allocation functions. Projections of future needs and of the production to meet those needs were undertaken, and the effort was made to balance the demands of both the government and the public. Conservation programs, and plans for increasing the production of those resources considered to be in short supply, became matters of concern as well. Further serving to homogenize the various industries and to reduce competitive differences among firms was the practice of exchanging trade and statistical data among competitors. As Clarkson summarized it, "The industries gave not only the ordinary statistical data, but revealed trade secrets, special processes, and improved methods, which, being cleared through the sections and the war service committees, enabled their competitors to improve quality or speed up production."[11]

Some of the more prominent business leaders to serve with Baruch on the WIB and its related committees were Alexander Legge of International Harvester Company; George N. Peek of Deere and Company; Robert S. Lovett of the Union Pacific Railroad; Herbert B. Swope, brother of the man who was later to become one of the principal architects of the NRA, Gerard Swope of General Electric; J. Leonard Replogle of Cambria Steel Company; Clarence Dillon of Dillon, Read and Company; Howard E. Coffin of Hudson Motor Car Company; Walter S. Gifford of AT&T; Elbert Gary of United States Steel; Daniel Willard of the Baltimore and Ohio Railroad; and Julius Rosenwald of Sears, Roebuck and Company. Other business representatives closely associated with the war effort and serving in government positions included Edward R. Stettinius (assistant secretary of war), Russell Leffingwell (assistant secretary of the treasury), and Dwight Morrow (member of the Allied Maritime Transport Council), each of whom had been—or later became—associated with J. P. Morgan. John D. Ryan (assistant secretary of war) was of Anaconda Copper Corporation; Charles M. Schwab (head of the Emergency Fleet Corporation) was of Bethlehem Steel; and Frank A. Vanderlip (head of the War Savings Stamp campaign) and Samuel McRoberts (chief of the procurement section of the ordinance division) were president and vice-president, respectively, of the First National City Bank. Mention must also be made of Baruch's right-hand man—a man who had been an executive of Moline Plow Corporation and was later to direct the NRA— Hugh Johnson.[12]

For purposes of this book, the significance of the WIB experiment lies in the exposure of the business community to a system of political coordination, under business direction, of those economic functions that are ordinarily thought of as being best left to the disciplines and pressures of the marketplace. The economic order and allocation of resources that are the products of the impersonal and informal market pricing mechanism were abandoned in favor of formal, political means of ordering economic activity. More importantly, the business community discovered in the WIB the basic machinery for a more permanent system for an effective business direction of economic life.

The anticompetitive impact of the WIB has been acknowledged by both Clarkson and Baruch. Clarkson observed that "[c]ompetition in price was practically done away with by Government action. Industry was for the time in what was for it a golden age of harmony."[13] Baruch was equally laudatory: "Many business men have experienced during the war, for the first time in their careers, the tremendous advantages, both to themselves and to the general public, of combination, of cooperation and common action, with their natural competitors."[14] Baruch also noted the implications of the WIB experience for trade association activity:

> In line with the principle of united action and cooperation, hundreds of trades were organized for the first time into national associations, each responsible in a real sense for its multitude of component companies, and they were organized on the suggestion and under the supervision of the Government. Practices looking to efficiency in production, price control, conservation, control in quantity of production, etc., were inaugurated everywhere.[15]

The WIB was viewed by certain businessmen as not only essential to the war effort but as having the potential for helping to regularize competitive conditions once the war ended. Prior to becoming president of AT&T, Walter S. Gifford told a meeting of the United States Chamber of Commerce in September 1917:

> [W]e have never needed such organized industry as much as we need it now when we are engaged in this great war and we never have needed it as much as we shall need it after this war is over, when we shall be in the midst of a world competition of unknown proportions.[16]

Echoing this view was Alba B. Johnson, president of the Baldwin Locomotive Works, who declared:

For the last twenty years, this nation has been offering a great sacrifice on the altar of a false god. Happily through the war this false god has been over-thrown, temporarily, at least. This false god of whom I speak is the principle of unlimited destructive competition. The foundation on which the temple of this deity has been raised is the Sherman antitrust act, and the results of this act have meant the sacrifice of millions of dollars of American business. If there is any one thing this war has determined it is that the Sherman act will not stand the strain of a national crisis. The Government itself has come to realize this fact, and recognizes that business must be conducted on the basis of a reason-able profit. And the only way to determine a reasonable profit is through a conference of all concerned in any particular business.[17]

Shortly after the war's end, the Electrical Manufacturers' Council met to discuss the matter of the peacetime continuation of the organizational struc-ture employed by that industry during the war. Some of the benefits identi-fied by industry leaders included conservation, uniform accounting systems, standardization, and the general coordination of the industry. In the words of one industry member, the objective was the retention of "the same coop-eration that we had during the war," which cooperation, he went on, would require the changing of existing laws.[18]

As the historian Robert Himmelberg has pointed out, many business-men were not only desirous of modifying the antitrust laws in order to per-mit trade agreements among competitors but of continuing the WIB in order to protect industries from postwar price adjustments.[19] In connection with such an objective, Bernard Baruch recommended to President Wilson that the board be continued in existence, an action that Baruch felt Wilson could take as part of his general war powers. Wilson declined.

With a Wilson-decreed end of the WIB scheduled for 1 January 1919, a number of proposals were made to get the board to approve industry agree-ments that would control prices and/or production. The priorities commis-sioner of the WIB, Edwin B. Parker—who was later to become president of the United States Chamber of Commerce—went so far as to propose that a majority of the firms in an industry be allowed to establish production quo-tas for each firm in that industry. All of these proposals were rejected by the board, not because of any philosophic opposition to them, but out of a con-cern that such actions might later be invalidated by the courts, thus subject-ing the board to public criticism.[20]

Not surprisingly, one of the leading business advocates of industrial self-regulation under government supervision was Bernard Baruch. In his report to President Wilson on 3 March 1921, Baruch recommended that an organi-zation along the lines of the WIB be maintained, in skeletal form, in peace-time. Such an organization (to be broken down into section or commodity groupings and to maintain the other basic WIB departmental headings) would, "in the event of an impending crisis, . . . immediately . . . mobilize all of the industries of the nation."[21]

Baruch, a financier closely associated with the Guggenheim copper interests, praised the degree to which American industry had been fashioned into a system of "cooperation" more attuned to the modern needs of the business community. His analysis of the basic policy changes in government and business relationships helped set the tone for business thought in the years leading up to the New Deal:

> The processes of trade have so changed their nature that the older and simpler relations of Government to business have been gradually forced to give way before certain new principles of supervision. We have been gradually compelled to drift away from the old doctrine of Anglo-American law, that the sphere of Government should be limited to preventing breach of contract, fraud, physical injury and injury to property, and that the Government should exercise protection only over noncompetent persons. The modern industrial processes have been rendering it increasingly necessary for the Government to reach out its arm to protect competent individuals against the discriminating practice of mass industrial power.[22]

Grosvenor Clarkson endorsed Baruch's sentiments in these words:

> Here we see the beginnings of the application in peace of the idea of nationally directed industrial strategy. It is plain that we are to confront nationally directed commercial strategy by our competitors carried to such an extent that it is doubtful if we can successfully meet it without some reorganization of the Government and a delegation of authority that Congress will be reluctant to make. The control of shipping, the tariff, taxes, railway tariffs, and foreign finance need to be centralized in some administrative body, as they were more or less centralized in the War Industries Board.
>
> How to maintain the price benefits of free competition, and obtain the benefits of the economies that can be effected only by association and united effort, is a difficult problem. However it may be solved, the fact will remain that the War Industries Board was the pioneer revealer of the immense wastes of production as generally conducted, and the greatest demonstrators of the possibilities of economies. In the long run economy must find a way to prevail. Tremendous wastes of service and material cannot be tolerated in the lean and laborious years that are before the world.[23]

Although the end of World War I brought with it the termination of the WIB, the experiences with the board produced favorable reactions from many business leaders, who saw in the mobilization of businesses into industrial groupings a workable means of rationalizing the economy in peacetime. The WIB provided American business with an experiment in pervasive, systemwide national economic planning; it went beyond the more familiar forays into the regulation of only a specific industry and encompassed virtually the entire productive capacity of the American economy. To the delight of many within the business sector, it was learned that such an agency could not only effectively control business decision-making but could itself be controlled by business interests. The experience of having thousands of autonomous business units integrated into a system subject to unified control—a system capable of regulating the allocation of resources, the amount of production, the prices of goods and services, and the content of trade practices—was something these business leaders would not soon forget. Their rhetoric continued to express concern for the problems of overproduction, price cutting, unfair trade practices, and other status quo-threatening consequences of a freely competitive economic system. With the war concluded, leaders from a number of industries undertook a campaign on behalf of a system of "cooperation" and "self-regulation" for American industry. World War I may not have made the world safe for democracy, but it did give encouragement to some business leaders that a system of "business cooperation," subject to legal enforcement by the government, could become a functional reality in order to make competition safe for business. Robert Cuff has concluded:

> The war crisis . . . intensified the commitment of business ideologues to prove the virtues of corporate capitalism. . . . With a properly rationalized state system directed by businessmen in government, America would be able to combine the traditional genius of individualism and free enterprise with the modern efficiency of administrative centralization and state regulation.[24]

Toward Conservative Collectivism

Postwar business efforts to stabilize economic relationships must be considered in the broader context of the development of "collectivism" as the underlying social premise in American life. The 1920s are part of that critical period discussed by the historian James Gilbert in his study of the development of collectivist thinking, a phenomenon he relates to the emergence of "a new industrial civilization in which the giant business organization was the dominant force."[25] As Gilbert has demonstrated, the architects of twentieth century American collectivism had patterned their ideas on the industrial corporation as the central organizational tool. Any form of collectivism is, after all, "conservative" in nature, being premised on the establishment of static, rigidly structured social relationships designed to restrain any influences that would pose the threat of substantial change. A symbiotic relationship thus developed between the forces of "social reform" and those advocating the conservation of existing economic institutions and relationships. In twentieth-century "liberalism," declared the historian James Weinstein, many business leaders saw "a means of securing the existing social order."[26]

Twentieth-century society had become increasingly characterized by large-scale political, economic, and social institutions. The individualistic and diffused forms of social organization had pretty well given way to highly structured and centrally managed institutional systems. The interplay of group forces replaced individual decision-making as heretofore autonomous persons became subordinated to collective, organized authority. Just as political power was moving from the local to the national level, so in the business sector the individual entrepreneur was becoming less significant than the large, nationally organized corporation. This centralizing trend in social organization was well expressed by the economist Simon Patten, who declared: "The final victory of man's machinery over nature's control of human society was the transition from anarchic and puny individualism to the group acting as a powerful, intelligent organism."[27] This movement toward increased institutionalism transcended—or, perhaps, one should say absorbed—such matters as ideology or class interests: it was not just political or corporate, socialistic or private-capitalistic organization that was emerging, but *organization* itself.

While it is not the purpose of this book to thoroughly explore the origins of either large, dominant business firms or large, centralized government, some mention needs to be made of such phenomena, particularly since an expansion of organizational size and authority was occurring within both sectors during the years here under study. At least three separate explanations can be offered for such parallel organizational growth: (a) the emergence of national—rather than regionalized—industries, which generated larger and fewer business firms, was the inevitable consequence of technological and organizational changes that were occurring within the economy. Because centralized political authority could be utilized to help provide the conditions necessary for such a transformation (e.g., a single, nationally uniform body of laws would not only preempt the diverse and often inconsistent laws generated by state governments but could help to standardize competitive trade practices so as to reduce the range of permissible competition), the more dominant business firms found it useful to their interests to help expand the powers of the federal government. Under this explanation, *business* purposes would have the *primary* role and *governmental* purposes a *secondary* role in the mutual expansion of both sectors. A powerful national government was, according to this view, a byproduct of the expansionist and centralizing trends taking place within the business sector.

(b) A second explanation is that the federal government had its own institutional interests to promote, which it accomplished by expanding and centralizing its powers at the expense of both state and local governments. Large, nationally organized industries found it expedient to influence federal policies in order to further their own economic ends. According to this interpretation, the business sector was only taking pragmatic advantage of an expanding political system. As such, the *political* system would be the *primary*, and the *business* system the *secondary*, cause of the parallel patterns of growth within these two sectors.

(c) A third explanation is that there was a *symbiotic* aggrandizement of the size and authority of business and political organizations. Under this view, the interests of the larger, nationally organized firms in having a large national government providing the legal framework within which to operate fed the expansionist interests of the government itself. Likewise, the enlargement of the powers of the national government were conducive to business interests in a number of ways. First of all, larger business firms can more easily spread the fixed costs of government regulation over their larger outputs than can smaller firms, so the larger firms gain a comparative economic advantage that can be utilized in their pricing practices. Secondly, parties with a concentrated economic interest in the formulation of government policies will have a greater incentive to influence the direction of such policies in furtherance of their ends than will those with a diffused economic interest.[28] Thus, it could be maintained, the adversarial relationship that might superficially appear to exist between the business and political systems cloaks an underlying symbiosis that permits each sector to expand the range of its interests in mutually supportive ways. A corollary of this explanation can be found in John Kenneth Galbraith's notion of "countervailing power."[29] According to this notion a large national government developed in response to, and as a check upon, the growth of large national industries.

My own interpretation of such developments would be found in a combination of (a) and (c) above, although such an explanation is not crucial to the validity of the research herein. I am inclined to the view that a system of large, nationally organized industries *required* a large, national government to direct, enforce, and protect dominant business interests from the destabilizing uncertainties of continuing technological and organizational innovations that would find expression in a freely competitive environment. In a sentence, large national—and multinational—corporations as we have come to know them in the twentieth century would not have been possible without the coercive backing of a powerful federal government[30] and, concomitantly, the emergence of the highly centralized federal government would likely not have taken place without the impetus provided by the business system itself.

Such interpretations do not, of course, fully explain the processes by which the business system managed to evolve from smaller, localized firms into larger, nationally organized corporate enterprises. In asking such a question, we must be mindful that size is always a relative term and, furthermore, that business efforts to restrain freely competitive market processes predate the twentieth century; they are as old as the business system itself. Nevertheless, throughout most of the twentieth century, there has been a prevailing orthodoxy about the presumed advantages of organizational size. As William Letwin has demonstrated, by the late nineteenth century, many economists—caught up in the effort to apply Darwinian ideas to social behavior—began to look favorably upon industrial combination as the inevitable consequence of evolutionary growth. Even some monopolies came to be regarded as socially beneficial.[31] Many came to believe that combinations were an assurance of greater economic efficiencies. In the words of Hans Thorelli, "The exaggerated belief in a direct and universally applicable proportionality between size and efficiency corresponded well to the climate of general economic thinking prevalent among business and political leaders."[32] Such assumptions were easily refutable by a basic understanding of the biological sciences, from which field the evolutionary metaphor had been derived. Nevertheless, such thinking underlay the merger movement, which reached its peak in America during the years 1897 to 1903.[33]

Whether the emergence of a system of large, nationally organized industries was either inevitable or desirable is a question about which debate may be had. But *that* such a system developed is a matter of fact, about which it needs to be asked: *why?* The business historian, Alfred Chandler, attributes such development to a combination of technological innovations and organizational changes. In his view, "the new generators of power" (e.g., electricity) and new technologies (e.g., the automobile, and instruments powered by electricity) were "the dominant stimuli to innovation . . . which created new products and processes."[34] It was in "the newer and most technologically complex industries" that the impetus for increased concentration was most prevalent, for within such industries "size had real economic advantages," and "the necessity of assured supplies . . . encouraged vertical integration."[35]

Whether such increased concentration developed out of a desire to achieve monopoly power—as is so often assumed—or only in order to better coordinate and integrate productive processes so as to foster greater efficiencies is a question beyond the scope of this inquiry. Drawing upon Chandler's work, Oliver Williamson has suggested the latter explanation. Williamson notes that "[s]pecialization by function" is, depending upon the size of the firm, "the 'natural' way by which to organize multifunctional activities" so as to realize "both economies of scale and an efficient division of labor."[36] Because, for manufacturers, "[i]t became profitable to realize . . . scale economies only when a low-cost distribution system appeared" and because existing distribution systems were not capable of handling the volume of traffic needed in order to realize such advantages, "manufacturers integrated forward into marketing."[37] As Chandler has postulated, national marketing practices produced the consolidation of manufacturing "in fewer and larger plants," which led to a departmentalized structure whose success depended upon "careful coordination" and reliable systems of information.[38] In the process, firms became more vertically integrated, while competition, in turn, led other firms to follow suit, causing "many American industries [to become] dominated by a few large firms."[39]

The net effect of such changes, according to Chandler, was to cause firms to rely less upon the informal processes of the marketplace to regularize conditions, and more upon the control mechanisms afforded by organizational hierarchies. As he states the matter, "the visible hand of management replaced the invisible hand of market mechanisms,"[40] because "administrative coordination became more productive and more profitable than market coordination."[41] He then adds:

The advantages of internalizing the activities of many business units within a single enterprise . . . could be achieved only when a group of managers had been assembled to carry out the functions formerly handled by price and market mechanisms. Whereas the activities of single-unit traditional enterprises were monitored and coordinated by market mechanisms, the producing and distributing units within a modern business enterprise are monitored and coordinated by middle managers.[42]

Chandler illustrates this transformation by drawing upon the railroad industry. Prior to the railroad, the prevailing methods of transportation such as horse-drawn wagons and canal barges were not sufficiently powerful enough to generate the volume of traffic, for any carrier, that would "require the services of a large permanent managerial hierarchy" to coordinate subunits within a firm.[43] With the appearance of the railroad, however, enterprises "grew large enough to require the coordination of the activities of several geographically contiguous operating divisions."[44] Through a variety of informal means, the managers of various railroads began cooperating with one another to coordinate and integrate their multifaceted operations. Over time, such "constant consultation and cooperation . . . made possible an administrative coordination of transportation" that was not only "more efficient than prerailroad market coordination" but also became the organizational model for other sectors of the economy, particularly in transportation and communication.[45]

It is important to remember that the business community, like any other abstraction, does not exist as a monolith and, consequently, not all industries—or firms within specific industries—underwent such changes or experienced them to the same degree. With such a caveat in mind, Chandler tells us that the modern enterprise was "the institutional response to the rapid pace of technological innovation and increasing consumer demand," the consequence of which was seen in the decline of the "small traditional enterprise" and the growth of the "modern multiunit business enterprise."[46] While the firms Chandler studied were to develop decentralized forms of organizational structures,[47] "as the large enterprises grew and dominated major sectors of the economy, they altered the basic structure of these sectors and of the economy as a whole."[48]

There have been other explanations offered for the emergence of dominant business firms. Thorstein Veblen has focused a good deal of attention on the separation of "workmanship" from "salesmanship" that accompanied the demise of handicraft production and the emergence of larger-scale machine industry. The "increasing scale and efficiency of technology" helped to transform the role of the *craftsman*—who was adept at both the commercial and technical aspects of his business—into that of the employed *workman*. When "the ownership and control of the industrial plant passed out of the hands of the body of working craftsmen," business decision-making came to be controlled by managers who exhibited "proficiency in pecuniary management and the acquisition of wealth." As a consequence, the emphasis in business enterprise was less upon "technological mastery and productive effect" and more upon making money. Such transformations led, further, to the practice of absentee ownership, a phenomenon facilitated by the use of the corporate form of organization.[49] In his view, "the corporation came into use as a means of increasing the scale on which industry was carried on." Improvements in "mechanical facilities" and other "industrial arts" have produced changes "in the material conditions of life" that have further contributed to the larger scales of business organization.[50] One of the consequences of all of this, according to Veblen, has been the erosion of traditional ideas of competition by substituting "competitive *selling*" for the "competitive *production* of goods."[51] While "[f]ree competition still stands as the popular ideal to which trade and production ought to conform," it has remained the primary purpose of political authorities in the advanced nations "to safeguard the security and gainfulness of absentee ownership."[52] Whether this explanation derives from historical fact or only ideological conviction need not concern us at this point.

Veblen does offer another explanation that deserves some attention. He had earlier characterized the business system as an expression of "the machine process," which "conditions the growth and scope of industry, and . . . inculcates habits of thought suitable to the industrial technology."[53] Such thinking is purely mechanistic in nature; "materialism" and "efficiency" are among its highest values, and a "standardization of conduct" is enforced upon those subject to it.[54] Political and business practices became dominated by such thinking, with the result that "the machinery and policy of the state [were] in a peculiar degree drawn into the service of the larger business interests."[55] (This would be an expression of the earlier explanation for the emergence of large business and political institutions.) While business leaders may continue to genuflect before the altar of free competition, they "neither are inclined, nor will business competition permit them, to neglect or overlook any expedient that may further their own advantage or hinder the advantage of their rivals."[56] The relevance of this interpretation to the events under study herein should become evident.

If, as many believed at this time, such large-scale business organizations were both unavoidable and wholesome, and yet led to a greater concentration within industries, how could the benefits of free and open competition be maintained? These questions became an important part of the debate over government antitrust and other regulatory practices.[57] Many felt that the public interest could best be served by *regulating* rather than *prohibiting* such combinations.[58] The 1904 annual report of the United States Bureau of Corporations reflected this widely held view of the large corporation as an "industrial necessity" produced by the "irresistible tendency toward combination." Accordingly, the bureau urged various regulatory proposals by which *reasonable* and *unreasonable* methods of combination might be legally distinguished.[59]

According to no less an authority on the subject than Thurman Arnold, even the antitrust laws took on a ritualistic role in the struggle to rationalize the demands of large-scale industrial organizations with the traditional values of individualism and free competition. The "machine process" identified by Veblen led to a specialization of production that made large organizations inevitable. "In order to tolerate" such conditions, said Arnold, "men had to pretend that corporations were individuals."[60] The antitrust laws helped to create the illusion that corporations could be thought of as "persons," as moral agents whose conduct could be subjected to the same standards of "reasonableness" as anyone else. Such laws

> became the great myth to prove by an occasional legal ceremony that great industrial organizations should be treated like individuals, and guided by principle and precept back to the old ways of competition and fair practices, as individuals were. . . . [The antitrust laws] have stood as a great moral gesture which proves that in a nation of organizations individuals really are supreme; or, if not, they are going to become so very soon through the intervention of the Federal Government.[61]

As a consequence, "the antitrust laws, instead of breaking up great organizations, served only to make them respectable and well thought of by providing them with the clothes of rugged individualism."[62] John Munkirs has likewise characterized early-twentieth-century antitrust decisions as being more ceremonial than substantive in nature, declaring that "[s]ociety's response to the expanding dichotomy between cherished economic beliefs concerning what economic reality ought to be and actual economic conditions was to create a series of judicial and legislative rituals."[63]

Joseph Schumpeter has pointed out another change that occurred within the business system: the shift of control of corporate organizations from "owner" to "managerial" groups. Such a transformation has also been identified by Chandler, Veblen, and Adolf Berle and Gardiner Means, among others. Schumpeter believes the outlook of owners is affected more by long-term considerations, while managers are influenced by shorter-term interests. He concludes that this shift leads to a decomposition of the conditions supportive of free-market capitalism. The result is the evolution of a "managerial" mentality that Schumpeter describes in these terms:

> [T]he modern businessman, whether entrepreneur or mere managing administrator, is of the executive type. From the logic of his position he acquires something of the psychology of the salaried employee working in a bureaucratic organization. . . . Thus the modern corporation, although the product of the capitalist process, socializes the bourgeois mind; it relentlessly narrows the scope of capitalist motivation; not only that, it will eventually kill its roots.[64]

In Schumpeter's view, the evolution of capitalism "tends to automatize progress" and thus "tends to make itself superfluous."[65] The transformation results in the demise of the more venturesome owner-entrepreneur and the flowering of the more conservative, security-oriented administrator. Entrepreneurs rarely put together great enterprises with their money alone. The interests of lenders or investors are usually involved in any business organization, as evidenced by almost all large corporations. Bankers, not being renowned for their daring, and stockholders, desirous of preserving the present value of their interest in the corporation, have relatively cautious outlooks. In time, the entrepreneur—whose innovative, risk-taking, creative skills gave birth to the firm—comes to be regarded with suspicion and distrust by investors and creditors, who view his "freewheeling" methods as "irresponsible" and a threat to the enterprise. In order to insulate the assets of the firm from his more hazardous pursuits, the entrepreneur is removed from his position of control and replaced by the "prudent" and "fiscally responsible" manager. Such a change need not be hostile, however, as many entrepreneurs lack any interest in administering what they have created and are content to move on to other creative pursuits. Hired to preserve and protect the interests of the institution from risky decision-making, the manager is steeped in the methods of cost accounting, organization charts, projections, and paperwork systems, and regards the guaranteed rate of return on investment as preferable to the risks associated with actions that could as likely bankrupt the firm as multiply its value.

A related problem that arises when the control of corporations shifts from owners to managers has been observed by Adolf Berle and Gardiner Means. After noting that the "[o]wnership of wealth without appreciable control and control of wealth without appreciable ownership appear to be the logical outcome of corporate development,"[66] they point out how such a division of interests can generate a conflict of purpose between these two groups. The interests of the owners may lie in the distribution of corporate earnings, while those of the managers may rest in the pursuit of other ends (e.g., personal profits that come at the expense of the corporation, the prestige or power interests associated with their corporate positions, or, as Chandler has noted, the reinvestment of profits in the firm in order "to keep the organization fully employed").[67] Such cross-purposes have a tendency to reduce the role of profits as a means of fostering corporate efficiency, a phenomenon that is particularly evident in corporations in which ownership is so broadly dispersed as to make organized opposition to current management rather ineffective.[68]

While Chandler acknowledges the separation of the *management* from the *ownership* of the modern business enterprise, he differs with Schumpeter about the short-term outlook of managers. According to Chandler, "managers preferred policies that favored the long-term stability and growth of their enterprises to those that maximized current profits."[69] Chandler also does not share Schumpeter's pessimism about the innovative traits of managers. Quite the contrary: he regards the development of modern organizational structures as a crucial, innovative response to economic and technological conditions. It appears that Schumpeter and Chandler are not so far apart, however, in their conclusions about the more cautious, stability-seeking attitudes of managers. Chandler has noted the preference of managers for conditions that would "maintain the long-term viability of their organizations,"[70] an outlook that also served as the underlying premise for post–World War I business efforts to stabilize competitive relationships.

Schumpeter's thesis has been endorsed by business leaders themselves, but never more clearly than by Walter S. Gifford, a president of AT&T who, in 1926, addressed himself to "the changing character of big business." Gifford distinguished the earlier "pioneering" era, with its "captains of industry," from the later period, with its need for "statesmen of industry." The pioneers were men who "had to create their own precedents, invent their own methods, brush aside the inertia of less vigorous spirits, and drive directly to their goals." Such men trusted, in his view, to "luck and speculation" but were able to create "an unrivalled system" of industrial production.

While, according to Gifford, such men served a purpose in the scheme of things, he noted the necessity for "corporation managers" to take control of the modern business organization. "Their task," he declared, "is less to carve out a place for their business than it is to carry forward a highly organized undertaking already established. They must conserve what has been built, and steadily add to it." The maintenance of "this more stabilized condition" required the abandonment of the attitudes of the past. Decisions came to be based more upon "deductions from . . . probabilities" than upon risk taking and speculation. In a word, "nothing that can be foreseen is left to chance." Although Gifford discounted the danger, he did acknowledge that a stabilized environment could turn the business corporation into "a sort of bureaucracy, where men become so secure in their jobs that they will lose energy and initiative."[71]

What was occurring within the American economy at this time can be partially explained by the law of entropy and the more recently emerging science of "chaos." Chaos theory is helping us to become more aware of the interplay between systemic structure and destabilizing processes in maintaining healthy, viable systems. As we shall see, however, it was just such interplay that the more dominant members of the business community found unacceptable. As a consequence of work being done in chaos theory, we are beginning to appreciate the deeper meaning of "order," for within conditions of seeming irregularity and randomness can be found recurring patterns. What we have come to call "chaos," in other words, contains a deep hidden order. Smoke from a cigarette may rise rather smoothly for a few inches and then reach a point where it breaks up into turbulence. One sees the same phenomenon at work in the eddy of a river, or the heartbeat of a patient with arrhythmia, or a sharp rise or fall in the Dow Jones industrial average on a given day: a regularity that suddenly jumps into chaos.

Until recently, it was thought that these shifts from relative constancy to discontinuity reflected a change from an ordered to a disordered system— that the system was "falling apart" in some way. Because these chaotic conditions represented a movement from *linear* to *nonlinear* behavior (i.e., an additional unit of input produces *not* a *corresponding* increase in output, but a change that is *disproportionate* to the increased input), the ability to predict—and, thus, control—such conduct was lacking. Because we have been conditioned to think that what was not controllable was, therefore, disorderly, we convinced ourselves that such nonlinearity meant confusion and unruliness. But after modern computers made it possible to study the dynamics of such processes, it was discovered that these unpredictable, nonlinear systems were nevertheless exhibiting a kind of recurring regularity organized around points known as "strange attractors." (The pricing system for a given product in a given market might be characterized as a "strange attractor," for instance, for the behavior of market participants.) Furthermore, chaos scientists were discovering that such turbulence provided the environment within which creative change and growth occurred. Rather than proving that *equilibrium* conditions are necessary for the survival of systems and that *disequilibrium* is a threat to their survival, as the accepted wisdom would have it, the study of chaos is revealing just the opposite.

The second law of thermodynamics informs us that orderly systems move inevitably from states of *order* to *disorder;* every closed system is ultimately doomed by the processes of entropy. For an *open* system, however, such disintegration can be temporarily delayed by a system's ability to absorb energy (or *negative* entropy) from outside itself. Whether this externally derived energy is in the form of money, new technology, information, or other resources capable of temporarily reversing this entropic decline, systems must be prepared to *change* if they are to remain healthy and viable. Indeed, unless more order is brought into a system from its environment, it will soon experience entropic death. For the purposes of this book, it can be said that the survival of any business firm—or an entire industry, economic system, or even civilization—is dependent upon maintaining an unceasing resiliency, a capacity to accommodate itself to the inevitable changes occasioned by our entropic world. Insofar as they imply the maintenance of stability, equilibrium conditions are incompatible with this need to resist entropy, for stability is a resistance to change, and change is precisely what any healthy system must do if it is to avoid entropic death.

None of this is to suggest that *all* change is necessarily beneficial to a system, or that negentropic changes might not be so minuscule in nature as to be initially unobservable. Clearly, a business firm could introduce a new product for which there was great sales resistance, and the result could be disastrous (e.g., Ford Motor Company's "Edsel"). Another firm might continue making minor adjustments to its product lines in order to accommodate changing consumer preferences, without giving much external appearance of having changed at all. Change, in other words, can be *destructive* as well as *creative*. What the study of chaos informs us is that, in any complex (yet seemingly stable) system, a bifurcation point will be reached at which turbulence and randomness begin to be exhibited. While systems will endeavor to *anticipate* such changes, with practices designed to prevent fluctuations, complex, nonlinear behavior does not lend itself to prediction. When such fluctuations *do* occur, a healthy system must be prepared to respond in ways that *reduce*—rather than *accelerate*—entropy.

The distinction between *static* and *dynamical* systems can be seen in the analysis of marketplace pricing. While it is commonplace—particularly in short-term analyses—to speak of "equilibrium" prices in a free market, it is more realistic to think of prices fluctuating around a price level that econo-

mists label "equilibrium." (Again, the language of "chaos" might characterize this point around which prices fluctuate as the "strange attractor" for the
prices and production of a given commodity.) The continuing adjustments in
supply and/or demand that accompany such price changes—and tend to keep
prices fluctuating *around* an equilibrium price level—is an example of the
*dis*equilibrium operating within dynamical systems. Once again, the adjustments may or may not be dramatic in nature; compare, for instance, the
1929 collapse of the stock market to the more common drops in the Dow
Jones index. It is the *sensitivity* to environmental changes, coupled with a
resiliency to adjust to such changes, that differentiates static and dynamical
systems.

Disequilibrium is a condition to which any system—organic or inor-
ganic—must respond creatively by moving to higher levels of order (that is,
by generating negative entropy); otherwise it faces the entropic death inherent in stabilized systems. Far from just learning to *tolerate* such disequilibrium,
healthy systems—whether we are considering *firms* or entire societies—will
actively *promote* such conditions in order to generate the change necessary
for their survival.

A system, then, does not promote *order* by becoming *stable*. It is the
point at which a system goes into turbulence or chaos when new information generates significant instability that it can pursue either of two courses
of conduct. It can make no changes, in which case such instability will lead
to a further entropic disintegration; or it can respond to such turbulence by
developing more complex patterns of orderliness. Such processes have been
well analyzed by two pioneers in the study of chaos, Ilya Prigogine and Isabelle
Stengers. In their discussion of what they call "dissipative structures,"[72] they
demonstrate how nonequilibrium conditions provide the environment within
which new forms are developed that permit systems to achieve the greater
complexity required to overcome entropy. Such systems manifest "order
through fluctuations,"[73] and maintain their resistance to entropy by constantly renewing themselves.

The health of any system, then, is to be found in a kind of "creative
disequilibrium."[74] The resiliency to respond to changing conditions is enhanced by the system's capacities for autonomous and spontaneous behavior. Indeed, the degree to which one manifests such resiliency could be considered a measure of the health of that system. What this means, of course, is
that we must begin to rethink the nature and meaning of individual freedom:
rather than regarding such a condition as little more than a subjectively held
preference, we must begin to think of it in terms of its organizational and
social necessity. Because equilibrium conditions are, by definition, devoid of
the new energy required to sustain these processes, the entropic implications
of designing and protecting stabilized systems seems evident.[75]

These dynamics are at work within the business system. A business organization is created, and its initial successes in attracting investors and customers infuse energy into the firm. Under the leadership of an innovative entrepreneur, these investments and earnings are used to develop a more complex system of order that, presumably, will generate even more investments and earnings. Such continuing successes mean that the firm is overcoming entropy. With other firms operating under the same constraints—so the theory goes—an unrestrained system of competition will assure that the most innovative and efficient firms will continue to resist entropic forces and survive, while those that do not will perish. Thus a system of free competition exists *not* as a kind of game contrived by ambitious men and women of commerce to amuse themselves, but as the social expression of our most commonly held need: to overcome entropy and survive.

There are, unfortunately, influences at work within firms that seek to counteract these continuing needs to resist entropy. A healthy, resilient system will respond to changes in its environment by modifying *its* behavior so as to develop more effective strategies to overcome entropy. An institutionalized system, on the other hand, will generally endeavor to change its *environment*—including the behavior of other systems—so as to bring such environment into harmony with its interests. Such were the responses to competition made by most major business interests not only during the period here under study but in the preceding and following years as well.[76] Organizational size appears to be a major factor influencing the kind of response. As Prigogine and Stengers point out, "the more complex a system is, the more numerous are the types of fluctuations that threaten its stability."[77] The larger and more structured the system, in other words, the more frequent are the responses such a system must make in order to maintain its vitality.

The following example may help to illustrate the point being made. Let us imagine a firm—the Consolidated Buggy Whip Manufacturing Company—that has, until quite recently, been the nation's leading manufacturer of buggy whips. With the advent of the automobile, however, most buggy whip manufacturers have left the business and gone into other fields, perhaps the spark plug or tire business. But Consolidated doesn't really get the message until, one year, its catastrophic drop in earnings threatens it with bankruptcy. A great deal of entropy, energy that is unavailable for productive work, has built up within the company. There might be, for instance, an inefficient allocation of resources for product advertising rather than for research into new product lines. Consolidated is now in a state of internal chaos, or nonequilibrium. In a completely free market, its options would seem to be limited to two choices: (a) to do nothing and go out of business, completing its entropic collapse; or, (b) to move into a completely new—and more profitable—product line. But in a system in which political institutions are able to intervene in the market on behalf of the interests of business firms, Consolidated has yet another option: to try to persuade the government to act on its behalf to obtain benefits it has been unable to secure by its own efforts. Perhaps it will be able to maintain an antitrust action against the automobile manufacturers; perhaps it can get the government to subsidize the manufacture of buggy whips; or, as is more relevant to the topic here under study, perhaps it can get Congress to enact legislation defining its competitors' conduct as consisting of "unfair trade practices." Should it succeed in any of these efforts, Consolidated will have, at least temporarily, overcome its entropy, but *only* by transferring *its* entropy to others, namely, its more efficient competitors and/or the consuming public.

Schumpeter's use of the phrase "Creative Destruction" suggests his anticipation of the more recent work in the study of chaos. An orderly system can survive only by remaining resilient within a constantly changing environment, only by a willingness to take the risks of changing accepted practices when the consequences of doing so are uncertain, and only by understanding that stability and equilibrium conditions are incompatible with creative processes. If, as Schumpeter argues, firms tend to get transformed from owner-controlled to manager-controlled enterprises, and if manager-controlled organizations are more cautious and conservatively disposed in their decision-making, then such tendencies would suggest the presence of countervailing pressures to the commonly feared accumulation of organizational size and power. Whereas the prevailing view has been that such countervailing influences must be exerted from *without*—in the form of government regulation—entropy and chaos theories suggest a more spontaneous source of such pressures arising from *within the business organizations themselves!* As Prigogine's and Stenger's analysis suggests, it may be that the very success of any firm generates internal influences that make it increasingly difficult for larger firms to sustain themselves. Such a conclusion finds some support in one study showing that, of the one hundred largest firms in 1909, only thirty-six continued among the top hundred as of 1948.[78]

The processes by which individual organizations have evolved must be considered here. As firms become institutionalized, they transform themselves from organizational *tools* for the accomplishment of some common purpose (e.g., to generate profits for their investors who, in turn, are using the firm as a means of producing negative entropy in *their* lives) into an entity that becomes *an end in itself,* its own reason for being. I have partially defined an "institution" elsewhere as *"any permanent social organization with purposes of its own."*[79] Increasingly, the leadership of such institutionalized firms becomes more interested in preserving the existence and the market positions of their firms than in continuing the never-ending cycle of negentropic innovation and renewal. While any institution may well employ creative strategies in efforts to further its interests, increased organizational size carries with it *tendencies* for the structuring of behavior and for the conservation of beneficial arrangements. While there is no determinism at work here, all too often the need to remain resilient and creative in order to resist entropic forces gives way to illusions of maintaining equilibrium conditions by short-circuiting the processes that foster vital changes.

In his study of bureaucracy, Anthony Downs has identified some of the institutional dynamics to which the American business system has been subject. In his view, *"All organizations tend to become more conservative as they get older, unless they experience periods of very rapid growth or internal turnover."*[80] Furthermore, internal pressures are brought to bear upon organizational officials to get them to become "conservers," who are "essentially change avoiders."[81] As a consequence of such conservative influences, as the organizations grow older "they tend to develop more formalized rule systems covering more and more of the possible situations they are likely to encounter."[82] Such rules "increase the bureau's structured complexity," which reinforces its "resistance to change" and makes it less able to adapt to the changed conditions it faces.[83] Other factors help to maintain such inertia: as higher officials intensify their control over subordinates, the latter will increase their efforts to subvert such controls, while officials will resist any changes that diminish "resources under their own control."[84] Further, as any organization increases in size, *"the weaker is the control over its actions exercised by those at the top"* and *"the poorer is the coordination among its actions."*[85] While Downs notes that such inertia has socially beneficial consequences as well (for example, stabilizing social practices and maintaining various "cultural values"),[86] its adverse impact upon the organization's capacities for effecting change outweigh such benefits.

The societal implications for the institutionalizing and structuring practices under study in this book go far beyond matters of economic concern; they include the decline and collapse of civilization itself. While it is not my purpose to go into a complete analysis of such a topic, an understanding of the consequences of our organizational practices would be incomplete without at least some brief mention of it. The historian Carroll Quigley[87] has explained such declines as the consequence of a civilization's "instruments of expansion"—which he identifies as those organizations engaged in invention, saving, and investment—becoming *institutionalized.* When such systems are transformed from being the *means* by which the interests of the civilization are produced and become *ends* in themselves, they have become institutions. By developing purposes of their own, such institutions become interested in creating conservative environments in which threats of any substantial change are restrained in favor of maintaining the stability of the institutions themselves.

These "instruments of expansion" can take many forms, depending upon the nature of the civilization. While modern industrial societies would employ such instruments as technology and the production and distribution of goods and services, other civilizations might find their "instruments of expansion" in the sciences, medicine, the arts, agriculture, or navigation. Whatever the concrete forms such instruments may take, when they become institutionalized and structured they lose those qualities that are essential to the continued growth and expansion of the civilization. Having transformed their purposes from being the creators of the values upon which their civilization rests to becoming ends in themselves, institutions begin to exhibit ossification and an unwillingness to adapt themselves to the kinds of changes any healthy organism must exhibit if it is to remain vibrant.[88]

The historians Arnold Toynbee—in his "challenge and response" analysis of the emergence, growth, and collapse of civilizations[89]—and Will and Ariel Durant[90] have reached similar conclusions. Toynbee has observed, for instance, that "[g]rowth is achieved when an individual or a minority or a whole society replies to a challenge by a response which not only answers that challenge but also exposes the respondent to a fresh challenge which demands a further response on his part."[91] A civilization begins to break down, he goes on, when there is "a loss of creative power in the souls of creative individuals" and, ultimately, "a tendency towards standardization and uniformity" within society.[92]

The Durants share this interpretation. In their view, whether a given civilization will continue to develop or decay depends largely upon whether—and how—challenges to existing situations are met. This, in turn, depends upon "the presence or absence of initiative and of creative individuals with clarity of mind and energy of will . . . capable of effective responses to new situations. . . ."[93] They then add: "When the group or a civilization declines, it is through ·. . . the failure of its political or intellectual leaders to meet the challenges of change." As with organic systems, "civilizations begin, flourish, decline, and disappear—or linger on as stagnant pools left by once life-giving streams."[94]

While a system of open and unrestrained competition provides the disequilibrium within which creativity and innovation could flourish—and thus maximizes the opportunities for individuals, firms, and civilization itself to resist entropy and thrive—these same conditions are looked upon as threats by those firms that have come to regard the stabilization of their institutional interests as a purpose that preempts the broader survival needs for change and growth. Apparently unaware that healthy organisms can continue to survive only by remaining in *non*equilibrium states that generate more creativity and that equilibrium conditions are synonymous with death itself, the officials of such firms begin to design and assemble structures to restrain these processes of change. Rather than having to endure the constant competitive turbulence caused by other firms pursuing *their* strategies for resisting entropy, they have sought a less variable trade climate. Their efforts to resist change have taken many forms: voluntary agreements among competitors; political restraints in the forms of tariffs, import restrictions, and laws that standardize product designs, employment policies, and sales practices; and the more recent development of government regulatory agencies whose principal purpose is to enforce an economic stability conducive to the interests of major commercial and industrial institutions. Such have been a few of this century's contributions to institutionalizing our society's "instruments of expansion." As William Lazonick has suggested, we might learn from the British "the dangers of the static, competitive equilibrium model" of economic systems. In his view, a major problem in the economic life of twentieth-century Britain "was that 'statical equilibrium' rather than 'organic growth' was *too* representative of economic reality."[95]

As we shall see, much of the American business community was actively involved, during the years 1918 to 1938, with further structuring those practices by which the production and distribution of goods and services depend. In increasing numbers, businessmen began to identify open competition as "wasteful" and "destructive." In the perceived turbulence of such conditions, some even spoke of the "death" of firms. Under such conditions, one's first impulse might be to empathize with their desire to preserve their existence by attempting to stabilize such discord. But such empathy begins to wane when one considers not only the adverse consequences of such efforts on other firms and individuals, but on broader societal interests as well.

Policies designed to preserve the interests of existing business institutions have only contributed to the entropic decline to which the present American economic system may be destined. In endeavoring to protect their institutional interests from the chaotic fluctuations and uncertainties of an unrestrained competition, business leaders are inadvertently generating the processes of decay and ossification that prevent systems from remaining resilient and innovative. American industries that are no longer able to compete with their more efficient foreign competitors; factories and transportation systems that make up a spreading "rust belt" across many parts of the country; a continuing recourse to taxpayers as involuntary (and unsecured) "creditors" to bail out increasing numbers of failed commercial and industrial interests; and a continuing decline in the quality of life for most Americans—these are a few of the more visible symptoms of an economic system whose apparently terminal condition may yet be reversed by a change in our thinking as to what it is important for us to preserve. One thing seems rather certain, however: as an understanding of entropy and chaos would allow us to predict, and as Quigley's historical analysis demonstrates, unless there is a reversal of these governmental policies, the processes of change that are essential to a system's being able to successfully resist entropic tendencies will continue to be thwarted and, with it, will likely come the collapse of the American economic system.[96]

THE BENEFITS OF SIZE RECONSIDERED

Because our behavior so often expresses our underlying metaphysical assumptions, it is worthwhile to raise the question of whether this century's attraction to large institutional systems has its origins in empirically based pragmatism or a kind of systemic determinism, or is only a reflection of belief systems about the presumed efficacy and/or inevitability of large organizations. In other words, has our world become institutionalized through the impersonal and irresistible interplay of social and economic forces, or because our thinking has convinced us that large organizational systems are generally advantageous?

If the study of chaos and complexity do not offer sufficient challenges to our assumptions regarding the advantages of increased size, recourse may be had to American business history. The presumed benefits associated with organizational size generally failed to materialize from the merger movement that was so popular at the turn of this century. In his early study of corporate reorganizations, Arthur Dewing concluded that the experiences of firms that had undergone consolidation attested to "the inadequacy of mere consolidation as a basis of economic efficiency."[97] In one study involving ten unrelated companies, Dewing observed that the combined postconsolidation earnings had averaged only 65 percent of the preconsolidation levels.[98] In Dewing's opinion, the reasons that most combinations failed to live up to their promoters' expectations involved "the difficulties attending the administrative management of a large business" and "the difficulties attending the creation of a business organization sufficiently powerful to dominate an industry in the presence of actual or potential competition."[99] Following the merger that created United States Steel in 1901, its market share fell from 61.6 percent in 1901 to 39.9 percent by 1920.[100] Likewise, the 1902 merger that produced International Harvester was followed by a drop in market share from 85 percent in 1902 to 64 percent by 1918.[101] Gabriel Kolko partially explains these declines in terms of the internal problems created by organizational size. In his view, "U.S. Steel . . . was a technologically conservative, increasingly expensive operation that illustrates the inadequacy of the dominant theories on the positive relationship between size and efficiency current since the end of the nineteenth century."[102] While many large firms were able to overcome such influences by remaining resilient and responsive to changed conditions, organizational size, per se, did not seem to afford the advantages expected.

Such a conclusion also finds support in a study by the Temporary National Economic Committee (TNEC) on corporate incomes for the year 1919, which showed "that the larger corporations earned less than the average of all corporations; that those with an investment of more than $50,000,000 earned the least, while those with an investment of less than $50,000 earned the most; and that earnings declined almost uninterruptedly, with increasing size."[103] In another study of profits from 2,046 manufacturing firms from 1919 to 1928, it was found that "those with an investment under $500,000 enjoyed a higher return than those with more than $5,000,000 and twice as high a return as those with more than $50,000,000."[104] It seems, then, large organizations are increasingly less capable of sustaining their market positions in the face of competitive challenges without the use of artificial restraints to control the behavior of other firms that pose threats to their established interests.

This is not to deny that many firms have been able to overcome these internal, countervailing influences. Chandler's research documents the effectiveness of the organizational changes that occurred throughout much of the business system.[105] Firms were, indeed, responding to the conditions in which they found themselves, and many were becoming organizationally more efficient. But to what extent did the artificial structuring of competitive relationships become an increasingly attractive strategy to large business organizations *because* of numerous dysfunctional factors associated with firm size?

Any consideration of the effects of size upon organizational behavior ought to include the landmark work of Leopold Kohr in challenging our culture's deeply engrained assumptions about the advantages of size. Beginning with the observation that "[w]henever something is wrong, something is too big,"[106] Kohr proceeds to make the case for what he calls "the *size theory of social misery.*"[107] In his view, "[o]nly relatively small bodies—though not the smallest, as we shall see—have stability. . . . [B]eyond a certain size, everything collapses or explodes."[108] Furthermore, "[t]he instability of the too large . . . is a *destructive* one. Instead of being *stabilized* by growth, its instability is *emphasized* by it. The same process, so beneficial below a certain size, now no longer leads to maturity but to disintegration."[109] Though his analysis preceded the work being done in chaos theory, it is evident that Kohr's conclusions are compatible with other studies in nonlinear dynamics. The allometric principle governing biological systems—namely, that there is an optimal size for the members of various species and that too much variation above or below this level will not allow the organism to function adequately—adds analogical support to the proposition that *dis*economies of scale operate to restrain organizational size. Furthermore, the studies of Dewing, Kolko, and the TNEC, demonstrating the disadvantageous consequences to firms that have gone through mergers and other consolidations, affords additional support for Kohr's basic thesis.

A more realistic understanding of the nature of organizational size, as well as of the purposes and economic consequences of government regulatory practices, might be served by further research and analysis incorporating these various strains. It may be that increasing the size of any organization tends to produce countervailing influences that foster inertia, conflict, communications breakdowns, inflexibility, and general instability. It may be, in other words, that large organizations tend, as a consequence of these internal counter pressures, to become less resilient, less capable of making satisfactory responses to changing conditions in the marketplace. What we may discover, in our application of chaos theory to organizational systems, is that government intervention and regulation, far from serving as a countervailing pressure to offset large-scale, dominant business firms, actually serves as a *deterrent* to the functioning of those hidden patterns of order that lie deep within the turbulence of a competitive marketplace—hidden patterns of order that militate against both organizational size and efforts to insulate firms from the processes of change to which their size makes them increasingly less capable of responding.

Conclusion

The conservative orientation of many members of the "managerial" groups influenced business thinking during the years that followed World War I. Charged with the authority and responsibility for profitably managing assets worth many millions of dollars, and faced with competition from radically new product lines and methods of production and distribution, and intense and aggressive trade practices by other producers and sellers, it is not surprising to find such business leaders seeking means of maintaining and regularizing existing conditions. Out of a desire to preserve the value of their organizations as going concerns, businessmen were attracted, in increasing numbers, to proposals for artificially structuring otherwise competitive relationships. It was neither the egoistic pursuit of power nor the promotion of abstract social doctrines that impelled business leaders to seek the fundamental alteration of commercial and industrial practices during the years in question. Motivations were grounded, rather, in concerns that were purely pragmatic in nature. To paraphrase Justice Holmes's classic observation of the history of the common law, the development of the American business system has been a product of *experience*, and not of theoretical design.[110] Businessmen (and nonbusinesspeople as well) have been attracted to systems of either unrestrained or regulated competition, depending upon the anticipated benefits they perceive in each. The high-flown rhetoric and appeals to "fairness" and "cooperation" and the recitation of the need for new principles of market behavior in order to bring the times into harmony with the changes and complexities wrought by the evolutionary forces of capitalism were, as we shall discover, window dressing for the merchandising of concepts designed to satisfy more immediate and material interests. From this perspective, the efforts of businessmen to modify and structure the competitive environment become neither a sinister conspiracy nor an ideological commitment, but only a pragmatic response based on economic self-interest.

Government regulation of economic behavior has largely been focused upon trying to stabilize the positions of various economic interests that have been responsible for fostering regulation, to the detriment of the processes of change that are necessary for the continuing health of all systems. As the study of entropy and chaos remind us, it is the processes of continual transformation and adjustment that represent the vitality and well-being of a system, while states of permanence and equilibrium are synonymous with death.

Of course, to the degree we have been successful in our endeavors, we tend to develop an attachment to what we have produced, as well as to the instrumentalities we have employed to produce them. As a consequence, our capacities to respond to changing conditions in our world are complemented by an attraction for stability. Most of us feel a need to accurately anticipate the consequences of our actions and to have our world function in a manner consistent with our interests. We seek to create environments in which purposeful, self-seeking activity can occur, and in this regard, businessmen are not unlike anyone else. They create those systems and foster those practices that serve to maximize their profits. As Robert Wiebe has suggested, "The desire for predictability," along with the "values of continuity and regularity, functionality and rationality, administration and management . . . required long-range, predictable cooperation through administrative devices that would bend with a changing world."[111] In such a way do organizations begin to get transformed into institutions.

This felt need for certainty and predictability in business decision-making is partially explainable in terms of Schumpeter's analysis. The more conservative, short-term outlook held by many members of the "managerial" classes has a tendency to find expression in demands for a business environment made secure from the uncertainties associated with a condition of unrestrained decision-making. The unhindered exercise of free choice by both buyers and sellers poses the continuing threat of change. The wants and innovative capacities of humans are boundless, and in a free environment the self-seeking motives of people will cause many to organize their resources in order to produce goods and services that can better satisfy those human wants than can existing goods and services. To the cautious businessmen with a managerial outlook, such a condition is inconsistent with the objectives of preserving existing institutions from the vicissitudes of the marketplace. In the past, such institutional pressures for stability came to dominate business thinking, and produced proposals for restricting the autonomous decision-making of firms.

As we have argued, such structuring of human behavior in order to maintain the status quo and to forestall the threats associated with free competition is totally inconsistent not only with the concept of human freedom but with the processes of growth and change required for any system seeking to overcome entropy. Freedom implies change, as decision makers continually adjust their behavior in response to altered conditions within their environments. In the long run, the failure to maintain such variability and resiliency will produce the entropic collapse of any system employing such a strategy. Such consequences are enhanced by the fact, as chaos theory informs us, that the behavior of complex systems is unpredictable, meaning that the best strategy for survival consists in remaining flexible in the face of changing circumstances. But the prospects of change become increasingly unacceptable to those charged with the shorter-term responsibilities of managing and preserving the assets of business organizations. Therein lies the paradox: the *survival* of firms depends upon maintaining a competitive environment in which the threat of *extinction* is a continuing possibility. Such considerations, arising within the context of the major changes taking place within the economy, were central to business efforts to achieve "self-regulation" in the years following World War I.

Frederick Lewis Allen has characterized the general state of the reform movement at the end of World War I as one in which, due to the enormity of the war itself, "the wish to regulate and control business and finance was thoroughly played out."[112] This statement fails to fully account for the postwar interest among men of commerce and industry in restructuring the business system along collectivist lines. What emerged from the intellectual community was a set of premises consistent with business purposes, namely, the creation of "a collective society to control the forces of economic change," subject to the direction of those "social entrepreneurs . . . who would work out the generalized schemes for regulating that new society."[113] The fundamental question confronting business leaders throughout the 1920s has been well stated by Gilbert as "[w]hether an antiquated individualism or a new collectivism would emerge to mold this new industrial society."[114] Encouraged by their wartime experiences with the WIB, many businessmen began the peacetime task of mobilizing themselves on behalf of the latter proposition.

2

Trade Associations
and Codes of Ethics

> The group's accepted scheme of life is the consensus of views held
> by the body of these individuals as to what is right, good, expedi-
> ent, and beautiful in the way of human life.
> —Thorstein Veblen

Postwar efforts to change business motives from the singular pursuit of firm
profits to the broader consideration of industry interests began with the trade
associations. Trade associations went back many decades prior to the 1920s,
but they took on added significance during World War I, serving as the principal mobilizing vehicles for the WIB. When the war ended and businessmen
contemplated extending into peacetime the benefits derived from wartime
industrial organization, it was only natural that their attentions should be
drawn to the trade associations. Because the trade associations had their
own industry-oriented self-interest and were subject to the control of industry
members themselves, they provided attractive machinery for those desirous
of advancing a collective view of the conduct of economic life. In contrast
with the decentralized individualism of prior decades, the trade associations
represented the emerging group-consciousness in industry, the coordinating
arm of the new institutional order. In place of some vague abstraction, the
trade associations gave visibility and a sense of reality to the various industries, and for this reason they were indispensable instruments in the development of an industrial perspective among businessmen.

In December 1918, the U.S. Chamber of Commerce held a conference in
which representatives of the National Association of Manufacturers (NAM)
actively participated. It went on record in favor of the creation of trade
associations and urged all businessmen to join and support their respective
organizations.[1] Taking such advice, many industries lost little time getting
organized into trade associations, whose activities extended from efforts to
create "cooperative" attitudes among competitors to the enunciation of
specific "codes of ethics," to proposals for politically structured industrial

controls. Throughout the postwar years, various business representatives endeavored to fashion the most effective means for stabilizing and harmonizing trade practices, efforts that more often than not centered around the trade associations. Any effort to understand the transformation of business attitudes toward competition must include an examination of such industrial groupings.

TRADE ASSOCIATIONS AND THE "NEW COMPETITION"

The trade association movement had many promoters, but there were none more enthusiastic in their support than Herbert Hoover. While still secretary of commerce, Hoover offered this assessment of the centralizing trends within the business system:

> I believe that we are, almost unnoticed, in the midst of a great revolution—or perhaps a better word, a transformation—in the whole super-organization of our economic life. *We are passing from a period of extremely individualistic action into a period of associational activities.*

Hoover shared the view of a number of business leaders that the trade association could not only establish collective standards of competitive behavior but could enforce those standards against the "small minority who will not play the game," those few who "drive many others to adopt unfair competitive methods which all deplore." In his opinion, the trade association was "the promising machinery . . . for the elimination of useless waste and hardship."[2]

Hoover went on to discuss the motivations of the business community to regularize competitive practices:

> Ever since the factory system was born there has been within it a struggle to attain more stability through collective action. This effort has sought to secure more regular production, more regular employment, better wages, the elimination of waste, the maintenance of quality or service, decrease in destructive competition and unfair practices, and ofttimes to assure prices or profits.[3]

The political scientist Theodore Lowi has stated the proposition more briefly: "In history and in theory, the law of the commercial marketplace is competition. The trade association seeks to replace this with an administrative process."[4]

The campaign to create an environment conducive to a greater degree of business "cooperation" was not without some rather sophisticated rationales. One of the principal theoreticians for a system of industry-regulated competition was Arthur Jerome Eddy, who captured the imagination of business leaders with a book, originally published in 1912, titled *The New Competition*.[5] Asserting that "Competition is War, and 'War is Hell'," Eddy went on to outline a program for altering the fiercely competitive conditions of the day through the use of the "open-price" system. Eddy, who envisioned a neoguild system for business, favored the grouping of each trade and industry into separate organizations, the purpose of which would be not to *fix*, but to *report*, prices, productive capacity, wage levels, "and all competitive practices."[6] The members would file with their association all inquiries, bids, and contracts, and such information would then be made available to other members. A critical factor in the open-pricing system was that no firm was required to agree to any price range or level, nor was it prohibited from altering its price structure once it was filed with the association. Firms making any such changes were required, however, to immediately report such changes. Through such a system, which attracted a great deal of business support, it was felt that business could be purged of an element considered sinister by many: secret prices.

It will become evident, in reviewing specific trade association "codes of ethics," that pricing policies of competitors ranked as one of the primary sources of business discontent. Eddy recognized that concern when he summarized the advantages of the open-price association as including the elimination of "vicious bidding," "secret bidding," and "secret rebates, concessions, and graft."[7] Turning his attention to the role that the legal system would have in his program of "cooperation by publicity," Eddy anticipated the conclusion later reached by other business leaders concerning the need for enforcement of trade standards against recalcitrants: "Men are so perversely constituted they seem to prefer compulsion to cooperation; they call upon the state to compel them by law to do what they ought to do for themselves, to frame rules of conduct they should voluntarily devise for their own protection."[8]

The inherent contradiction of *mandatory* enforcement of *voluntary* codes was to plague the trade association movement throughout the 1920s. Under Eddy's plan, legal assistance would be sought not only for purposes of publicizing all competitive practices but for "the suppression of all dishonest, fraudulent, oppressive and unfair business methods."[9] Eddy recommended the establishment of a federal commission, to be coequal with the Interstate Commerce Commission, to administer and enforce the law. Enforcement would be facilitated by a requirement that every corporation engaged in interstate commerce obtain a license from the federal commission.

Among the trade practices that Eddy proposed to make punishable offenses were the following: (1) failure of a firm to keep accurate records of all sales and purchases; (2) secret rebates and commissions; (3) billing at other than actual terms of sale; (4) false or misleading statements regarding costs, sales, and prices charged to others; (5) refusal to tell one buyer when lower prices have been charged to others for similar goods; (6) selling at or below cost; and (7) selling to one man or locality on terms better than those charged to a competitor or to other localities.[10]

Eddy foresaw the trade associations playing a central role in helping to enforce the provisions of the law and, in turn, the proposed commission having supervisory powers over the associations as well as the individual firms. Such powers would include authority "to review the acts of the association, if necessary revise and fix prices and conditions of purchases and sales, award damages, enforce penalties, [and] dissolve the association."[11] Eddy's ideas concerning the control of pricing policies of business firms contain the same thread of logic that became interwoven in the statements of business leaders, association "codes of ethics," and governmental programs such as the Trade Practice Conferences and the National Industrial Recovery Act.

There were many business leaders who, although committed to the idea of trying to mitigate the competitive tempo, had certain misgivings about the use of the trade association to accomplish that purpose. In addition to the enforcement problems, many expressed concern that the use of trade associations to regulate trade practices within industries would constitute a violation of the antitrust laws. Past Supreme Court decisions, including the *Trans-Missouri Freight Association* case,[12] left business in doubt as to the permissible scope of trade association activity. As a consequence, rather than face either criminal prosecution or the abandonment of the association concept, some business leaders began advocating the amendment of the antitrust laws to allow for industry-wide agreements regulating trade practices. The U.S. Chamber of Commerce had conducted a referendum of its membership in 1919 on just such a question. The results showed almost 97 percent favoring congressional review of the antitrust laws; nearly 75 percent favoring the establishment of general business standards "to be administered by a supervisory body"; and nearly 72 percent favoring "an enlarged Federal Trade Commission" as the appropriate supervisory body.[13]

Concerns over the legality of effective trade association practices were not confined to the business community. Conflicts arose within the Harding administration between Attorney General Harry Daugherty and Secretary Hoover over the question of whether the statistical reporting practices of associations violated the antitrust laws. Daugherty—who apparently sensed a good deal of public animosity toward trade association practices—insisted upon an interpretation of the Sherman Act that would have all but emasculated statistical programs. Accordingly, he began a number of antitrust prosecutions to test his views in the courts. Hoover, on the other hand, favored statistical interchange not only as a means of promoting efficiency but for encouraging a more general stabilization of commerce and industry. Though he believed that competition should be the controlling influence in economic life, he was persuaded that cooperative activities among competitors could be harmonized with that purpose.[14]

By the mid 1920s, the U.S. Supreme Court had established rather clear parameters for permissible trade association activity. The "open-price" system came under attack in the *American Column & Lumber*[15] and *Linseed Oil*[16] cases. The trade associations involved had been receiving and reporting statistical information on the activities of their individual members, who were required not only to file periodic reports with the associations but to make their books available for association audit. The associations further endeavored to predict future pricing and production levels and made recommendations concerning future trade practices. In the *American Column & Lumber* case, the Court held such activities to be violative of the Sherman Act; it concluded that they had contemplated a "harmonious" competitive relationship, maintained not by "fines and forfeitures" but by "business honor and social penalties,—cautiously reinforced by many and elaborate reports, which would promptly expose to his associates any disposition in any member to deviate from the tacit understanding that all were to act together under the subtle direction of a single interpreter of their common purposes."[17] In the *Linseed Oil* case, the Court concluded that the purpose of the "open-competition" plan "was to submerge the competition theretofore existing among the subscribers and substitute 'intelligent competition,' or 'open competition'; to eliminate 'unintelligent selfishness' and establish '100 per cent confidence,'—all to the end that the members might 'stand out from the crowd as substantial co-workers under modern co-operative business methods.'"[18]

Following these two decisions, the U.S. Chamber of Commerce announced its support for the principle of allowing trade associations to engage in effective statistical reporting. Consistent with the results of its earlier referendum, the Chamber proposed abolition of any legal restraints upon such reporting. It is not clear whether the Chamber was advocating the *collective* reporting of the data for the industry as a whole or whether, as in the *American Column & Lumber* and *Linseed Oil* cases, it was urging a form of reporting that identified individual firms. The latter position can reasonably be inferred from the Chamber's own language that spoke of the reporting of "actual prices in closed transactions." Such a stand is also consistent with the prior practices of a number of trade associations that found individualized reporting a more effective source of intraindustrial pressures for trade practice conformity. On the other hand, the Chamber discouraged the use of such data for purposes of "concerted action" by association members.[19]

In two 1925 decisions—the *Maple Flooring*[20] and *Cement*[21] cases—the Supreme Court upheld the reporting activities of two trade associations. Although, in *Maple Flooring*, the association's past practices bore a great deal of similarity to those previously declared illegal, the association had altered its system in an effort to comply with the rulings in *American Column & Lumber* and *Linseed Oil*. In *Maple Flooring* and *Cement*, the associations continued to report on such matters as production, sales, and prices, but instead of identifying individual firms in their reports, they provided only aggregate, industry-wide figures. Further distinguishing their practices from the earlier cases, these associations avoided recommending future pricing or production policies, and broadly distributed their statistical data by including customers and public agencies as recipients of the same information sent to association members. The Court, drawing a clear distinction between these two pairs of cases, declared:

> Competition does not become less free merely because the conduct of commercial operations becomes more intelligent through the free distribution of knowledge of all the essential factors entering into the commercial transaction. . . . Persons who unite in gathering and disseminating information in trade journals and statistical reports on industry; who gather and publish statistics as to the amount of production of commodities in interstate commerce, and who report market prices, are not engaged in unlawful conspiracies in restraint of trade merely because the ultimate result of their efforts may be to stabilize prices or limit production through a better understanding of economic laws and a more general ability to conform to them. . . .[22]

At first glance, the Court's opinion in this case could be read as an apology for trade association efforts to restrain competition. Such a response, however, fails to consider the paradox that a condition of so-called perfect competition and effective industry methods to cartelize trade are often evidenced by identical factors. Both are premised, in part, upon identical prices in a market in which all participants have access to complete information. Thus, just as identical prices can be interpreted either as evidence of industry price-fixing or of "perfect competition," the dissemination of detailed pricing and production information can be regarded as either *fostering* or *inhibiting* competition.

By 1925, then, the business community had a fairly clear view of the boundary line separating lawful from unlawful trade association activity. If the information was *past*- rather than *future*-oriented, was presented as *aggregate*, industry-wide data rather than as *individualized* firm practices, was distributed broadly rather than just to association members and, above all else, made no effort to recommend future pricing or production decisions to industry members, the reporting system would likely meet with Court approval. But these very limitations frustrated industry efforts to stabilize competitive trade practices. Having historical, industry-wide data was of some benefit in business decision-making, but it was of little help to the industry in combating price declines. Industry members desired an effective means of exerting pressure on the notorious "10 percent," or what one trade association official called "the chiseling minorities,"[23] who would not "play the game." Being able to identify the price cutters in an industry, having access to the critical pricing, production, and cost factors of one's competitors, and being able to present such information in a way that would suggest, to industry members, the kinds of decisions that would encourage price stabilization—*this* is what interested businessmen and provided the underlying motives for the statistical reporting activities of trade associations. So much had the Supreme Court's decisions minimized the value of such practices that, of the 150 trade associations acknowledging their use of "open pricing" in 1921, only 33 maintained the system in 1929.[24]

Trade association efforts to promote competitive stability in the 1920s were not confined to such formal arrangements as "open-pricing" plans. Trade associations, trade publications, business leaders, and related organizations devoted a great deal of effort to the enunciation of business principles designed to foster a more "cooperative" business environment. A very general statement of principles, cast in the spirit of many already existing association codes, was announced by the U.S. Chamber of Commerce in 1924. The Chamber's statement extolled "fair dealing" and a "fair profit" and criticized "waste in any form" and "excesses of every nature" (the latter including "inflation of credit" and "overstimulation of sales"). Another provision decreed: "Unfair competition, embracing all acts characterized by bad faith, deception, fraud or oppression, including commercial bribery, *is wasteful, despicable, and a public wrong. Business will rely for its success on the excellence of its own service.*" The statement closed by supporting "*lawful cooperation* among business men," urging them to so conduct their businesses as to "*render restrictive legislation unnecessary.*" By September of that same year, some 270 trade associations and other business organizations had ratified the Chamber's declaration.[25]

An elaboration upon these basic principles was offered by Edwin B. Parker, who, as chairman of the Chamber's Committee on Business Ethics, outlined his views as to what was meant regarding "unfair competition": "[T]he seeking of a business advantage through efforts directed to harm a competitor is unethical and wasteful and will receive the unqualified condemnation of all right-thinking men. Whatever form such efforts may take entails economic waste and is repugnant to the public interest." The principle of "lawful cooperation," Parker declared, was based upon standards that were "essential to the intelligent conduct of business under such restrictions as will prevent abuses." Though he did not specify the "abuses" he had in mind, the anticompetitive flavor of many of these provisions left little doubt as to the benefits anticipated by the Chamber from adherence to the spirit of such principles.[26] The distaste for unrestrained competition was voiced a few years later by Parker in a talk to the Chamber: "Business believes in wholesome competition, but competition is not primitive strife. Business knows that competition may become not the life of trade but in truth the death of the traders. Piracy masquerading as competition is piracy none the less."[27] The same sentiment was expressed by F. M. Feiker, vice-president of the McGraw-Hill Company, who suggested that "cut-throat competition" results in "waste to the consumer" and "takes business scalps in a truly savage fashion."[28] Wilson Compton, an officer of the National Lumber Manufacturers Association, offered similar views on the nature of competition:

> Competition is not fair or free if it is not equal. And it cannot be equal between competitors of such widely different financial strength, sales facilities, and bargaining power as exist to-day in the various industries among the hundreds of thousands of separate individual selling units which are constantly besieging the same buyers, seeking the same business, in the same markets.[29]

While one writer described the changing business atmosphere as one where "suspicion and injurious 'cut-throat' competition give way to a spirit of friendly co-operation and of confidence,"[30] Magnus W. Alexander, president of the National Industrial Conference Board (NICB), provided a more detailed account of the hoped-for consequences. Viewing business as "more than a medium for making profits by any means," Alexander declared that the spirit of cooperation "aims to develop self-government in business, not because it fears the growing weight of the club of government, but because it believes that industry, if it wills so, can be a more effective policeman and judge of its affairs than can government." The effectiveness of such policies would, according to Alexander, depend "on the spirit of the people and its government to give these molders [i.e., businessmen] a free hand within the limitations set by legal and moral law."[31]

The NICB was, throughout the 1920s, a major promoter of effective methods of "business cooperation." Begun in 1916, it served during World War I to help coordinate wartime economic planning. The NICB played the role of political activist, research publicist, and public relations proponent for American industry. It also had a primary role in the establishment of the War Labor Board. Its efforts on behalf of intraindustrial cooperation have been characterized by Robert Brady as the promotion of "unit thinking." In the words of one trade association president, the NICB was responsible for "bringing about uniformity of thought and action among employers, woefully lacking in the past. We are thinking together."[32]

The consistency of purpose, the "uniformity of thought and action," implicit in notions of "cooperation" and "self-regulation" can be seen in an examination of the statements of business leaders during this era. Edwin Parker, for instance, declared that "the one certain way in which business can escape the burden of government control and regulation is by self-regulation." This principle of self-regulation was, according to Parker, bringing the nation into "The New Era of Business," which he described as "the era of fair play, of better understanding, not alone between business and the public, but among the various branches of an industry." To this end, Parker envisioned the creation of a trade relations committee—employing a vertical structuring of manufacturers, wholesalers, and retailers of each industry— to develop machinery of "self-government" in order to prevent trade "abuses" from becoming trade "customs." Such a plan would, Parker maintained, "promote rather than restrict competition," and he went on to suggest a procedure for implementation that was similar in format to the Trade Practice Conferences held under the auspices of the Federal Trade Commission.[33] Similar positions were expressed in a resolution by the U.S. Chamber of Commerce,[34] by Chamber president Lewis E. Pierson,[35] and by former Chamber president Julius H. Barnes.[36]

It is quite clear from Parker's remarks that he was looking beyond a system of "self-government" that existed only on a plane of ethical expression, and that he contemplated a condition under which such standards could be *enforced* against members of the industry who violated them. Such "self-government" was praised by a noted trade association attorney in these terms: "Business self-government, simply because it is self-government and not government imposed from an outside authority, is creating standards of conduct and measures of enforcement that are far more strict than any that have ever before been prescribed by governmental authorities or by the courts."[37] The same sentiments were expressed by trade association executive Hugh P. Baker,[38] U.S. Chamber of Commerce president John W. O'Leary,[39] and Maryland governor Albert C. Ritchie—a man who had not only served as legal advisor to Bernard Baruch and counsel to the WIB but was later given serious consideration as an alternative to Franklin D. Roosevelt for the 1932 Democratic presidential nomination.[40]

The success of the "cooperation" movement in helping to rationalize competitive practices was attested to by Lewis Pierson, who observed that during the preceding quarter-century American business had abandoned "the out-worn notions of unrestricted competition."[41] The "cooperation" that business hoped for was synonymous with the development of attitudes of respect for the positions of one's competitors. Many business leaders sought to persuade—or compel, if need be—businessmen to abandon the aggressive, risk-taking, market-challenging practices that threatened other established firms. This was a "conservative," status quo-defending endeavor in the purest sense of the term. In order to secure each firm from having to be continuously responsive to competitive threats, all were being asked to refocus upon the *industry*, rather than upon their individual *firms*, as the object of their self-interest. By stabilizing prices and trade practices, and by lowering the intensity of competition, business leaders hoped to create an environment in which no firm needed to fear substantial loss of business as a result of its inability to meet the test of a more rigorous, revenue-lessening competition.

Reflecting their desires for an effective system of price stabilization, business leaders identified "overproduction" as a cause of the inconstant competitive conditions within various industries. In the eyes of one observer, "[o]verproduction . . . has its origin in the rate of industrial expansion," a condition that was accelerated not only by increased "use of power machinery and technological improvements" but by the demands of World War I. Such productive machinery, he went on, "is being operated without brakes or governor."[42] John E. Bassill, vice-president of Tubize Chatillon Corporation, found just such a mechanism of control in the Federal Reserve Board, which, he noted, can help to stabilize production—and, thus, prices—by restricting credit during periods of economic growth.[43] Such monetary policies, which continue to play a central role in government economic planning, afford another example of the recurring conflict between institutional interests in stabilizing environments in furtherance of their ends, and individual and societal interests in fostering the processes of "creative disequilibrium." Whether appealing to a spirit of "cooperative" competition or more formal government programs, most of the business community was, during the time period under consideration here, preoccupied with efforts to restrain a vibrant economy.

It must be emphasized that the sentiment underlying the business campaigns against competition was more attuned to trying to stabilize competitive conditions (for example, eliminating sharp fluctuations in production and prices) than in trying to establish monopolistic or oligopolistic practices. Efforts to achieve such stability included pooling arrangements, mergers, associational activities, and, particularly in the steel industry's use of the infamous "Gary dinners," informal "price understandings."[44] That such voluntary arrangements were almost entirely unenforceable—and, in some instances, raised the specter of antitrust prosecution—did not diminish the efforts of industry leaders to find some effective means of generating more stable competitive environments.

Writers of the 1920s confirmed that the American business community was seeking, through expanded trade association activity, an effective method of stabilizing pricing, production, and sales practices within the various industries. The *New York Times* observed that "an entirely new sort of government is being established in the United States," consisting of

> the sum of a large number of separate and unrelated agreements between self-governing economic groups to regulate their own concerns, to make rules for their own members, and even to punish those who violate them. It will be a government of voluntary cooperation, of self-determination along natural economic lines. . . . It is a pooling of the accumulated knowledge of the best way to do things in every field of industry and the formulation of that knowledge into a definite code backed by the sanction of all the interested parties. But this code is not usually compulsory, nor is obedience to it imposed under penalty of fine and imprisonment. On the contrary, it is a voluntary consensus of opinion followed by mutual agreement. Those instances in which it is compulsory are cases in which the original voluntary agreement has subsequently been written into the statutes of the several states.[45]

Much the same conclusion was reached in a 1926 article in the *Outlook,* which noted that "American business . . . is making progress toward capacity for self-government" and is recognizing the principle of operating businesses according to the "common-sense rules of restraint, fair play, and consideration for the rights of others." The growth of the institution of "codes of ethics" by trade organizations was looked upon as "proof . . . that American business would like to be self-governing in some better sense than that of every man for himself."[46] One trade association official declared that "business has had to recognize the weakness of the individualistic theory and adopt a policy of cooperation,"[47] while Haley Fiske, president of the Metropolitan Life Insurance Company, added his praise for trade association activity that had helped "to enable members, especially the weaker ones, to stay in business in what is characterized as 'a deplorable competitive situation.'"[48]

THE CODES OF ETHICS

The trade association "codes of ethics" were generally considered, within the business community, important instruments for efforts to stabilize competitive relationships. Business attitudes toward these codes were reflected in the NICB's observation that "the defects of the competitive system . . . are grounded in the inherent nature of competitive organization and control," which, it went on, "arise from uncoordinated pursuit of competitive advantage." Pointing to the "economic waste and industrial instability" that had carried "competitive struggle to destructive lengths," the board's study concluded that the trade associations had provided more effective machinery for the formulation and enforcement of trade principles, with the "somewhat elastic standards . . . giving place to more rigid codes."[49] The content of these codes expressed, quite well, the anticompetitive attitudes that had developed within the business community as a response to vigorous economic behavior and the threat of change.

The majority of trade associations during the 1920s enunciated a "code of ethics" or "code of fair competition" as an expression of the minimal standards of competitive conduct desired by the firms in a particular trade or industry. Although a few of these codes attempted to establish enforcement machinery, most involved a combination of abstract statements of principles and condemnation of specific trade practices. The language of the codes was couched not so much in the legal rhetoric of penalties, fines, and injunctions as in the language of moral and ethical persuasion. The appeal was to one's conscience, sense of ethics, or desire for approval and acceptance by one's competitive peers. The "unfair," the "questionable," and the "unethical" were to be eschewed in favor of the "fair," the "wholesome," and the "responsible." While such codes lacked any ultimate sanctions for enforcement, it would be a mistake to assume that they were intended, within the industries themselves, only as boilerplate. They served to reinforce within the minds of businessmen the new industry-oriented premise inherent in "cooperative competition." The codes echoed the spirit of "cooperation" and were designed to promote those conditions that would serve to stabilize businesses, protecting them from the vicissitudes of change to which, increasingly, firms were unwilling to have to respond.

The business world had long considered many types of competitive practices to be "unfair." Albeit some of these practices involved outright fraud and dishonesty (such as misbranding of merchandise or misrepresentation of product quality or package contents), it is evident that most of the practices complained of by businesses did not involve cheating *customers,* but were those that intensified the level of competition within an industry. Of greatest concern were the more aggressive practices through which some members of the industry were able to attract more business to themselves (and thus away from other members) by offering inducements to customers. Although one may rightly condemn as "dishonest" those practices in which a customer receives less than what he bargained for, the same charge cannot be leveled against sales practices that are attacked for their tendency to shift buyer preferences by reducing prices. In fact, the very effectiveness of the trade practices complained of were brought about and sustained by the ability of the firms employing them to satisfy customer demands on terms better than those of their competitors. The essential factor to keep in mind regarding a study of business code making is the overriding concern of businesses to protect *themselves*—not the *customer*—from the effects of aggressive competitive practices. The expression of concern for the customer was largely window dressing to gather public support and "legitimacy" for what was little more than a campaign to ease the burdens of free competition from the shoulders of firms at a competitive disadvantage.

Most association codes began with broadly worded declarations on behalf of a more polite and gentlemanly form of competitive behavior. Such language sought to incorporate the "golden rule" into business dealings or advocated a policy of "live and let live" among competitors. One code seemed to embrace every positive human emotion:

> Always to deal with each other in a true spirit of justice, amity, courtesy and tolerance, and in pursuance of the elementary conception of right and honorable business conduct which should and must prevail in a society built upon the sure foundation of a democracy, organized in harmony with the most enlightened civilization in history, and finally directed to preserve individual opportunity and free and fair competition in the enhancement of the general welfare.[50]

Others were less pretentious in asking their members not to "discredit or injure the industry,"[51] or "unjustly discredit a competitor's product."[52] They urged, instead, that they "practice clean, honorable competition"[53] and "respect the rights of competitors."[54] Other abstract propositions of competitive civility can also be found in the codes.[55]

The reactions of members of the business community to vigorous and effective methods of competition can be gleaned from the specific language within various codes. By looking to the precise trade practices complained of, as well as to the conditions being put forth as exemplary of a more "cooperative" spirit, one can better understand the direction being taken in business thinking. The crucial analytical point to be considered in examining the association codes is to determine both the intent and the effect of the specific practices condemned therein. Broad statements seeking to encourage greater "cooperation" might be designed only to promote personal, harmonious relationships among the members of an industry—without any motive to restrict competitive practices—or might be concrete evidence of cartelizing sentiments among businessmen. Only by looking to the particular prohibitions can an accurate judgment be made. In so doing, it can be seen that while a certain camaraderie was desired, such "fellowship" was looked to as a means of satisfying objectives more *economic* than *social* in nature.

Just what the "recalcitrant minority" was doing that so displeased the other members of an industry might be better understood by focusing upon one practice regarded by many as "unethical": that of wholesalers doing "direct selling" to consumers. The members of the Eastern States Retail Lumber Dealers' Association were desirous of curbing this practice and, in order to bring economic pressure to bear upon the wholesalers, entered into an agreement to report to the association the names of any offending wholesalers. Such names were then circulated, on a "blacklist," to members of the association. While wholesalers did not wish to offend their retail customers, a few were nevertheless willing to risk exposure in order to increase their sales. In doing so, they earned for themselves a place on the "blacklist," not because of any failings of character ordinarily associated with "unethical" behavior, but only because of a failure to respect the expectations of their competitors. The retailers, of course, complained that the wholesalers enjoyed a cost advantage that permitted them to offer lower prices to the consumers and that this made the practice "unfair." But whatever the practice complained of—whether the "direct selling" here or the growth of "chain stores" denounced by the independent retailers, or the "price cutting" almost universally condemned by association codes—each reflected a more efficient method of doing business that, one way or another, would result in lower prices. When the U.S. Supreme Court held this "blacklisting" system to be an unreasonable restraint of trade under the Sherman Act,[56] it only added to the frustrations of companies trying to control the aggressive appetites of their competitors.

PRICING POLICIES UNDER THE CODES

Because prices were of central concern to business interests, a great deal of attention was paid by trade association codes to those practices that had a tendency to *lower* prices or encourage price *instability*. Since competition is presumed to be of social value and ordinarily involves two or more sellers trying to persuade customers to do business with them by the use of such inducements as lower prices, it is difficult to see who, other than an unsuccessful competitor, is injured by low prices. Nevertheless, trade associations have helped to create an all-too-common impression of "price wars," "price cutting," and "cutthroat competition" as being inimical to the general welfare and symptomatic of demoralized business conditions.

Just as trade associations attacked *low* prices for products because of their tendency to reduce industry revenues, some also assailed *high* prices paid to suppliers of raw materials for their tendency to increase production costs within the industry. This was demonstrated in a number of codes, such as that of the International Association of Milk Dealers, which prohibited the bidding up of raw milk prices paid to suppliers by "[i]nvading the competitor's territory . . . and seeking to withdraw a competitor's supply by paying or offering to pay patrons heretofore delivering to such competitor a higher price than he currently pays or offers to other producers," or obtaining supplies of milk through offering "special inducements."[57] Other trade associations attacked bidding "extravagantly on raw material that has been sold, in order to make trouble for a competitor," as well as paying too high a price for equipment taken in as trade-ins.[58]

Typical of the provisions contained in a number of other codes are those in the code of the American Bottlers of Carbonated Beverages. It contained a pledge by its members to charge a fair and reasonable price for their products, adding: "My desire shall not be to undersell my fellow bottlers, but to contend with them for first place in the quality of my products and the service I render my patrons."[59] Further expression of the fear of lowered prices was found in the code of a leading textile trade association: "The manufacturer should scrupulously avoid price cutting without regard to costs or to the lowering of profits in the industry to dangerous levels." It noted, "Legitimate competition is the life of the industry, but unscrupulous competition is injurious to yourself, to your competitor, and to your industry."[60] Yet another association praised "intelligent cooperation" as preferable to "[i]gnorant, irresponsible and profitless competition," and then offered the observation,

Nothing so shakes the confidence of the Public as the knowledge that only through haggling and bargaining can it be sure of obtaining the lowest and presumably fairest rates; nothing is so unfair to the unsuspicious and trusting customer; nothing is so damning to the effort to establish confidence and goodwill and to carry on our business legitimately and honestly on a plane of fair dealing with equal advantage to all.[61]

Raising the specter of "predatory price cutting," a number of association codes moved to condemn "below cost" selling practices. Some codes declared as unethical the "[s]elling or offering to sell below cost or at less than a fair profit, to force a competitor out of a field."[62] Another provided that "none of the products of this industry should be sold, knowingly, below a price which would return to the manufacturer the cost of production plus a fair percentage of profit."[63] Few trade associations would have taken exception with one retail group that spoke of a "fair profit based on the cost of doing business, plus a fair return on his investment" as being "the right of every merchant." Nor would many have quarreled with the assertion that it was unethical "[t]o sell or offer to sell under a competitor's price in order to beat him out of a sale or force him out of business."[64]

The "Declaration of Principles" of the National Retail Coal Merchants Association went further and provided a more specific statement of what it considered fair pricing. It began with the assertion that the retail coal merchant *is entitled to a fair return on his investment* of capital and service. We believe in open competition unrestricted by municipal or Government regulations. Retail prices must be based upon cost plus fair profit. We therefore favor individual determination of prices on the basis of mine price plus transportation charges plus cost of retailing plus a fair return on investment of capital and service, no more and no less.[65]

In a more emotional statement concerning pricing policies, the National Association of Retail Grocers, which had gone on record opposing "factory stores" as "un-American," supported the principle of the "minimum resale price" or other methods of "standard price control" in order to protect all concerned from the actions of the "reckless price-cutter" who engages in "trade piracy."[66] A general condemnation of selling below cost was contained in a number of other codes.[67]

"Selling below cost" had a number of possible interpretations. The most implausible was that a business would undertake the production and sale of goods at a price that did not cover both *fixed* and *variable* costs. Except as a measure for accomplishing such purely short-term purposes as ridding itself of surplus inventories, or the quite limited "loss-leader" retailing practice of reducing prices sharply on one item in order to induce patrons to shop with them, it is rather apparent that no business would have adopted a long-range policy based on intentionally incurring losses. If a firm had inadvertently offered its goods at below-cost prices, it would not have taken long for that business to correct its error.[68] In fact, if a business had been unable to cover its variable costs, it would have (unless one adheres to the theory of "predatory price-cutting") shut down production until such time as the market price for such goods increased to some point above the level of its variable costs. Though a firm might have continued to produce and sell its goods at a price that covered *variable* costs but not its already incurred *fixed* costs, no additional production would have taken place if the firm had not anticipated recovering at least its variable costs.

Thus, little purpose would have been served by code provisions seeking to ban the selling of products at prices beneath the variable costs of the seller, prices that would reduce profits to the firm. The motivation to maximize profits would limit such selling. But trade associations were not simply seeking to condemn such an uneconomic practice as subvariable cost pricing. Selling "below cost" was understood to mean, as a number of codes spelled out, the selling of goods and services at prices that did not cover variable costs plus a properly allocated share of both fixed costs and "fair rate of return" on investment.

The fear of the so-called predatory price cutter has been one of the most popular criticisms of business behavior and continues to find expression in the study of competition and monopoly. This theory is premised on the belief that a firm would find it advantageous to intentionally sell its products at a price that would not return its costs in order to force prices down and, ultimately, drive its competitors out of business. The predator is supposedly able to accomplish its purposes by isolating a single market for the price cutting, funding its endeavors through a "war chest" created, in part, from the monopoly profits realized elsewhere by such methods. After having eliminated its competition, so the theory continues, the predator would be in a position to raise its prices, this time to a level that would allow it to enjoy monopoly profits in that market.

The fear of predatory pricing rests upon questionable grounds. In the first place, what some might regard as predatory behavior can bear a remarkable resemblance to a highly energized competition.[69] Secondly, there are definitional problems as to what would constitute predatory pricing. Phillip Areeda and Donald Turner have offered a definition that has provided a focal point for the debate: "A price at or above reasonably anticipated average variable cost" should not be regarded as predatory.[70] While there have doubtless been instances in which the practice, so defined, has been engaged in, the economic disadvantages to the *predator* in following such a course of action would seem to minimize any public policy concerns for such behavior. If a firm wants to eliminate its competition, it is less costly to buy out other firms than to try to drive them out of business through predatory tactics. After all, any firm engaging in such practices will have to incur greater losses than the intended victim, and since the firm practicing predation presumably enjoys the larger market share, its losses will be significantly greater than those of the victim. Further, there is too much risk associated with the employment of such methods. For instance, one cannot be certain that the intended "victim" will play the game: it might shut down until the predator ceases its tactics, thus incurring a temporary loss of business, but without suffering the destructive losses contemplated by the predator. The "victim," after all, has a significant investment in *its* enterprise, and cannot be expected to passively allow itself to be driven out of business without making some rational response. But even if the victim is driven out of business, its assets will likely be sold to other firms or be taken over by the victim's creditors, leaving the predator with yet another competitor to attempt to drive out of business. And if the predator overcomes all of these obstacles and actually begins to enjoy monopoly profits, its very success will invite new competitors into the market.[71] It is conceivable, of course, that any particular firm might engage in predatory tactics by mistake (e.g., by a miscalculation of its costs, or a lack of awareness of other alternatives), but as a conscious strategy for eliminating a competitor in order to maximize the profits of the would-be predator, the practice would not represent an economically rational strategy.[72]

The only conceivable effect, if any, of a code provision attempting to outlaw "predatory price cutting" or "selling below cost to force a competitor out of business" would be to maintain prices at a higher level than would otherwise have prevailed under aggressive competition. The pricing policies of a firm are, after all, determined on the basis of what serves to maximize its profits, *not* what can be done to injure the business of a competitor. If the lowering of a price will increase the sales volume, reduce unit costs, and increase the profits of the firm, then the decision will likely be made to lower the price. The attack on "predatory price cutting," then, is not directed against the *motives* of the lower-priced firm but toward the *effects* that the profit-seeking pricing policies of one firm have upon its competitors. The businessmen who value the goodwill of their competitors more than likely interpret the admonitions against "below cost" and "predatory" pricing as warnings to keep up prices.

The attempt by some producers to obtain business — after having initially made higher bids—by undercutting the lower bids of their competitors was another common source of complaint that found its way into many association codes. The basic contention was that the firm submitting the low bid had "won" the right to the order and ought not be subject to any further competition from its rivals. The only circumstances under which such an occurrence could arise, of course, would be between the time the bids were submitted and the offer had been accepted by the person inviting the bids. Once accepted, a binding contract would come into existence, which would adequately protect the position of the firm whose bid had been accepted. Under such conditions, there would be a disincentive for the party inviting the bids to negotiate with the successful bidder's competitors for a lower price. Thus, code provisions against seeking to undercut the bid of a competitor were aimed *not* at the practice of inducing a buyer to breach its contract with a competitor (for which, under the common law, both the buyer and the firm inducing the breach would be liable in damages), but at a business seeking to undercut a rival's *offer* that had not yet ripened into a contract. Once a firm had submitted its own bid, in other words, and that offer had not been accepted by the firm inviting the bids, that firm should not then lower its bid in order to meet or undercut the offer of a competitor. Such an attitude was consistent with the belief popular among many businessmen that the process of "bargaining" was demeaning, an attitude that also found expression in the "open-pricing" systems.

Characteristic of code provisions dealing with this situation was that of the Northwestern Lumbermen's Association, which stated: "The seller who offers a lower price for equal quality and quantity should get the order. It should not be given to his competitor who reduces his bid to meet competition or to undersell a competitor."[73] One association had a provision enjoining the quoting of "ridiculously low prices on business that has been placed"; another prohibited quoting "fictitiously high prices" at the start of a transaction and later lowering them; yet another warned its members: "[D]o not oversell your own merchandise," adding that "It is unethical to continue a solicitation after an order has been placed, or to influence a sale by price reduction or other inducements."[74]

Another form of price competition that consistently drew the wrath of a sizeable portion of the business community was the granting of rebates and discounts to customers. Because the effect of rebates and discounts was to lower the effective price to the buyer, the essence of business objections to such practices was the same as that attending other forms of price reduction. The fundamental concern was well expressed by Charles Gibson, chairman of the board of Gibson-Snow, Inc., who observed that "any dealer who is constantly getting an added discount . . . is the more strongly tempted to cut the price of his goods."[75]

One trade association code pledged itself against "the giving of free goods, secret rebates and those things which have a tendency to cheapen my products, as well as to demoralize the industry I represent."[76] Still another association prohibited, in its code, "the allowance of secret discounts or rebates," as well as "[g]iving away goods or samples other than is customary in such quantities such as to hamper and embarrass competitors or to have virtually the effect of rebates."[77] Other codes attacked "all methods of rebating," "deduction of excessive discounts," "unjust returns of merchandise," and "all other sharp practices."[78]

The question of rebates and discounts became entangled in another issue, that of price discrimination. The existence of price discrimination was but a reflection of the fact that different buyers are likely to have different intensities of demand. Under such circumstances, a profit-maximizing seller would have an incentive to offer his product to different buyers at different prices. Stated another way, the firm that offered a lower price to one buyer than to another did so not to inflict injury upon or to indulge a bias against the buyer paying the higher price, but for the purpose of concluding transactions with buyers of different demand preferences and different bargaining positions. Although the practice of price discrimination tended to evoke strong emotional reactions, nonuniformity in pricing is but the response of a seller seeking to maximize his profits in a market of nonuniform buyers.[79] The question has been asked:

Has it not been a common method of transacting business for generations to strike an independent bargain in each negotiation? And if the exploitation of some buyers, less crafty than others, occurs, is the seller responsible for their weaknesses? How, under a regime of private property and free exchange, impute moral delinquency to those who take full advantage of the weak bargaining power of other parties voluntarily dealing with them, or of their own superior strength in the market?[80]

Price discrimination had been strongly opposed by many business interests desirous of eliminating cost differentials among competitors. Such differentials provided some firms with a comparative advantage over others in their pricing policies, a fact no more evident than in retailing, where the independent retailers found themselves up against the more efficient and ever-increasing chain stores who had been the principal beneficiaries of price discrimination. While Section 2 of the Clayton Act[81] addressed itself to the question of price discrimination, the courts had—up until the *Van Camp*[82] case in 1929—given a narrow interpretation to the section, holding that price discrimination was unlawful only if it tended to lessen competition between the *seller* and *its competitors,* not between the *buyer* and the *buyer's competitors.*[83] Even though the Supreme Court broadened the scope of Section 2 in the *Van Camp* case, business support for stronger legislation dealing with price discrimination was to continue, culminating in the enactment, in 1936, of the Robinson-Patman Act.

Another selling practice that found almost universal condemnation in the codes was what was referred to as "commercial bribery." Generally, this involved a seller offering a gift, commission, or other form of remuneration to the agent of a buyer in order to induce that agent to place an order with the seller. The gist of the "offense" has been stated as follows:

> Whenever there is inducement to an employee to act contrary to the interests of his employer, or to an agent to act contrary to the interests of his principal, the transaction savors of corruption. And the trader who seeks thus to promote his sales is engaged in an unfair method of competition.[84]

Concern over this practice was expressed by Williams Haynes, president of the Drug and Chemical Markets in New York City and long an opponent of "commercial bribery." He defined the offense as "[t]he secret giving of commissions, money and other things of value to employees of customers for the purpose of influencing their buying powers." Haynes had great praise for a bill, then in Congress, that would have provided fines or imprisonment for acts of "commercial bribery," as well as immunity from prosecution to the first member of the "conspiracy of silence" who would, under oath, report this "evil" to a federal district attorney. That reaction against such so-called bribery was motivated by the price-reducing tendencies of such practices can be seen in Haynes's particularization of offenses, which included not only the "cash bribe" but also "special rebates, double invoices, coupons redeemable in goods, elaborate presents, extra commissions for quantity orders or quantity sales." As a contrast to such "evils," Haynes was attracted to the "fixed price" in retailing, a method that had led to the abolition of "haggling barter" and, Haynes might have added, helped to foster the practice of "administered pricing" that has served to make economic transactions less subject to the individual influences of bargaining and negotiation.[85]

"Commercial bribery" was widely attacked by business and industry leaders. A number of codes had prohibitions against "graft," "bribes," "bonuses," or "commissions" to persons in the employ of a buyer,[86] while some codes condemned "long-term credits" and "excessive entertaining" as forms of "commercial bribery."[87] Although, on the surface, the trade associations addressing such practices might be held up for praise for seeking to protect the integrity of the fiduciary relationship existing between a customer and his purchasing agent, it is highly unlikely that such a consideration was the motive behind those code provisions. After all, the customer would ordinarily be protected by the dealings of his agent in securing "commissions" for his placing of business because, under common law duties relating to principal and agent relationships, the agent, as a fiduciary, was required to account to the principal for any benefits he received from a third person with whom he was dealing for his principal. On the other hand, such payments to purchasing agents may not, in fact, have constituted a violation of a principal-agent relationship. The principal may, for example, have had an understanding with his agent that the latter could retain such bonuses as a form of extra compensation; or such payments might, in fact, have been turned over to the principal by the agent. In such cases, the only real objection that a seller's competitors could have had to the practice would be that, like a rebate, it tended to lower the effective price of the product or service to the buyer.

ASSESSING THE TRADE ASSOCIATIONS

In reviewing the many trade association codes of ethics, one is impressed by the degree of specificity and certainty with which offenses were defined. Not content with the expression of glittering bromides, business associations wanted their codes to serve as bills of particulars for their industries so as to leave no question in the mind of a competitor what behavior was enjoined. The anticompetitive nature of such prohibitions is rather evident: the establishment of and adherence to trade standards, including pricing and sales practices of the sort discussed herein, have a tendency to *standardize* the conditions under which competition will take place. By eliminating certain practices from the scope of permissible activity, variations in competitive methods are reduced. This, in turn, introduces a greater degree of predictability and stability in trade relations. Under conditions of free and unrestrained competition, there will be a wide range of trade practices and pricing policies to which the firms in an industry must be prepared to respond in order to successfully compete. Firms will have an incentive to be innovative and inventive, conscious both of reducing costs and expanding markets. Because all firms would be subject to such conditions, the intensity of competition among them would be very great, with the more aggressive members of the industry engaged in practices that the others might not have to emulate, but would have to take into account and respond to in formulating their own policies.

It must be remembered that the period here under study was, as Taeusch and others have noted, characterized by significant changes in the structure and content of various industries as well as the organizational forms and methods of doing business. Many business leaders sought to respond to the threats posed by such changes by reducing the vigor with which they were exhibited in competitive practices. By standardizing trade practices, the innovative and aggressive firms would lose their comparative advantages over the firms less willing or able to maintain the more energized pace. Competition would thus become less threatening, reducing the responses firms would have to make to their more aggressive competitors.

The established firms would, quite understandably, find such competitive restrictions particularly beneficial, for a newer firm would, in order to attract customers away from the older firms, have to offer significant inducements. This is a problem always faced by a newcomer. The existing firms enjoy an immense advantage by virtue of their goodwill and established positions, a situation that can be overcome only by recourse to the most effective competitive methods. But if competitive methods become fairly standardized, and the newer firm is required to adhere to the same patterns as the established firm, the newcomer will find itself at an even greater disadvantage: it will have been deprived of the means of offering the necessary inducements to attract customers away from the established firms. Add to this the disadvantage of being labeled an "unethical" businessman if one should have the temerity to attempt such an assault on the industry's "establishment," and one can readily see the attraction existing firms had to efforts to standardize trade practices. One prominent industrialist, Owen D. Young, chairman of the board of both General Electric and the Radio Corporation of America, expressed his attraction for such standardization:

I am very hopeful that as time goes on we will become standardized, not only as to machinery, but that we may also become standardized in regard to conduct to the point that we will have sufficient confidence in ourselves so that we will know that we do not and dare not violate the standards of the group.[88]

Rexford Tugwell, an economist who was later to become one of the principal architects of the New Deal, characterized the role of trade associations as being, in part, to coordinate and regularize conditions within various industries. That function was accomplished, to some extent, by the exchange of trade information, which had the effect of spreading "throughout industry very quickly knowledge of the latest processes and to bring each unit or business in the trade more rapidly up to the standard of the best." In his view, the overall effect of the association movement was "to facilitate voluntary coordinations," an influence with a "general effect on the regularization of the necessary mutual adjustment between supply and demand."[89]

THE FAILURE OF VOLUNTARY RESTRAINTS

The business community has had within it those who have been quite resourceful in attempting to devise workable systems for modifying the intensity of competition in their respective industries. Such attempts, when voluntarily undertaken, have generally proved ineffective.[90] The history of the trade association codes of ethics reveals that, in spite of the good intentions that accompanied their establishment, these efforts to short-circuit the competitive processes were also doomed to failure. As the pioneer student of business codes, Edgar Heermance, has observed:

> The difficulties in the way of a trade agreement come both from the companies that are outside the combination and from those that are in. To control production, it is necessary to hold in line substantially all the producing units. . . . There seems to be something in the nature of an agreement which tempts the weak-kneed competitor to break it, in order to reap an immediate advantage.[91]

The conflict existing between the *individual* interests of the firms in an industry, and the *collective* interests of the industry itself (as represented in the trade associations) is explained by economist Mancur Olson's analysis of collective action.[92] Under conditions of perfect competition (in which prices are uniform and no single firm can, by altering its production, significantly influence the price level), each firm will have a profit-maximizing incentive to increase its production and sales. As each firm is operating under the same incentives, the combined effect will be a lowering of prices. Assuming an inelastic demand curve for the industry, its total revenues will decline. In spite of such declines in prices and industry revenues—in fact, even if each firm has advance knowledge of such consequences—each will have an incentive to increase its production until such time as the price level falls below the costs of production. As long as there is a net gain to any firm in putting an additional unit on the market, it will do so regardless of the effect on the industry as a whole. Olson thus summarizes the point: "[W]hile all firms have a common interest in a higher price, they have antagonistic interests where output is concerned."[93] He continues: "[S]ince the larger the group, the smaller the share of the total benefit going to any individual, the less likelihood [there is] that any single individual will gain enough from getting the collective good to bear the burden of providing even a small amount of it."[94] Relating Olson's analysis to the inquiry before us, "the fact that profit-maximizing firms in a perfectly competitive industry can act contrary to their interests as a group"[95] helps explain the failure of voluntary efforts to restrain the pursuit of individual self-interest.

The inherent conflict existing between individual and collective interests was elaborated upon by Olson:

> A group of profit-maximizing firms can act to reduce their aggregate profits because in perfect competition each firm is, by definition, so small that it can ignore the effect of its output on price. Each firm finds it to its advantage to increase output to the point where marginal cost equals price and to ignore the effects of its extra output on the position of the industry. It is true that the net result is that all firms are worse off, but this does not mean that every firm has not maximized its profits.

Further,

> [I]t is now generally understood that if the firms in an industry are maximizing profits, the profits for the industry as a whole will be less than they might otherwise be. . . . [T]his is true because, though all the firms have a common interest in a higher price for the industry's product, it is in the interest of each firm that the other firms pay the cost—in terms of the necessary reduction in output—needed to obtain a higher price.[96]

Other factors—previously considered in the discussion on so-called predatory pricing—contributed to the failure of voluntary attempts to restrain competitive activity. First, such agreements were almost never entered into by all members of a given industry. The proverbial "10 percent" who would not agree with the policies of the rest of the industry would continue to employ aggressive competitive methods that, to the degree they were successful, would draw customers away from the firms holding out for higher prices. Second, even if all firms in the industry had adhered to an agreement moderating trade practices, to the degree such an arrangement succeeded in keeping prices above a competitive level new entrepreneurs would see the profitability of entering that industry and selling at a lower price.

The firms that agreed, in principle, not to engage in certain trade practices undoubtedly did so in the hope that, by their assent to a "code of ethics," their competitors would be less inclined to engage in such practices. But whether one's competitors abided by the agreed-upon standards or not, each firm would find it to its benefit to continue to increase its production and sales so long as the market price exceeded its costs of production. Even assuming the best possible case for the anticipated consequences, namely, that all firms would be better off if each would adhere to price-maintaining code provisions, the fact that each individual firm would be better off violating the code made such efforts unworkable. In the end, these voluntary restraints failed because, being voluntary, there was no way to compel firms to abandon the pursuit of their self-interest.

The policy implications in all of this have been spelled out by Olson. He concludes that "unless the number of individuals in a group is quite small, or unless there is coercion or some other special device to make individuals act in their common interest, *rational, self-interested individuals will not act to achieve their common or group interests.*" While, as Olson states, all firms have an interest in the *benefits* arising from collective action, it will always be to the interest of each firm to have others pay the *cost* (e.g., by reducing production in order to promote higher prices). Olson summarizes the point: "The larger a group is, the farther it will fall short of obtaining an optimal supply of any collective good, and the less likely that it will act to obtain even a minimal amount of such a good. In short, the larger the group, the less it will further its common interests."[97]

Consistent with Olson's analysis, voluntary efforts to restrain the pursuit of firm self-interest in favor of securing industry objectives met with failure. This failure led many business leaders and trade associations—particularly those in industries that had experienced relatively low profit levels in the 1920s—to support political solutions to what was considered the problem of "profitless prosperity." Employing a study by Ralph C. Epstein that demonstrated the relative profit levels of different industries, Robert Himmelberg has concluded that business leaders in such lower-profit industries were the strongest advocates not only of revision of the antitrust laws but of "legalized cartelism" following the onset of the Great Depression.[98] They were not, however, the only members of the business community to seek answers to their problems in legislative halls.

While some 1920s contemporaries maintained that the principal motivation for "self-government" came from a desire by business to avoid government regulation,[99] Olson's appraisal offers a more realistic explanation. Businessmen saw in a condition of free and unrestrained competition a threat to stable prices, the preservation of existing markets, and the maintenance of the value of their assets. Free competition was viewed as an invitation to the forces of change, a condition inconsistent with business desires for stability and permanency. Group interests suffered as individual firm interests were being maximized, all to the ultimate benefit of customers who enjoyed lower prices. Many business leaders began to understand that the collectivizing demands of the new institutional order required a partnership with the political state. The coercive machinery of government not only helped assure adherence to group schemes to subvert market processes and render competition less effective, but provided the mucilage to hold otherwise autonomous business units in line.

3

Political Alternatives

> If any portion or class of society is sheltered from the action of the environment in any essential respect, that portion of the community, or that class, will adapt its views and its scheme of life more tardily to the altered general situation; it will in so far tend to retard the process of social transformation.
>
> —Thorstein Veblen

Trade association experiences with codes of ethics suggest the presence of market influences that tend to neutralize voluntary efforts to restrain competition. As long as there are no legally enforceable restrictions on entry or trade and pricing practices, the inherent antagonisms between *individual* and *group* interests will render industry-inspired restraints ineffective. As long as compliance was truly voluntary, with individual firms free from the compelling influences of fines, injunctions, damage actions, or jail sentences, the costs of noncompliance were minimal and would be incurred whenever the anticipated benefits of doing so were greater than the costs associated with compliance.

This lack of enforcement machinery in association codes caused many business leaders to direct their attentions toward developing more effective methods of securing compliance with business standards desired by the more influential members within the various industries. The business community had discovered that firms would not sacrifice their individual interests to group interests unless there was coercion to make them do so. Unable to accomplish the trade-practice desideratum through codes resting upon voluntary compliance, a number of business leaders and trade associations considered compulsory measures. The journalist John T. Flynn noted the inherent weaknesses in voluntary systems of "self-rule" and pointed to the seemingly inevitable attraction of political means for realizing competitive stabilization:

> They [trade associations] are harassed by the unwillingness of those rebellious and adventurous spirits who refuse to accept their rule. They are forever running

77

into the disturbing fact that while a trade may, after a fashion, "rule itself," it
cannot rule some other trade which is in collision with it. . . . It is this very
weakness which sends trade associations to Congress and the legislatures every year with appeals to the government to join them in some program of
regulation. But the practice of regulating others is habit forming. It is a mania.
. . . As soon as men find themselves in a game they begin to invent rules for that
game, and the more extensive and complicated the rules become. At first they
depend upon a certain spiritual pressure operating through the law of honor to
support the rules. But very soon they seek more effective means of getting the
rules obeyed. This involves a kind of force.[1]

A "self-regulation" that was couched in the voluntary-sounding par-
lance of "cooperation" soon gave way to proposals that envisioned more
formal and pragmatic methods for compliance. Business attitudes toward
"self-regulation" underwent a transition from favoring purely voluntary efforts to restrain market practices to favoring those that were involuntary in
nature. The phrase ultimately came to encompass the notion of trade associations establishing business standards that would be subject to legal enforcement by such associations employing the power of the government.
Thus, by the late 1920s, many business leaders would have agreed with Bernard Baruch that the cooperative experiences of the World War I years "should
be stimulated and encouraged by a Government agency, which at the same
time would be clothed with the power and charged with the responsibility of
standing watch against and preventing abuses."[2]

A vehicle used to develop support for the emerging doctrine of industrial "self-regulation" was the artificial polarization of the alternatives of
"government control" and "self-regulation." To an impartial observer, it
might appear that the only question had to do with whether business decision-making was to be regulated by the state or by the consensus of the
members of a given industry. The alternative of individual firms making their
own decisions, in response to their individual assessments of market conditions, was never afforded; quite the contrary, such a state of affairs was
characterized as the very "evil" to be exorcised. This evaluation of business
attitudes was shared by John T. Flynn, who, in discussing the meaning of the
concept "let business rule itself," observed:

This is one of those fair-sounding but ambitious phrases which may mean very
much or very little. It may be innocent enough provided we can agree on its
intent. But when we say business should be left to rule itself we must be quite
certain what we mean by business. . . . If this little war-cry is devised for no
deadlier purpose than to demand self-rule for the individual factory or store,
then we need not quarrel with it, for it means nothing. One thing is certain: no
one intends to permit the individual business man to rule himself as independently as in the old days of free competition. Let no one suppose that those

who want business to rule itself have any notion of letting the individual business man go scot-free of regulation. They wish him to be supplied with plenty of discipline. They propose, however, that this regulation shall come not from the government but from business itself.[3]

The NICB, which had contributed much to the development of support for the regulation of business from within, characterized this "power of self-regulation" as "the real basis for hope of the preservation of the competitive system" and then noted that, even though government regulation had its benefits, the role of trade associations in helping to eliminate unfair trade practices had a great deal more to do with the "transformation, now going on, from cut-throat warfare for profits toward a more chivalrous competition."[4] It is fairly apparent that, to the NICB, the "preservation of the competitive system" involved the preservation of the positions of existing firms and that aggressive sales practices and pricing policies that threatened these market positions had to be eliminated. Sharing this view was O. H. Cheney, vice-president of the American Exchange Irving Trust Company, who asserted:

The new competition cuts across old distributing lines, and so must the new cooperation. The sooner every trade association activity becomes integrated into the organized activity of the whole industry, the sooner it will be ready to fight constructively in the new competition. Regardless of inter-distributor competition, every factor within an industry must fight together; and regardless of inter-commodity and inter-industrial competitions, all industries having common interests must understand and help each other.[5]

The NICB, in a study of the role of business organizations in helping to provide stability and to minimize competitive practices, noted the problem of "reconciling freedom and authority" and sought to strike a middle position between the "extremes" of "individualistic policy of unfettered and unregulated competition" that had produced "waste" and "ill-will," and the alternative of "authoritative control of industry under official bureaucratic forms." The system of "voluntary cooperation" was seen as a "synthesis of freedom and authority" that could provide for the "autonomous regulation of commercial practices," through which the "trade associations may come to share with the government itself, as in the days of the medieval guilds, the responsibility for eliminating unfair and predatory competitive conduct."[6]

The medieval guild is a perfect analogy for the system that was sought by many business leaders in the 1920s. The essence of that earlier practice was that a given trade or industry was considered not as a composite of independent and free-acting firms engaged in the same line of economic activity,

but as a collectivized unit comprising the members of such trades who func-
tioned under the centralized, legally enforceable direction of the guild itself.
The guild was a self-contained entity, representing the will of the dominant
members of that trade and having the power to regulate the practices of the
members to make certain that no activity was engaged in that would be
disruptive of the positions of other members. As the economist Ludwig von
Mises pointed out, the guild "enjoys full autonomy; it is free to settle all its
internal affairs without interference of external factors and of people who
are not themselves members of the guild."[7]

The guild system was enjoying a resurgence of popularity in England
and continental Europe at this time, and American business leaders were
beginning to see in the corporate state an attractive alternative to the disruption of unencumbered competition. Many businessmen were convinced that
competition became "undesirable" whenever it had the effect of disrupting
existing market relationships or threatening the position of a competitor.
Business leaders sought to persuade one another of the "community of interest" each had in the elimination of those aggressive practices that endangered the status quo.

That the realization of such objectives depended, ultimately, upon the
exercise of state power to enforce industry-desired standards had become
evident to many within the business community. Of course, many business
leaders had, long before the 1920s, come to embrace political solutions to
economic problems and to regard the role of government as complementary
to business purposes. Julius Barnes observed, "So sound are the fundamen-
tals of American business that the spirit of courage, confidence and enterprise could be revitalized quickly by intelligent team play between Government
and industry." He then added: "The manifest quick response of the processes of industry to government policies, wise or unwise, emphasizes the
growing interdependence of Government and industry in this country."[8]

The growing acceptance, by business leaders, of this "interdependence
of Government and industry" became increasingly evident. Indicative of this
emerging sentiment was the infatuation many businessmen had with one of
the principal champions of guild socialism, Italian premier Benito Mussolini.
Julius Barnes, Willis Booth (vice-president of Guaranty Trust Company),
James Emery (counsel for the NAM), Lewis Pierson, E. H. H. Simmons (president of the New York Stock Exchange), Elbert Gary, Thomas W. Lamont
(head of J. P. Morgan), Otto Kahn (of Kuhn, Loeb and Company), and Andrew W. Mellon were some of the more prominent men of commerce and
industry to see in Mussolini the quality of leadership needed for the solution
of economic problems. Gary's enthusiasm was such that he declared, "We
should be better for a man like Mussolini here too." Kahn characterized
Mussolini as a "patriotic realist," adding "I bow in homage [to him]." Mellon

regarded Mussolini as "a strong hand to reestablish the Italian Government upon sound principles." Pierson was so mesmerized by Mussolini as to hail his restoration of "the ideals of individualism," while Lamont referred to himself as a "missionary" for Italian fascism.[9]

The case for an extended political authority for enforcing industry trade standards was advanced by other businessmen. In a somewhat emotional speech to the annual meeting of the U.S. Chamber of Commerce in 1928, Edwin B. Parker expressed his support for government enforcement of such "self-regulatory" rules. Parker urged that the business community be "purged of those pirates whose acts stigmatize and bring business generally into disrepute. . . . Ruthless and selfish initiative must be curbed in the public interest and in the interest of legitimate business." Although, according to Parker, "business can, and is prepared in effect to legislate for itself in eliminating unfair, uneconomic and wasteful trade practices, including all forms of unfair competition," business nonetheless lacks "both the machinery and the power" to enforce business-promulgated standards of business conduct or to discipline those who would "demolish the canons of sound business practices." The enforcement of such "sound business practices" would, in Parker's view, occur "when the appropriate Government agency has, after full hearing, approved such rules as in the public interest."[10]

The interrelationship of cooperation and government enforcement was also observed by Francis H. Sisson, vice-president of the Guaranty Trust Company, who wrote: "[W]e are urgently in need of cooperation, not only among our industrial, commercial, transportation and financial interests, but also between the government and these important elements in our economic life." While Sisson recognized that "[s]tringent government control" would be a "deadly menace," he commended the idea of a "cooperation" between business and government, under which "competition that causes economic waste would be eliminated," resulting in "a high sense of justice and fairness." Projecting the beneficial effects of cooperation onto a world market, Sisson declared: "[W]e cannot adequately cooperate outside of the United States if we are compelled to indulge in costly and wasteful competition within our borders."[11] Similar sentiments were voiced by Gordon C. Corbaley, president of the American Institute of Food Distribution, who espoused the right of manufacturers to eliminate "destructive competition" by controlling "excess productive capacity." Corbaley also recommended the establishment of a national administrative board to coordinate industrial activity.[12] Meanwhile, Lewis Pierson prophesied, five years before the enactment of the NRA, that "[t]he day . . . is not far distant when organized business, organized labor, and a comprehending government will unite for the intelligent teamwork that alone can solve our newer problems."[13]

The turbulence wrought by the significant organizational and industrial developments discussed earlier and the unrestrained, aggressive practices of one's competitors reinforced business understanding of the proposition later put forth by Mancur Olson: that the competitive self-interests of individual firms will work to the detriment of the collective interests of the industry itself "unless there is coercion . . . to make individuals act in their common interest." The centralizing demands of the new industrial order that had been impressing its character upon American society caused many business leaders to begin experimenting with various political formulas to reorient the perspectives of businessmen.

TRADE PRACTICE CONFERENCES

One of the initial efforts of trade associations to obtain some degree of government approval and enforcement of codes of business practices involved the "trade practice conferences" established and conducted by the Federal Trade Commission. The FTC had frequently received complaints from industry members concerning trade practices that were so pervasive within particular industries that it would have been fruitless to attempt to deal with them on the basis of formal proceedings against each firm engaging in the practices. Consequently, as early as 1919 the FTC began inviting members of specific industries to participate in conferences designed to identify trade practices that were felt by "the practically unanimous opinion" of industry members to be unfair. As already noted, individual firms were unwilling to adhere to more passive trade standards, not only for the self-interest motivations mentioned by Mancur Olson but for the correlative reason that they knew their competitors would also deviate from agreed rules. While the earliest conferences were initiated by the FTC itself and were without any specific statutory authorization, it did not take long for trade associations and industry members to see in such machinery an effective method for the enforcement of those rules which, it was hoped, would stabilize the conditions so many had found so intolerable. The conference procedure was, apart from the enforcement offered by the FTC, rather close in concept to the trade association "codes of ethics," making it a readily acceptable political alternative to the more disappointing voluntary efforts. As a result, the trade practice conferences received the active support of the U.S. Chamber of Commerce and other trade groups throughout the 1920s and up into 1931 when, as a consequence of the FTC suddenly reducing the scope of trade practice rules, many within the business community began actively promoting alternative programs, some of which were to ultimately become part of the New Deal's National Industrial Recovery Act.[14]

The basic procedure governing a trade practice conference involved the

FTC inviting the members of a specific industry to attend a conference, at which a discussion of trade practice problems and proposed solutions would take place under the general supervision—though not the direction—of a representative (ordinarily a commissioner) of the FTC. Complaints regarding existing conditions and proposed rules to deal with such conditions came from industry members themselves, with the commission playing a role more akin to that of a moderator than that of an ultimate authority. Industry members were then invited to express themselves as to the fairness or unfairness of specific trade practices. In the words of the FTC, "If the practically unanimous opinion of the representatives of the industry condemns a given practice . . . [it] is given great weight by the Commission in considering such practices."[15] It must be emphasized that such industry expressions did not obligate the FTC to follow any of the recommendations made at the conference. Though such expressions were purely "advisory" in nature, it is also correct to point out that, to the degree they represented a consensus of opinion within the industry, they tended to have a great deal of influence with the FTC as statements of the "common law" for that industry. The commission's attitude toward such declarations was stated rather succinctly: "The effect is that the weight of opinion of the industry has been communicated to the Commission and that thereafter the Commission will feel it to be its duty in case complaints are made to it of a continuance of the condemned practices on the part of any member of the industry, to issue its formal complaint. . . ."[16]

It is understandable, then, that the business community saw in the trade practice conferences a greater potential for the enforcement of industry standards than what had existed in the trade association-formulated codes of ethics. Despite the commission's having acknowledged that the enforceability of rules emanating from such conferences would ultimately be subject to judicial review, any experienced legal counsel could give adequate assurance to his clients—at least at this point in time —that the courts would tend to give a stamp of prima facie "reasonableness" to rules that represented the nearly unanimous thinking of industry members who had participated in the formulation of such rules under the auspices of the FTC.

The rules that came out of the conferences and were approved by the FTC fell into two categories: Group I rules and Group II rules. Group I rules were considered by the commission as expressions of the prevailing law for the industry developing them, and a violation of such rules by any member of that industry—whether that member had agreed to the rules or not— would subject the offender to prosecution under Section 5 of the Federal Trade Commission Act as an "unfair method of competition."[17] Although a number of business leaders and trade association executives were fond of speaking of the "voluntary" nature of the trade practice conferences, there was no question as to the binding nature of Group I rules on all members of a given industry, regardless of whether a particular firm had ever "voluntarily" chosen to be bound by such rules. As one chairman of the FTC put it, "[T]he Commission undertakes to enforce compliance [with Group I rules] by proceeding against all violators, whether they have subscribed thereto or not. . . ."[18]

Contained within Group I were rules that dealt with practices considered by most business organizations to be the more "disruptive" of stable economic conditions. Generally included were prohibitions against inducing "breach of contract; . . . enticement of employees; . . . espionage; . . . disparagement of competitors; . . . commercial bribery; . . . price discrimination by secret rebates, excessive adjustments, or unearned discounts; . . . selling of goods below cost or below published list of prices for purpose of injuring competitor; misrepresentation of goods; . . . use of inferior materials or deviation from standards; [and] falsification of weights, tests, or certificates of manufacture."[19] While some of these rules involved efforts to restrain fraudulent practices that would harm consumers, most were clearly directed toward competitive practices that, it was feared, would have a harmful effect upon the competitors of firms employing such methods.

Group II rules, on the other hand, dealt with practices that the courts or the FTC had not generally held to be unlawful per se. They usually were practices that were objectionable to members of a specific industry but were not universally regarded as "unfair methods of competition" within the meaning of the Federal Trade Commission Act. Even though the FTC considered the violation of a Group II rule to be an unfair method of competition, this class of rules was considered binding only upon the firms that had actually agreed to them, a fact that prompted FTC chairman Abram F. Myers to observe that the absence of enforcement against nonsigners was "a serious stumbling block" to business efforts on behalf of self-regulation.[20]

The basic content of trade practice conference rules, whether of the Group I or Group II variety, did not generally differ from the trade association codes of ethics. What did differ, of course, was that the FTC now afforded a means for the enforcement of such rules, with the categorization of rules into either Group I or Group II determining how and against whom such rules would be enforced. To illustrate the point, a trade practice submittal of the National Petroleum Marketers Association, adopted in 1920, contained a provision outlawing cash discounts and secret rebates.[21] The trade practice rules for the oil industry, adopted the same year, provided for uniform agency and tank rental agreements, with minimum rental rates established. Cash discounts were also prohibited. The 1928 rules for the petroleum industry in Virginia required, as a Group I rule, the posting of and adherence to selling prices, along with the prohibition of any discounts, while the Group II rules sought to discourage the direct sale of petroleum from bulk plants into the buyers' trucks. The millwork industry rules, adopted in 1928, required adherence to published prices by all manufacturers.[22] A trade practice conference for the motion picture industry, held in 1927, resulted in a code that banned, among other practices, "commercial bribery" and "paid commercial advertising from motion picture exhibitions" (Group I), as well as "fake motion picture acting schools" and "deceptive titles" (Group II).[23] The grocery trades, responding to the intense competition generated for the most part by the chain stores, adopted proposals seeking to restrict such price-lowering practices as "secret rebates," "free deals," "premiums, gifts, or prizes," "selling . . . below delivered cost," and "price discrimination."[24] That such rules and proposals were principally reactions against the very aggressive competition taking place within these industries, and not a "moralistic" response to corporate fraud and corruption, will be more evident from the examination of specific industries in subsequent chapters.

Based upon the past efforts of many businessmen to foster more sedentary methods of competition, the tendency of trade practice conference rules to prohibit the more energetic competitive modes was rather predictable. As Kittelle and Mostow have noted:

> A study of trade practice submittals and rules issued prior to 1930 indicates that businessmen, in requesting conferences, were not always motivated by a desire to help the consumer. Many were unquestionably hopeful of achieving some measure of price-fixing or control over production or the channels of distribution; and some of the early rules went rather far toward making this hope a reality.

They added what, by now, should be rather apparent, namely, that businessmen, in seeking the prohibition of certain practices, "were all too prone to regard as 'unfair competition' almost any kind of active competition that discommoded them, particularly if it related to price."[25] A similar conclusion was drawn by Robert Himmelberg, who declared that "the codes became potential instruments for limiting competition. The blanket prohibition of price discrimination would have the effect of preventing a seller from shaving prices to win a new customer, and thus eliminate one of the leading inducements for price competition."[26]

The role that the trade practice conference played as a tool for business self-regulation was noted by M. Markham Flannery, director of trade practice conferences for the FTC: "Never in the history of American business has there been a time when self-regulation has received more intensive consideration." Discussing the role of trade practice conferences in the self-regulatory scheme, Flannery pointed out what others had observed: effective self-regulation was dependent upon the establishment of rules that could be enforced against violators, a function for which the conferences were best suited.[27] Edwin B. Parker praised the trade practice conference as "an expeditious and economical means of eliminating the use of unfair methods of competition," adding that such "voluntarily" adopted rules would, when ratified by the FTC, become "the rule of business conduct for that industry." Such a procedure, Parker concluded, "offers to business an opportunity in good faith to set up simple machinery in each trade, diligently to seek out the abuses which unquestionably exist to a greater or less extent in every industry, and to take effective measures to eliminate them."[28]

Echoing these views was O. H. Cheney, who observed that "about the only way to regulate business effectively is to let it regulate itself by giving the best thought and character in an industry a chance to come to the top, and to back it up with the police power of the Commission."[29] In his opinion, then, the "self-regulation" was presumably to be subject to enforcement by the federal government and was not to be "voluntary" in the sense that any recalcitrants could avoid adhering to the standards developed by members of the industry.

Retailer Lincoln Filene's appraisal of the trade practice conference procedure was that "it was a definite forward step in the general movement to make industries 'self-regulating' so far as unfair trade practices are concerned, and to tie in the self-regulating process with the only federal administrative body then in existence to cooperate with and to enforce the conclusions of the industry." Filene saw in such procedures the possibilities for FTC activity in areas in which the NRA later became involved. In his view, trade practice standards upon which an industry could not reach agreement could be determined by the FTC itself. The consequence of following such principles would be, according to Filene, "to build a structure of lasting value to business and to the community," one that would be consistent with his long-held goals of competitive regularization for the retailing trades.[30]

LOOKING AHEAD

A number of proposals for the establishment of regulatory machinery, patterned on variations of the trade practice conferences, were made by business leaders during the postwar decade. One such plan, put forth in 1924 by Bernard Baruch, envisioned the creation of a so-called Court of Commerce. Such a court would, in his mind, provide business with a tribunal for seeking to stabilize business conditions. The procedure employed would be much like the seeking of a declaratory judgment. Businessmen would appear before the court "with such questions as whether in time of overproduction and low prices they could cut down production and fix a price." Baruch favored the use of such a court over the FTC (which he described as "an inquisitorial body"), for such a court "would encourage such practices of cooperation and coordination in industry as would be found to be clearly of public benefit." Such a court would also "be clothed with the power and charged with the responsibility of standing watch against and preventing abuses."[31]

A proposal similar to Baruch's had been made in 1919 by Rush C. Butler, chairman of the Federal Trade Committee of the U.S. Chamber of Commerce, who, criticizing the effects of the Sherman Act, recommended that Congress establish an administrative agency whose job would be to determine, in advance, "whether or not agreements between competitors in restraint of trade are or are not unlawful."[32] He recommended such an arrangement for the internal problems of the coal industry in particular. Suggestions like these by Baruch and Butler demonstrate the relationship business "cooperation" bore to the maintenance of business stability through restricted production and pricing practices. As long as the business agreements contemplated in these proposals were truly voluntary in nature (i.e., firms were not to be legally compelled to adhere to any industry determined trade standards), the proposals of Baruch and Butler, at least at this point, only seek to remove any taint of antitrust illegality from agreements made between or among firms. As such, no real harm can be discerned in their suggestions. It is evident, however, that the business leaders advocating systems for the stabilization of competitive conditions were not always meticulous in distinguishing the voluntary from the involuntary means.

In May 1930, Baruch took the opportunity to renew his support for a courtlike system of "self-regulation." Drawing upon what he considered to be the favorable atmosphere created through the WIB, Baruch told the Boston Chamber of Commerce that American business needed "a common forum where problems requiring cooperation can be considered and acted upon with the constructive, nonpolitical sanction of the government."[33] Noting that effective means of restraining "excess production" were prevented by existing laws, Baruch went on to suggest that a "tribunal invested like the Supreme Court" be established. He added:

It should have no power to repress or coerce but it should have power to convoke conference, to suggest and to sanction or license such common-sense cooperation among industrial units as will prevent our economic blessings from becoming unbearable burdens. Its sole punitive power should be to prescribe conditions of its licenses and then to revoke those licenses for infringement of such conditions.[34]

Among business leaders, apparently contradictory meanings were attached to such concepts as "voluntary," "nonpolitical," and "noncoercive."

While Baruch spoke of the "nonpolitical" nature of such a proposed tribunal and would even have denied it the "power to repress or coerce," he went on to talk of a licensing procedure as the "sole punitive power" of the tribunal. In other words, each individual business would have been required to obtain a license from this agency as a condition to doing business. This license, and with it the right to conduct business, could have been revoked in the event a firm failed to abide by the rules established by the tribunal. That such a system could hardly be considered "noncoercive" would be evident from the moment a dissenting businessman, stripped of his license by the tribunal, sought to continue operating his business.

Baruch's plan was, in effect, but a reiteration of the same basic regulatory structure he had advocated since the cessation of the WIB. It was, in format, identical to his 1924 proposal for a Court of Commerce. The idea of having some sort of an "industrial court," composed of members of the business community, had intrigued many business leaders, including such men as the noted retailer John Wanamaker, who earlier proposed a plan for a "Supreme Bench" of businessmen that was similar, in many respects, to that offered by Baruch. Along the same lines, the president of the Wool Institute proposed "a special supreme court for industry" that would "interpret the economic law governing state, interstate and national transactions."[35]

In a policy recommendation that was consistent with the prevailing sentiments of many business leaders for a greater politicization of competitive relationships, Rexford G. Tugwell proposed

> [t]hat industrialists move faster than they have in the past toward close association, so that, without compulsion from any governmental body, a general scheme and a definite program, for economic affairs, on a national scale can gradually emerge, with inter-business and inter-industry controlling bodies responsible for coordination and maintaining the smooth flows of goods and services.

Tugwell then observed,

> [W]e linger in the past, with our clumsy governmental machinery for control hopelessly out of date. We muddle where we ought to clarify; we obstruct where we ought to encourage. Governmental controls ought to be brought to bear where voluntary ones break down, where, in fact, the interests of the public conflict with those of a super-coordinated industry.[36]

In order to achieve the level of maturity that he felt industry must attain, Tugwell declared that one of the requirements was "the need to socialize industry, which means to make it serve social ends rather than individual ones." He then asked: "[I]s industry becoming socialized? As we move toward greater associationism, toward a generally closer-knit fabric of relations, it seems inevitable that socialization should accompany the movement. The identity of social with group interests grows greater as the group grows larger."[37] Tugwell concluded that "there still remains a clear tendency toward associationism of a kind which arises out of normal technical processes. And when this happens, it is always more possible to achieve coordination among producing groups than it was before."[38]

Tugwell's observations are significant in that they were premised upon the same influences identified by Mancur Olson, and they recognized the progression from *voluntary* to *political* means of regularizing trade practices. There is certainly no deterministic influence at work here: business and trade association leaders could well have confined their efforts for moderating competitive influences to agreements, understandings, and appeals to "business ethics." In fact, many were undoubtedly content to approach the question informally, without recourse to political intervention. Nevertheless, the historical development of legislative efforts to realize commercial and industrial stabilization was generally preceded by voluntary programs that, upon failing to accomplish their intended objectives, were superseded by appeals from many business sources for more effective measures.

What business leaders were seeking in their proposals for "self-regulation" was a system for moderating trade practices in order to maintain stable, predictable, nonthreatening business conditions. This process has been referred to as "rationalization," a concept more specifically detailed as

the process of associating together individual undertakings or groups of firms in a close form of amalgamation, and ultimately of unifying, in some practicable degree of combination, whole industries, both nationally and internationally; with the allied objects . . . of increasing efficiency, lowering costs, improving conditions of labour, promoting industrial cooperation, and reducing the waste of competition, these objects being achieved by various means which unification alone makes in full measure available—the regulation of the production of an industry to balance the consumption of its products; the control of prices; the logical allocation of work to individual factories; the stabilization of employment and regularization of wages; the standardization of materials, methods and products; the simplification of the ranges of goods produced; the economical organization of distribution; the adoption of scientific methods and knowledge in the management and technique of trades as a whole; and the planning and pursuit of common trade policies.[39]

H. S. Person, managing director of the Taylor Society and an advocate of "rationalization," observed rather prophetically that, as of 1930, "there has been . . . no situation in the United States sufficiently critical to generate the emotional impulse for a positive step in the direction of rationalization."[40]

That the "situation" of the Great Depression had already begun to provide the "emotional impulse" that was to culminate in the New Deal National Industrial Recovery Act experiment was evident from the nearly unified voice with which business leaders increased their appeals for "self-regulation" in business.

BUSINESS IN THE GREAT DEPRESSION

While it is convenient to use 24 October 1929—"Black Thursday"—as the benchmark inaugurating the Great Depression, a proper understanding of this economic crisis demonstrates a series of events, along a continuum beginning at least as early as 1921 and running well into the New Deal years, that must be understood in order to fully grasp the cause and effect factors associated with the depression. Nevertheless, the popular reaction to the "great crash" of the stock market justifies the use of this date for gauging the attitudes of business leaders toward the depression and their proposals for dealing with it. Did the depression bring with it any change in business philosophy toward stabilizing and rationalizing competitive conditions? What policies were advocated by business leaders, and how do they compare with suggestions for economic reform put forth in prior years?

The principal contention of this study is that the business community had become increasingly sensitive to the creation of an environment that would insulate firms from the adverse consequences of aggressive competition. If this assessment is correct—if business was, indeed, pursuing policies designed to preserve the positions of existing firms—then one might expect an intensification of such efforts during the catastrophic depression years.

While the impact of the depression injected a new sense of urgency into their appeals, it does not appear that leading businessmen made any significant deviation from their desire for a system of industrial "self-rule" under federal supervision. The depression gave additional strength to the arguments on behalf of the restructuring of competitive relationships, but it did not alter the basic content of their proposals. If anything, this time period served as a catalyst for the conversion of the idea of "self-regulation" into the concrete proposals that ultimately became the National Industrial Recovery Act.

There is no universally accepted explanation for the cause of the Great Depression. Interpretations have ranged from Milton Friedman and Anna Schwartz's[41] view that the depression was occasioned by erroneous Federal Reserve monetary policies to Peter Temin's[42] suggestion that consumption and investment changes following the stock market crash were to blame, to Henry Simon's[43] contention that such factors as government-created instability in commercial banking and the abandonment of competition through increased government intervention were to blame, to Charles Kindleberger's[44] view that the depression had foreign origins. Herbert Hoover[45] shared Kindleberger's explanation, although he attributed the primary cause of the depression to World War I. One must add to the list John Kenneth Galbraith's[46] identification of such factors as insufficient advances in investment, the maldistribution of income, and corporate and banking structural deficiencies, as well as such questionable explanations as psychologist John J. B. Morgan's[47] "manic depressive psychoses of business."

The cause of the Great Depression has also been characterized—certainly in the popular mind—by the over-production of goods, a condition that has generally been attributed to the failure of businessmen to make accurate predictions. This time period has been used to help propagate the notion that a market economy cannot be self-regulative, but must be subject to political supervision and direction. But, as another economic historian has demonstrated,[48] the period leading up to the depression was not marked by overproduction in the sense that businessmen failed to properly anticipate consumer demand. Rather, there was an "overbidding" of costs associated with the production of certain types of goods; the costs ended up being too high in relation to the selling prices of the goods themselves. This "malinvestment," resulting in the overproduction of certain specific goods (and not of all goods throughout the economy) was sired, in this view, not by the absence of political intervention, but because of it, in the form of the inflationary expansion of credit and the supply of money. Far from serving as a model of the dysfunctional nature of market disciplines, the Great Depression is seen as a classic example of the adverse effects of deviating from the market and imposing political direction upon the economy.

Regardless of the origins of the problem,[49] many industries found themselves in the depression years with stocks of unsold goods, a situation for which the standard textbook response is a reduction in prices in order to clear the market. Up until this time, it had been accepted policy for governments not to interfere with such market readjustment mechanisms. Following the 1929 crash, however, the Hoover administration intervened to prevent price declines, a move which retarded economic recovery.[50] Such price-stabilizing policies happened to coincide with business efforts to eliminate sharply fluctuating prices. The depression did create surpluses in many industries, but for other industries there was a decline in demand as a result of a general ordering of buyer preferences during the depression. The aggressive competitive practices of the predepression years, coupled with falling prices that, in part, characterized the market's attempt to reestablish equilibrium, served to intensify the demands of many businessmen for some method for effectively controlling competition.

Many business leaders, during the early depression years, would doubtless have been in agreement with the prescription offered by Wallace B. Donham, dean of the Harvard School of Business:

> Our new group of business men must develop and enforce a group conscience if the evolution of business ethics is to be speeded up; a group conscience which will hold not only the individual but the whole group to both personal and group responsibility for relations with the rest of the community. When this degree of solidarity is accomplished, and when business has to this extent acquired the ability to enforce its own sanctions, and not till then, will business have assumed the leadership which has been forced on it by science.[51]

Donham's statement serves not only to summarize the development of business attitudes toward intraindustrial relationships, but is a fitting prologue for what was to follow.

As 1929 drew to a close, many businessmen continued their expressions of concern for the development of cooperative attitudes among competitors. One trade association executive condemned the businessman who operated his business "in entire disregard of the effects on his competitor and the rest of the industry,"[52] while another executive lamented price discrimination and secret rebates, calling them "evils" that had resulted from "mass production, overproduction, high-power selling and national advertising." He praised the FTC's trade practice conferences as effective means for laying down and enforcing rules for industries, then offered this view of the modern businessman: "Instead of being the individualistic merchant of the old days, he must believe in the new spirit of cooperation."[53]

Proposed remedies for these trade conditions continued to find expression among members of the business community, with the emphasis tending to be on political solutions. Noting that "our profits are absolutely unprotected," one businessman proposed the establishment of "business ethics legislation" in order to "make it possible for fair practices to become a law in any industry when 80 or 90 per cent of that industry, together with governmental supervision, agree on a policy."[54] Perhaps the thinking of most businessmen was best summarized by Henry S. Dennison, president of Dennison Manufacturing Company: "We *must* manage ourselves if we are to gain on the past. No laissez-faire, no unchanneled and unimpeded course of nature, no invisible hand will do it for us. . . . [W]e now find ourselves in a period of growing social self-control."[55] Even though "laissez-faire" has never characterized the American economy, each succeeding generation speaks of its accretions to the ever-expanding regulatory apparatus as "bringing an end to laissez-faire." Dennison's remarks, while reflective of this approach, should not be taken as an accurate appraisal of predepression policies.

Business attempts to promote trade stability received a setback when, in

1931, the FTC—having become concerned that the trade practice conference procedures might have been subject to abuse by trade groups—undertook a major revision of the then-existing trade practice rules. In the eyes of
many members of the business community, this revision greatly restricted
the effectiveness of such conferences as a means of moderating competitive
practices. A publication of the influential NICB provides a terse summation
of the business response to the emasculation of trade rules by the FTC:

> It was this unilateral revision of codes to which members of various industries
> had subscribed under the impression that they represented something in the
> nature of a covenant, or contract, imposing mutual obligations, that brought
> to an end the second stage in the development of the trade practice conference.
> Chagrined by being left without official approval for numerous practices and
> activities which they deemed appropriate and useful in combating the current
> depression, and unconvinced of any real advantage from agreeing to abide by
> settled rules of law . . . business men lost their enthusiasm for these emascu-
> lated codes. What they wanted was not less but more of the same medicine.[56]

This assessment of business attitudes toward enforceable trade practice rules
is quite accurate. The quest for a workable system, undertaken long before
the onset of the depression, began to increase in intensity. Many business
leaders embarked on campaigns for alternative political resolutions of their
perceived problems of competitive instability. The groundwork was thus
begun not only for the NRA but for a close working relationship between
many businessmen and the New Deal philosophy of government-structured
economic behavior.

One of the most detailed blueprints for seeking to stabilize industrial
conditions—one that served as a precursor for the NRA—was put forth on
16 September 1931 at the National Electrical Manufacturers Association
meeting in New York by Gerard Swope, president of the General Electric
Company. Known, appropriately, as the Swope Plan, it envisioned the ultimate organization of all companies with fifty or more employees into trade
associations to be supervised by an administrative body of the federal government. These trade associations would be empowered to define "trade
practices, business ethics, methods of standard accounting and cost practice,
standard forms of balance sheet and earnings statement, etc." They would
also be permitted to

> collect and distribute information on volume of business transacted, invento-
> ries of merchandise on hand, simplification and standardization of products,
> stabilization of prices, and all matters which may arise from time to time relat-
> ing to the growth and development of industry and commerce in order to pro-
> mote stabilization of employment and give the best service to the public.[57]

The Swope Plan envisioned the adoption of a system of workmen's compensation, of life, disability, and unemployment insurance, and of old-age pensions (all ostensibly to gain the support of labor), but the primary impetus for the plan came from a desire of industrialists for a coordinated system to stabilize industry through rules made by trade associations and enforced by the federal government.

The Swope Plan, in other words, epitomized the thinking of an increasing number of business leaders as to the appropriate means for enforcing business-desired competitive standards. The plan contemplated that a majority of the members of an industry would enjoy the use of the coercive power of the federal government in establishing and enforcing rules against a dissenting minority. There would be no more futile appeals to a competitor's "conscience" or sentimentalized rhetoric about the "good of the group"; the Swope Plan proposed to give industry members, through their trade associations, the politically backed power to command. The rationale for the exercise of such coercive authority was expressed in the official explanation of the Swope Plan. Employing a definition of questionable consistency, it spoke of the "voluntary acceptance of decentralized *mandatory* government of industry. . . in association with the U.S. Government."[58] The *involuntary* nature of the plan was then spelled out:

> Probably the shoe of "coercion" will pinch most in the rules or plan set up by a Swope Plan trade association for stabilization of production and price. Life [sic] the farmer who will not limit wheat or cotton production, the individual manufacturer will in all likelihood bleat and bluster when he is asked to follow a given plan. The answer to this is the same answer that our forefathers probably gave to a citizen in a New England town when he objected to a "town meeting's" action: "Do your hollering and your arguing in due order and time when you exercise your prerogative as a free citizen by coming to the meeting and debate and vote; and then when the matter is decided by majority vote, obey the mandate. . . ." By this test, the plan for logical government in industry is in no sense a contravention of liberty, nor an interference by government in business. Business merely uses the government's aid in governing itself.[59]

In what, at the very least, must be considered a presumptuous undertaking, the following argument was advanced:

> How can coercion be "considerate and fair?" Only when the fullest technical opinion within a given industry agrees that it knows the interests of the moderately small producer better than he does. A man's peers can pass upon a man's needs more fairly than any others. Coercion in the coerced one's own best interests is no less considerate than a measure of coercion applied to an adolescent when all moral suasion has failed.[60]

Swope himself was an articulate spokesman for a collectivist viewpoint. Asserting that "industry is not primarily for profit but rather for service," Swope was a living example of the "managerial" mentality identified by Schumpeter. He adhered to the "trusteeship" theory of management, premised on a triadic responsibility to workers, investors, and the public. His thoroughly institutionalized outlook is represented in his declaration that the business organization has an overriding "duty of perpetuating itself." He acknowledged, as other business leaders had already done, that the environment of economic stability contemplated within his own Swope Plan was dependent upon coercive political structuring. In his words, "one cannot loudly call for more stability in business and get it on a purely voluntary basis."[61]

Business reaction to the Swope Plan was very favorable. Praise for it came from such noted business leaders as J. E. Edgerton, president of NAM; Silas Strawn, president of the U.S. Chamber of Commerce; and Magnus W. Alexander. Editorial support came from *Business Week*.[62] Among other business supporters of the Swope Plan were Cornelius Kelly, of Anaconda Copper,[63] and General Electric's Owen D. Young. Young declared: "We can in this country have organized economic planning with some curtailment of individual freedom which, if the plan be wise and properly executed, will tend to diminish economic disorder and the penalties which we pay."[64] Young made a more direct appeal for government control in these words: "We are now learning . . . that we must enlarge our restraints and controls over the economically powerful. . . . Business having failed to discipline itself, I see no escape from some direction and control by politics."[65] He added:

> Cooperation is required by the great majority of the participants and the coercion of the rest may ultimately be necessary. I hate not only the term but the idea of coercion, and yet we are forced to recognize that every advance in social organization requires the voluntary surrender of a certain amount of individual freedom by the majority and the ultimate coercion of the minority. It is not the coercion of the recalcitrant minority but the voluntary submission by the large majority which should impress us.[66]

He further noted that the surrender of individual freedom contemplated by such a plan could be made to either the government or to the "organized group," of which each individual member would be a part.[67] Why—assuming people to be motivated by self-interest—any individual would ever voluntarily choose to surrender some of his individual freedom in order to submit himself to the coercion of others is a point to which Young did not address himself.

Young had long been an advocate of government regulation as a means of safeguarding the interests of those engaged in commerce and industry. In his view, the important consideration was to have *more* effective regulation, not *less*. Speaking before the Senate Committee on Interstate Commerce on the subject of the communications industry, Young stated:

> [W]henever I have spoken about unifying communication services, either in the domestic or in the international field, I have always attached to it the proviso that adequate regulation and control shall be put into the government of such services and the rates to be charged therefor. I have no doubt but what effective regulation can be established, fair alike to the people rendering the services and to the people served. In fact, I may say that we must learn how to regulate adequately our public services in private hands, or there will be no alternative but the government ownership of such services.[68]

The supporters of "cooperative regulation" in business, then, largely took the position that such regulation, in order to effectively deal with intraindustrial problems, had to be made mandatory. Henry S. Dennison expressed this view:

> [I]t is necessary to realize that the field for purely voluntary action in the business world is a limited field. . . . [W]e must be willing to imagine a referee with a power and influence greater than that which any group from the business world would be willing voluntarily to grant him and to maintain in him.

Dennison went on to assert that if "business umpiring" was to go beyond voluntary activity and become truly effective, resort must be had to an agency such as the FTC.[69]

It is at this juncture that the legitimate business interest in stabilizing competitive conditions becomes an illegitimate exercise of group domination and coercion. So long as firms were not *compelled* by legal force to follow the restrictive schemes of their competitors, people in the market who thought such restraints to be excessive would be assured of at least the opportunity of competitive responses. The mechanism of self-interest that prevents voluntary restrictions of the market from being effective is negated once the threat of fines, injunctions, or imprisonment is interjected to dissuade one from pursuing that self-interest. In this sense, the regularization of competition and the stabilization of existing relationships through the employment of political sanctions does more than simply disadvantage the more aggressive competitors: it also serves to diminish the effectiveness of the market mechanisms as spontaneous, impersonal disciplinarians of economic behavior. To the extent that the survival of any firm—not to mention the health of the economic system generally—depends upon firms having the resiliency to respond to conditions of disequilibrium, legally enforceable restraints upon competitive behavior could only serve to foster greater entropy.

Variations on the Swope theme were offered by the NAM and by a special committee of the U.S. Chamber of Commerce.[70] Their respective proposals called for legislation that would allow sellers to enter into agreements covering such matters as production, markets, and prices. The Chamber committee reflected the collectivist outlook that had settled into business thinking by this time:

> A freedom of action which might have been justified in the relatively simple life of the last century cannot be tolerated today, because the unwise action of one individual may adversely affect the lives of thousands. We have left the period of extreme individualism and are living in a period in which national economy must be recognized as the controlling factor.[71]

The committee further recommended the establishment of a national economic council, composed of representatives of different sectors of society, that would serve in an advisory capacity to deal with economic problems. Such a council would function under the auspices of the Chamber of Commerce and would be "charged broadly with the responsibility of proposing policies and measures that will contribute to our economic wellbeing." The report concluded by advocating a reduction in working hours in industry and, consistent with the Swope Plan, proposed a system of unemployment insurance financed by state and local governments and private sources, along with workmen's compensation and old-age pensions.[72]

A resolution of the NAM, passed in the spring of 1932, noted that the prohibition by the antitrust laws of cooperative agreements between sellers had "fostered widespread industrial and social maladjustment." It went on to recommend that Congress amend this legislation to permit such voluntary agreements. The objectives of such agreements, according to the resolution, would include (among others) the avoidance of "destructive competition" and "wastage of materials," as well as the preservation of earnings. It thus incorporated the rhetoric of "conservation" that, as we shall discover in chapter 6, was exploited to further anticompetitive purposes.[73]

Francis H. Sisson, while noting that the antitrust laws served a valid purpose at the time they were enacted, declared that such laws had become a "stumbling-block in the path of economic progress." The public, he went on, had accepted free competition "as the panacea for all economic ills," but in the current trend toward consolidation such thinking needed reexamination. In his opinion, "[t]he economic forces behind the consolidation movement are irresistible; . . . the advantages of free competition, from the point of view of the people as a whole, are immeasurably out-weighed by those of cooperation."[74] Sisson then observed that the integration of business "can be achieved only through the sacrifice of the automatic regulation that free competition has always provided. For this automatic regulation must be substituted an artificial regulation dependent on human wisdom and foresight, and subject to the weaknesses of human nature."[75] Thomas L. Chadbourne added the thought that repeal or amendment of the Sherman Act was essential to curbing "the calamity of over-production and unwieldy surpluses."[76]

Another leading businessman, J. Harvey Williams, president of J. H. Williams and Company, reiterated many of these sentiments when, in 1932, he declared that "destructive competition" existed within all industries except those that were "so integrated or so dominated by a few large units that they [were] able to escape the blind competition and the general urge for volume regardless of profit." What was needed, Williams concluded, was the organization of industries into more effective systems of cooperation in order "to stabilize the industry at a fair profit." Drawing upon the examples of railroads, banks, and stock brokerage firms, he noted that while price competition had been all but eliminated from such industries, there was nevertheless a "tense competition" for business in the providing of quality and service. Williams then gave away the underlying motivation for the regulation of competitive practices when he admitted that bank interest rates and brokerage fees would undoubtedly be much lower if such institutions were subject to "the same kind of unbridled competition for volume to which we in industry are subject." In such a case, he added, "those elements of the public interest would not think that this cutthroat competition was such a good thing for the country." He then observed: "It is claimed that prices will go up if competitors are permitted to agree on prices. In so far as cost plus a fair profit is not being realized today, that probably is true; and to that I say, what of it?"[77] The same point had been made by another business executive who viewed what he considered subprofit selling as stealing from the industry itself. He urged the establishment of "a legalized fair selling price" and, in order to maintain such a price, suggested: "[W]hy not stabilize it and protect it, for only through a fair price can the profits of industry be conserved."[78]

APPROACHING THE NEW DEAL RECOVERY PROGRAM

As the depression wore on, business leaders became more militant in their proposals for stabilizing trade conditions. In his role as president of the U.S. Chamber of Commerce, Henry I. Harriman elaborated upon his thoughts on how to deal with businesses that did not choose to "cooperate" with his organization's proposal for recovery: "They'll be treated like any maverick," he said. "They'll be roped, branded, and made to run with the herd."[79] Harriman—committed to the idea of a form of central planning—approached President Hoover, urging him to recommend to Congress the Chamber's plan for self-regulation. Hoover, though long an advocate of government intervention into economic affairs,[80] refused Harriman, contending that such a program would lead the country into fascism or socialism. On 23 September 1932, in the midst of the presidential campaign, Harriman again urged Hoover to support the Chamber proposal, saying that Roosevelt had agreed to it and, if Hoover did not, a sizeable number of key business leaders would support Roosevelt. Hoover again refused Harriman's appeal. Although there is no way of determining the extent to which this reluctance cost Hoover business support, there is no question that Roosevelt enjoyed substantial backing from within the business community.[81] Roosevelt responded to this support when, a few weeks after his inauguration, he submitted his "recovery bill" to Congress. This measure became the cornerstone of the early New Deal. Like the Swope Plan, it called for the rehabilitation of American business through a government-enforced system of industry created "codes of fair competition."[82]

The superficial appearance of the legislation as systematically conceived conceals the backstage efforts of a variety of interests engaged in the drafting of a measure that would be marketable to industry, labor unions, and the political leadership. Spurred on by Senate passage of Senator Hugo Black's "share-the-work" bill—which provided for an outright statutory determination of the maximum number of hours an employer could work his employees in a week (namely, thirty)—business interests joined with administration and congressional leaders to prepare a substitute measure for industrial recovery. Business was not opposed to the idea of limiting hours of work. A Chamber of Commerce committee, headed by Paul W. Litchfield, president of Goodyear Tire and Rubber Company, had already endorsed the principle of permitting agreements among employers to limit hours and set minimum wages as a means for promoting recovery.[83] What the business community did find objectionable in the Black bill was the *political*—rather than the *business*—determination of standards, a point clearly made by Harriman.[84] As we have already seen, business and trade association leaders had long favored a "voluntary" system of "cooperative self-regulation" that, translated into more precise language, contemplated the establishment of machinery through which the dominant members of an industry could establish trade practice rules that all members of the industry would have to follow. It was implicit that business was to set the standards, with the government's role limited to that of providing the mechanism for enforcement. The Black bill was inconsistent with this premise. Many businessmen would doubtless have embraced Bernard Baruch's seemingly contradictory use (unless one understands the context in which it was used by business leaders) of the word "voluntarily": "While we agree fully that industry must voluntarily accept and ask for coordination, and that any appearance of dictatorship must be avoided, the power of discipline must exist."[85]

It was under such circumstances that at least three distinct groups began the task of drafting a recovery bill, with Assistant Secretary of State Raymond Moley, New York Senator Robert Wagner, and Undersecretary of Commerce John Dickinson serving as the nuclei for the groups. Moley worked rather closely with Hugh Johnson and Donald Richberg. One of the central provisions in their proposal was for federal licensing of business firms as a means of enforcement. Senator Wagner was assisted by various representatives of business, labor, and government. Two well-known trade association attorneys, David Podell and Gilbert Montague, helped with this draft, as did James Henry Rand of Remington Rand and Virgil Jordan, president of the NICB. The Dickinson group—made up of such advocates of government planning as Rexford Tugwell, Frances Perkins, and Jerome Frank—later merged with the Wagner group to draft a single proposal. These groups met at the White House with FDR and, after some prolonged negotiations, compromise, and rewriting, emerged on 15 May with a final draft of the bill. It was submitted to Congress two days later,[86] and received overwhelming support from the business community. Virgil Jordan seemed to reflect business sentiments when he declared:

> Contrary to the popular impression, there is nothing essentially revolutionary in the proposals contained in the Wagner bill. They represent rather a logical extension of principles of industrial control already implicit in the organization of American business. They merely offer an opportunity to work out those principles and for the first time to give them practical effectiveness.[87]

The NAM had also been active in the preparation of legislative proposals, having presented a draft of a bill to Secretary of Commerce Daniel C. Roper. The NAM's proposal contemplated the establishment of a federal agency along the lines of the WIB. Working in conjunction with trade associations, it would seek to accommodate production to demand and establish "fair" prices. The agency itself was to be composed of seven members: the secretary of labor, along with five representatives of commerce, finance, labor, agriculture, and the public, respectively.[88]

It is worthwhile to note that, while the administration's recovery bill represented the culmination of years of effort by business leaders and trade associations to establish effective machinery for the moderation of trade practices, it was by no means anathema to the policies of twentieth-century political "liberals." There has been a popular polarization of "progressivism-liberalism," on the one hand, and "big business-corporatism" on the other, a dichotomy whose demonstrated inaccuracy has diminished its intellectual respectability. The harmonious relationship between the economic policies long advocated by the business sector and the commitment of the "liberal" political and intellectual community to national economic planning became abundantly evident during the New Deal years. That persons such as Rexford Tugwell, Robert Wagner, Jerome Frank, and Robert LaFollette could so easily join forces with Henry Harriman, Gerard Swope, and Virgil Jordan in constructing a piece of legislation with such far-reaching implications for political intervention in economic matters is a reflection of the consistency of purpose between "liberal" and business policies. This point was acknowledged by Senator Wagner himself, who, referring to the recovery bill, declared:

> I think this bill is important as the first step toward that which the Liberals of this country have been preparing for years. It was a part of the platform of the 1912 Progressive Party, namely the necessity of a national planned economy. Until we have that, I venture to say that we are not going to have an orderly organized economic system. A good deal of the chaos and disorganization from which we are suffering now is due to this lack of planning.[89]

This is not to suggest that American businessmen were prepared to turn the policy and decision-making functions of this proposed agency over to men like Tugwell and LaFollette. Businessmen insisted upon the reservation of this function to themselves, this being what was meant by "voluntary" self-regulation. Any conflict between "liberals" and the more influential members of the business community was not over the question of whether this machinery for economic planning should exist. The contest was only over *who* should control such machinery. The basic objectives of both "liberals" and many key business leaders for the regularization of economic life were, indeed, quite harmonious. In the New Deal recovery program lay the promise for the realization of the structuring of economic activity long sought by what, at first appearance, might seem to be interests with diametrically opposed purposes.

The recovery bill also enjoyed the support of organized labor. With the right of collective bargaining spelled out in Section 7(a), as well as provisions for establishing maximum hours and minimum wages in labor agreements—or, in the absence of an agreement, having such matters subject to prescription by the president as a code of fair competition—labor leaders and their organizations joined forces with business to back the measure. Working on behalf of the proposal were William Green, president of the American Federation of Labor; W. Jett Lauck, of the United Mine Workers;

and Secretary of Labor Frances Perkins. Support for the principle of coordinated industrial planning also came from Sidney Hillman of the Amalgamated Clothing Workers and the American Federation of Labor's Matthew Woll. On the eve of its passage, the recovery bill was hailed by the A.F. of L. as "the most advanced and forward looking legislation for recovery yet proposed."[90]

Even though the president's recovery proposal had not yet passed Congress, business leaders and trade associations—with reasonable assurance of the measure's eventual passage—began detailing their plans for organizing and regimenting the members of their respective industries along the lines long advocated by business spokesmen. In the keystone of the New Deal, American business eagerly anticipated the dream of a system for controlling competition and bringing trade practices within more comfortable boundaries. The press and trade journals of early 1933 echoed the resolutions, the spirit of cooperation, and the pleas for less aggressive competition heard since the end of World War I, with *Business Week* editorially observing "a surprising unanimity among business men in favor of the general theory" encompassed in the recovery proposal.[91]

General business sentiment in 1933 was in agreement with the influential business leader, Alexander Sachs, who assessed the period as an era of "economic nihilism" that "cannot be permitted to go on."[92] Henry Harriman appeared to sum up the reaction of businessmen in referring to the recovery bill as the "Magna Charta of industry and labor."[93] NAM president Robert L. Lund declared that his membership approved the bill as a means for reorganizing business and eliminating "demoralizing dangerous competition." Lund asserted that American industry had always been in sympathy with the purposes of the bill as a means of permitting it to "police itself against ruthless competition in the form of unregulated price cutting."[94] The NAM did voice opposition to some of the provisions of the recovery measure; it believed that the general impact of the licensing, import controls, and—most notably—the collective bargaining sections might be detrimental to business recovery. The manufacturers' group was not, however, opposed to the principle of industry-determined and government-enforced "codes of fair competition." As Lund was quick to point out, "the purpose" of the bill had the "entire approval" of his organization.[95] The NAM had, in fact, passed resolutions favoring the creation of self-regulating trade and employment standards, with a government agency (the resolution suggested the WIB) to promote and supervise such industry agreements until the emergency was terminated either by a presidential declaration or congressional resolution. Paradoxically, the resolution went on to condemn "experiments in government."[96]

The "constant inconstancy" of a freely competitive economy continued to provoke business to seek more permanent, stable relationships. Silas Strawn told a meeting of the U.S. Chamber of Commerce: "If we continue to adhere strictly to the theory that competition must continue regardless of the fate of the producer, it may become so keen as to deprive him of any return on capital invested and deny a living wage to his employes."[97] Business desired, according to Paul Litchfield, that "the destructive competition which had marked industry in the past be done away with."[98] He added: "[W]ere we permitted to establish fair and reasonable prices through group agreements the best interests of the country, social and financial, would be served."[99] The illusion that *institutional* interests could be served by maintaining equilibrium conditions fueled efforts to preempt the autonomy and flexibility necessary for the preservation of the health of the economic *system* itself.

It became increasingly evident that business efforts to subject trade practices to the enforceable collective will of industry members, were about to pay off. In May 1933, President Roosevelt came before the U.S. Chamber of Commerce for what critics might have characterized as a victory celebration. So delighted was the Chamber with Roosevelt's policies that it planned to have his address broadcast live over network radio, but FDR rejected this proposal, saying that his remarks were meant not for the general public but for Chamber members only. The esotericism implicit in Roosevelt's exclusion of the nonbusiness public—like that prevailing in the old "Gary dinners"—was a fitting prelude to the corporate-state cartelism of the NRA.

Chamber members greeted Roosevelt with what was described as "an enthusiasm which can hardly be overemphasized." His talk got right to the heart of what businessmen wanted to hear when he declared:

> In almost every industry an overwhelming majority of the units of the industry are wholly willing to work together to prevent overproduction, to prevent unfair wages, to eliminate improper working conditions. In the past success in attaining these objectives has been prevented by a small minority of units in many industries. I can assure you that you will have the cooperation of your government in bringing these minorities to understand that their unfair practices are contrary to a sound public policy.[100]

Chamber delegates responded with resolutions endorsing the industrial "self-regulation" inherent in Roosevelt's recovery program. In the words of the *Wall Street Journal*, these delegates anticipated that such regulation would "free the public from the detriments of competition."[101] At the same time, the trade journal *Steel* remarked editorially: "Industry should welcome the opportunity to participate in the shaping of the national industry recovery act. . . . The majority of industrial executives will be willing to sacrifice certain rights and privileges temporarily for the benefits to be derived from sanely coordinated activity."[102]

Additional business praise for Roosevelt came following a later radio broadcast in which he further outlined his industrial recovery program. Thomas J. Watson of IBM declared that businessmen were "appreciative and very thankful for the constructive work which [Roosevelt was] doing in our interests." The pharmaceutical industry's R. E. Spicer asked that "reasonable price-fixing be promptly permitted" in order to "prevent continuous ruinous cut-throat competition in the retail drug and other business." E. S. Jouett, vice-president of the Louisville & Nashville Railroad, was more succinct in stating: "Your address was the greatest I have ever heard from any one." Even Henry Ford, a man often held up as the epitome of twentieth-century "rugged individualism," ran a series of newspaper advertisements across the country praising FDR in these words: "Having observed the failure of sincere efforts to haul us back the way we came, he designed a new method—new political and financial machinery—to pull us out the way we are going—forward."[103]

Business leaders were thus able to segue the predepression rhetoric of "industrial cooperation" into the general recovery theme. Gerard Swope made the now commonplace assertion that "isolation is no longer possible for any one company" and that the only long-range security for industry was to "build up a strong autonomous self-regulating organization." Then, employing a non sequitur that had become almost trite by this time, Swope declared that the only alternative to such industrial self-regulation was regulation by the government itself. This same thought was voiced by Paul Litchfield, of Goodyear Tire and Rubber, who warned that the failure to resolve the current crisis would lead to state socialism.[104] The contention that the enactment of legislation compelling firms to adhere to industry created codes was necessary to forestall regulation by the government not only fails for lack of evidence or logic, but also ignores the basic fact of this proposed industrial recovery legislation, namely, that it *would* subject business to government direction. Granted, the source of the code provisions would be found in the wills of businessmen instead of government bureaucrats or politicians; but the failure of any firm to adhere to code norms would ultimately result in having the recalcitrant offender subjected to injunctions, fines, or other penalties enforced by administrative agencies and the courts. To suggest such a system as an *alternative* to government regulation is an abuse of poetic license, to say the very least.

4

Under the Blue Eagle
and Beyond

For no form of co-operation, small or great, can be carried on
without regulation, and an implied submission to the regulating
agencies.

—Herbert Spencer

The National Industrial Recovery Act was enacted into law by Congress on
13 June 1933, and with it was created the NRA. Whether one chooses to
praise this piece of legislation as the epitome of industrial enlightenment,
tolerate it as a pragmatic response to the depression, or condemn it as a
blatant exercise of political power to enforce industrial cartels, the functional realities of NRA code making are rather clear. Much has been written
on this "partnership between government and business," but no more succinct appraisal has been given than that of James Walker, who declared:

> In total effect this legislation was revolutionary. It reversed the age-old Ameri-
> can philosophy of free, wide-open competition. It denied the individual busi-
> nessman final determination of many questions of managerial judgment. The
> majority of an industry acting with government, or government alone, could
> restrain him as to plant expansion, plant location, and use of productive ca-
> pacity. Price controls could be imposed and selling territory limited. While
> he was not forced to join in code-making, he was bound by code terms and
> implementation.
>   From June, 1933, to May, 1935, monumental efforts were made to fit our
> economy into this strange system. Businessmen dropped productive work to
> swarm like bees around Washington, making codes, amending them, and inter-
> preting their uncertain provisions. Bureaucracy grew in geometric progression.
>   In the end most of American business, as well as the majority of our indus-
> trial workmen, had been brought within code control. Upwards of 731 codes
> were established. To create and implement them the President promulgated 70
> executive orders besides which administrative orders were issued to the extent
> of about 11,000.[1]

The NRA can be summarized as a system in which the essential business decision-making and trade practices of American commerce and industry were brought under the government-sanctioned direction and control of trade associations. The structure involved segmenting business firms into appropriate trade groupings ranging from such grand industries as iron and steel, petroleum, automobile manufacturing, and cotton textiles, to such esoteric industries as lightning rod manufacturing, steel wool, mop sticks, and corncob pipes. It is virtually impossible to conceive of an economic transaction involving commercial or industrial activity that would not have come within the domain of one (or more) of these numerous industry classifications. Each grouping was subject to the rule-making activities of the principal members of the industry involved, with the entire process supervised by the NRA, a separate federal agency headed by a man who had long been one of Bernard Baruch's chief lieutenants, General Hugh S. Johnson.

Johnson's military background reflected the combative nature of the NRA system. Having once referred to the NRA as a "Holy Thing . . . the Greatest Social Advance Since the Days of Jesus Christ," Johnson characterized the workings of his agency in these words:

> I think industry can both run itself and govern itself and that the coercive power of political government will be necessary only to discipline units within an industry which depart from practices which the overwhelming bulk of that industry regard as unfair and destructive. . . . Is this regimentation? If it is, it is regimentation by the majority itself through the peculiarly American doctrine of majority rule. That is no more regimentation than any form of government which any community elects to impose upon itself for the common good.[2]

Johnson's enthusiasm for "regimentation" was infectious. Bernard Baruch took up the martial spirit, suggesting that the recovery program be looked upon as a war. Baruch even recommended the creation of NRA insignias for businesses to use to identify themselves as "soldiers against the common enemy within," and to differentiate them from those who "are on the other side." This martial attitude was also reflected in the Rubber Manufacturers Association's appointment of Newton D. Baker, the former secretary of war, as special counsel to aid the industry in drafting a code of fair competition under the NRA.[3]

The basic machinery of the NRA consisted of industry "codes of fair competition" that had been submitted by one or more trade associations determined to be "truly representative" of the trade or industry to be regulated. Following a series of preliminary conferences and public hearings, a final draft of a code was settled upon by the members of the industry. If it received the approval of the NRA administrator, the code was sent on to President Roosevelt to either approve, modify, or reject. From start to finish, the code-making process was a joint effort by industry representatives, NRA officials, and the president to prescribe binding rules of business conduct upon all members of an industry. While the NRA codes were not unlike the trade association "codes of ethics" in their anticompetitive spirit and intent, they enjoyed what their predecessors had not: legal enforceability.

As the code-making process began, a struggle for the alignment of power ensued within the various trades and industries. Intraindustrial relationships that had, prior to the NRA, been established by the impersonal influences of the marketplace now became subject to political determination. Firms and groups that had achieved success through offering goods or services to customers on terms more favorable than that of their competitors and that, in the process, challenged the market positions of such competitors now found their competitive advantages taken away from them. Such loss of advantage occurred *not* as the result of superior competitive policies or strategies by one's adversaries, but as a consequence of abandoning free exchange and substituting political coercion. This code-making process was later described by Marshall Dimock in this way:

> During the NRA days, all through trains to Washington were filled with groups of excited businessmen from the same line of industry working until late at night putting the finishing touches on what they wanted Washington to sanction—because once these codes were approved and had been signed by the President their provisions were legally enforceable as standards of fair practice.[4]

The homogenous nature of the trade associations and government during the NRA years was evidenced not only in the code-making functions but in the enforcement phase as well. Each code was placed under the administration of a code authority, the membership of which was generally composed of industry members and one or more nonvoting representatives from the government. Depending upon the internal structure of a given industry, trade associations themselves were often named as the code authority for an industry. Thus, in the case of the steel industry, the board of directors of the American Iron and Steel Institute became appointed as the authority for the steel code. In spite of the varying forms the code organizations took, industry representatives were the dominant forces in establishing and administering the codes of fair competition, with the secretary of the code authority, in most cases, also being the chief administrative officer of the trade association.[5] The historian Paul Conkin has characterized the NRA this way:

> The N.R.A. never really tried, in any extensive or coherent way, to force public goals upon an unwilling business community. It was the businessmen who dominated the early N.R.A., both in the writing of codes and in the operation

of the enforcing code authorities. Usually without direct price-setting, most industry codes achieved the same result indirectly by limiting production, preventing price cutting, and forbidding unfair competition.[6]

Whatever rationalization might otherwise be offered to explain business support for the creation of the NRA, one inescapable fact remains: the NRA was the logical culmination of the basic premise that businessmen had been expressing for many years, namely, that a condition of free and unrestricted competition had to be restrained in order to protect the market positions and profit levels of their firms. The ceaseless struggle against entropic forces was too troublesome to those firms whose institutionalization had made them less resilient. An enforceable system for compelling overly aggressive challengers to respect the positions of existing firms and to restrain the pursuit of their own self-interests had not only been called for by business leaders throughout the 1920s but resulted in an overwhelming amount of support by that sector for the legislation creating the NRA. The NRA was far more than a freakish aberration of economic history: it was the natural outgrowth and instrumental expression of the emergent principle of industry-centered business thinking.

COMPETITION AND THE NRA CODES

Statements by business leaders in praise of the newly created NRA began flooding the newspapers, trade journals, and trade association meetings. Business response was overwhelmingly favorable, the general tone being *not* one of resignation to an inevitable fate, but an enthusiastic support that, in some cases, bordered on irrepressible excitement. It is quite clear that a large number within the ranks of commerce and industry looked upon this venture into government-enforced "business self-regulation" with the expectation of realizing more than simply recovery from the depression. The same anticompetitive oratory that dominated business thought and policy during the 1920s and that underlay business efforts on behalf of political alternatives for industrial stabilization during the years preceding the depression flowered once again in expressions of business support for the NRA. Trade association officials enthusiastically began the task of rounding up industry members to get them branded with a "code of fair competition" that would effectively make all business firms subject to the will of the leading members of the industry. The attitude of businessmen toward the NRA was poignantly described by one business magazine:

Washington hotels rejoice and Cabinet members groan over the wild rush of business men to the capital to find out about the new industrial plan. They want to know everything, but mostly how to punish the rascal who has been cutting prices in their industry, and how to fix some nice new prices.[7]

The presidents of the U.S. Chamber of Commerce and the NAM reiterated their support for the new law, with Henry Harriman noting: "The act will permit legitimate business enterprise to lift itself above destructive competition which has prevented recovery." Robert L. Lund confirmed that "[i]ndustry at all times has been in sympathy with the declared objectives of the legislation."[8] Harriman, as we have seen, had long been attracted to the idea of a politically structured economic system and, in April 1933, had gone so far as to testify to a congressional committee that he favored amending the Constitution itself in order to grant to the president the power to control industry.[9] He elaborated his support for economic planning in a simplistic analysis that has since become the bromide of every pseudoeconomist: "[T]he laissez-faire economy which worked admirably in earlier and simpler industrial life must be replaced by a philosophy of planned national economy."[10]

Impassioned response to the NRA was expressed by a number of business leaders, including Harry Thayer, former president of Western Electric and long an advocate of "trade combination." Thayer confirmed that business support for the system contemplated under the Recovery Act was more than simply a desperate response to a desperate problem; he declared that the enactment of the NRA "seemed . . . to be almost worth the price of the depression."[11] Others in the electrical manufacturing industry expressed the hope that, even when the depression was over, portions of the NRA could be made applicable as a permanent tool for economic planning.[12] An official of the American Paint and Varnish Manufacturers Association stated that the new legislation "could readily eliminate abuses which [the association] has been fighting since its formation in 1899."[13] Not inappropriately, perhaps, the National Fertilizer Association looked forward to "cleaning up a number of bad trade practices."[14] Perhaps the attitude of business toward the developing "partnership" with the state was best expressed by one of the leading business publications in a May 1933 editorial titled "Toward Stability," which recounted:

The American business man at this moment is utterly weary of the ruthless competitive struggle. It has been too much for him; he has survived so far, but he is spent. He is willing, he feels just now, to surrender some part of his freedom of action to achieve a degree of stability.

It will take some pains to work out details. But the solution is not impossible and it is worth all the pains and time it may cost. Let industry formulate its own codes of practice. Each industry knows its own special needs, its own problems. Let the government supervise these self-formulated codes, first to see that they are fair to the public, second, to see that they are enforced on the unscrupulous fringe who will never cooperate voluntarily with the majority, and who, under the present system of free competition, can undo the progressive work of all the rest.

Limit this, if you like, to the period of the emergency. Once tried we predict the system never will be abandoned.[15]

One of the more energetic boosters of the NRA was Thomas Watson. His support ranged from employing IBM's in-house publication to promote the NRA to ordering company employees to participate in NRA parades. In his words, "We must do something to help them. We have no right to think or talk of the NRA failing. It is not going to fail."[16] Another supporter, the shipbuilder and NAM official C. L. Bardo, called the NRA "the most important legislation ever enacted," while Alfred I. duPont stated that he had always favored legislation that would set aside the antitrust laws and permit business to be conducted "as it should be, free from inordinate competition."[17]

Business leaders were generally hopeful that the system contemplated in the recovery bill would become a permanent institution even after the emergency of the depression was over. Some mechanism for enforcement was inevitable if, indeed, business was to be transformed from the myopia of individual firm self-interest to the farsighted perspective of the collective interests of the industries. Since the NRA allowed for both government enforcement and industry determination and control of code standards, the arrangement was understandably attractive to business leaders.

One of the more optimistic visions of economic organization was given by a trade association president and former Federal Trade Commission member, Nelson Gaskill, who foresaw "an economic sovereignty the like of which the world has never seen." The provisions of the recovery bill would become permanent, he predicted, and from it a "regulated competition or a systematized democracy will develop." Gaskill was of the view that the fierce competition of earlier years was being rejected by business and that such competition could be moderated through the use of licensing, under which existing members of an industry could effectively exclude the entry of new firms.[18]

It should come as no surprise to learn that the most popular code provisions in the various trades dealt with pricing policies. Over 70 percent of the codes provided for uniform methods for determining costs, established practices for the setting of minimum prices and eliminating "below-cost" selling, and prohibited "commercial bribery" and rebates. Fifty-nine percent of the codes set up a system of "open pricing"; price discrimination, defamation of a competitor, interference with the contractual relationships of a competitor, and "piracy" were other popular subjects.[19]

A forthright appraisal of the self-seeking efforts of business organizations in developing NRA codes was provided by Dudley Cates, an insurance executive who also served as an assistant to Hugh Johnson. Cates noted that "a substantial majority" of the codes had been able to restrain the "excessive competition" that had caused "unbearable hardship and shocking loss." All too often, however,

> the NRA has been cluttered up with a multitude of codes of another kind, proposed by naively hopeful business men whose attitude gives the lie to the theory that we are a race of rugged individualists. Accepting the law as an invitation to occupy front seats at the millennium, they deposited their problems on the Government's doorstep. Many of these codes go far beyond wage and hour provisions and other protection to labor rights, and propose the changing of trade rules which do not even remotely touch public interest. . . . Many of the pending codes have no purpose other than to destroy some strategic advantage gained by the foresight, the energy, or the skill of some individuals or groups, to the envy of their competitors. Imaginations have been running high in search of ways to capitalize the act for private advantage.[20]

The rubber industry's exploitation of the code-making process demonstrates the anticompetitive nature of the recovery system. Like so many other industries, the rubber manufacturers had experienced intense competition that had manifested itself in the form of lowered prices. In spite of voluntary efforts within the industry to curb such practices, price cutting continued to dominate the industry. Not unexpectedly, therefore, the tire manufacturers looked to the NRA for price increases for their products. Harvey Firestone identified the major problems in his industry as "secret prices and rebates, causing discriminatory prices and price cutting," and went on to advocate an open-price system as part of the industry's code. Firestone expressed particular concern with the sellers of the so-called special brand tires and sought to control their pricing practices, which included price cutting and large trade-in allowances on used tires. The "special-brand distributors," Firestone lamented, were able to undersell the independent tire dealers, putting pressure on tire manufacturers "to meet the prices of the special-brand tires or be eliminated from the business." The Retail Rubber Tire and Battery Trade Code, which declared destructive price cutting to be an unfair method of competition, was a fair reflection of the role the NRA codes played in realigning competitive relationships, providing some firms—through political means—with advantages over competitors that they had been unable to obtain in a system of free competition.[21]

The tendency of the code-making processes to indulge the price-raising preferences of industry representatives may have gratified the short-range desires of businessmen, but as a measure designed to get the economy out of the throes of the depression it was counterproductive. One of the major problems faced by many industries was that of clearing stocks of unsold merchandise. This problem is overcome in the marketplace by a fall in prices, which stimulates demand to buy up the surpluses. One very effective way to interfere with this adjustment mechanism is to maintain prices above free-market levels, thus preventing the clearance of surpluses that is necessary for economic recovery.[22] The use of the codes of fair competition—under what has been regarded as the keystone of the New Deal program—provided legal impediments to the adjustments of supplies to demand. Its counterproductivity, especially when considered in connection with the effect of such measures as wage-maintenance provisions,[23] constitutes one of the more damning indictments of politically based economic planning.

NRA codes dealt not only with pricing policies and other competitive practices but with the regulation of production as well. Since both the level and stability of prices were largely related to the amount of and fluctuations in production, business efforts to effectuate a more regularized environment placed a great deal of emphasis on production factors. This desire to stabilize production was particularly evident in the petroleum and textile industries, where fluctuations in production had been responsible for price instability. Production controls in the NRA codes involved setting maximum production quotas for each company, determining the maximum number of hours (whether on a daily, weekly, or monthly basis) in which production could take place, and/or establishing controls over new productive capacity for firms and/or production for the purpose of increasing inventories. Any number of variations or mixture of these control methods could be found in the codes. Out of sixty codes controlling the number of hours for the operation of plants and/or machinery, forty-three involved the textile industry.[24] There were only eight codes that established maximum production quotas, but these included the codes of such basic industries as cement, copper, glass containers, iron and steel, lumber and timber, and petroleum. [25]

Code restrictions on the creation of new productive capacity were prominent within the textile industries, iron and steel, petroleum, transportation, and the clay products, glassware, and cement industries. As the category implies, these provisions were designed to limit the construction of new—or the modification of existing—productive facilities or, in some cases, even to limit the entry of new firms, all for the purpose of further controlling production. The most important codes seeking to control the amassing of additional inventories were those governing the petroleum and cement industries.[26]

On the whole, one finds a very high correlation between the provisions of the NRA codes and the voluntary undertakings from prior years (such as the trade association "codes of ethics") regarding trade practices thought to be most harmful to the collective interests of industries. If one digs through the veneer of "social responsibility" rhetoric and the emotional appeals that surrounded the NRA, one is left with a collection of legally enforceable, politically imposed codes that kept the competitive behavior of business firms within the more comfortable and nonthreatening boundaries long desired by principal firms within the various industries. These interests, seeking to preserve the value of their assets by maintaining their market positions against the assaults of competitive interlopers, achieved through the NRA the long-sought objectives of having enforceable, industry-controlled cartels. The NRA, as much as anything else, symbolized the completed emergence of a collectively defined system of "business." It was a victory of organized industry over individual firms.

Paradoxically, in endeavoring to promote commercial and industrial stability, the NRA was enervating the very competitiveness that rendered firms—as well as the economic system as a whole—resilient enough to continue the negentropic processes necessary for their survival. Apparently unaware that the maintenance of equilibrium conditions was a denial of the dynamical and transformative nature of any healthy organism, most members of the business community seemed eager to relax the intensity of the continuing efforts to overcome entropy. Whatever long-term disadvantages might be visited even upon the firms advocating such policies were ignored as faith in the collective illusion of security intensified. That such political structuring was tantamount to fostering a hardening of the arteries, arthritis, and obesity within an otherwise healthy organism, was to be left to future judgments.

BUSINESS ASSESSES THE NRA

Business reaction to the NRA was by no means universally favorable. A great deal of opposition had developed, largely among smaller industrialists who did not have as much influence in the code-making process within their industries. There was also criticism of the administration of the NRA, with businessmen often addressing themselves to such problems as "bureaucracy" in general, procedural rigidities, arbitrariness, and an ineffectiveness occasioned by having an agency invested with too broad a scope of responsibility and too little authority.[27]

In spite of sizeable opposition, however, it is clear that a substantial portion of the business community favored the NRA concept. A referendum of the membership of the U.S. Chamber of Commerce, in late 1934, showed overwhelming allegiance to the idea of a compulsory system for regulating trade practices. While 87 percent of those responding favored the proposal for allowing the existing act to expire in June 1935 "in accordance with its provisions," support was also voiced for the following proposals:[28]

For enactment of new legislation prior to expiration of the N.I.R.A.	FOR AGAINST	78.1% 21.9%
To permit industry to formulate its own rules of fair competition, subject to government approval.	FOR AGAINST	95.2% 4.8%
To restricting the power of the government agency to approval or veto.	FOR AGAINST	94.6% 5.4%
To have rules of fair competition enforceable against all concerns in the industry.	FOR AGAINST	91.8% 8.2%

Such results would appear to indicate opposition to the administration of the NRA as then constituted but support for the principle of business-determined and government-enforced controls to restrict competitive trade practices to within parameters favored by the more influential members of an industry.

Continued support for the NRA came from a variety of business sources, including Pierre S. duPont, Gerard Swope, and General Motors's Alfred Sloan.[29] The National Association of Credit Men, an organization claiming a membership of some twenty thousand in the fields of manufacturing, banking, and distribution, announced the results of a poll of their membership that showed 57 percent favoring a continuation of the NRA. On the other hand, the board of directors of the Illinois Manufacturers Association, long an opponent of the NRA, adopted a resolution opposing the NRA's continuation in any form. The New York and Philadelphia Boards of Trade also favored the termination of the NRA.[30]

Simultaneously with its being freed from the era of prohibition, the brewing industry produced enthusiasts for the NRA. In the opinion of the influential Jacob Ruppert, the NRA restrictions were "a blessing and an opportunity."[31] William Piel added his endorsement, calling the NRA an exercise in "self-regulation," which he described as "the government willing to prosecute and punish code violators only at industry's own command."[32] One might question the willingness of members of this industry, having been legally put out of business for a time as the result of political intervention, to so eagerly embrace this latest exercise of political authority over the marketplace. Such an apparent anomaly, however, may be explainable as an expression of the short-range outlooks that too often characterize business decision-making.

Carleton E. Palmer, president of the pharmaceutical company E. R. Squibb

& Sons, had considered price cutting to be a major problem in his industry and called for "cooperation rather than destructive competition."[33] Since his firm has been one of the leading manufacturers of aspirin, the opportunity ought not be passed up to recall novelist William Saroyan's classic response to an unidentified aspirin commercial that closed with a reminder that "aspirin is a member of the NRA." "Maybe," Saroyan quipped, "the NRA is a member of aspirin," explaining that both were "deadening a lot of pain, but they [weren't] preventing any pain."[34]

With the statutorily created expiration date of June 1935 approaching, many business and trade association leaders undertook a campaign to extend the life of the NRA for an additional two-year period. Business rallies were held to promote such an extension, and the Business Advisory and Planning Council of the U.S. Department of Commerce—a body composed of industrialists—went on record favoring a two-year extension.[35] The NAM and the Congress of American Industry held a joint convention at which they adopted a platform calling, in part, for a one-year extension of a modified NRA agency. While the platform spoke of having codes of fair competition be "voluntary on the part of industry," it was rather evident that the same definition of "voluntariness" was being applied here as previously, namely, that a code should not be imposed upon an industry unless a majority of the members of that industry approved it. Having received the backing of such a majority, however, the standards "should be binding upon the minority."[36]

Two basic proposals for NRA extension were before Congress: one, a resolution offered by Senator Bennett Clark to continue the NRA to 1 April 1936; the other, a measure offered in the House by Robert Doughton for a two-year extension. While these measures were under consideration, a rally of some seventeen hundred businessmen was held in New York City to support the Doughton proposal because of its greater time-frame.[37] This position was also endorsed at a meeting of some fifteen hundred businessmen held in Washington, D.C.[38]

Other trade associations and business executives joined in supporting a two-year renewal of the NRA, with heavy support coming from those industries that, prior to 1933, had been most subject to intense competition. George Sloan, chairman of the Consumers' Goods Industries Committee, stated that the two hundred industries represented by his group favored the two-year extension proposal—rather than the alternative ten-month extension—adding that most of the objections to the NRA had come from a "minority element that has opposed the NRA from the beginning." This minority, he observed, came not from highly competitive industries but from those which had been "better able to prevent the effects of cut-throat competition without the aid of the Recovery Act." Spokesmen from such industries as retailing, clothing and textiles, coal, steel, paper, drugs, tobacco, and copper also endorsed such an extension. One trade association official spoke of the need for a "revised NRA" that would "adapt itself to the present day needs and not the economic society of fifty years ago." Noting opposition from some business interests, Donald Richberg was nevertheless moved to claim, in testimony before the Senate Finance Committee, that 90 percent of business wanted the NRA continued.[39]

In spite of the experiences of prior years, some business representatives believed that the NRA controls on competitive practices could be effectively maintained without government enforcement. A man who had served not only as counsel to several trade associations but as a member of the Consumers Goods Industries Committee as well was of the opinion that voluntary compliance could be had on such NRA code provisions as the filing of prices, control of production, minimum wages, maximum hours, and requirements for uniform discounts.[40] One executive indicated that businessmen were adhering to the labor standards established under the NRA in order to retain the advantages from the trade practice provisions in the codes. An abandonment of the wage and hour standards was implicitly threatened if the fair-trade provisions were eliminated.[41]

Consistent with the results of its prior referendum, delegates to the May 1935 meeting of the U.S. Chamber of Commerce adopted a resolution favoring the enactment of new legislation to "permit voluntary codes of fair competition by industries actually engaged in interstate commerce." Henry Harriman predicted that the NRA, in one form or another, would "become a permanent part of our economic policy" and urged a retention of the good sections and the elimination of the bad portions of such legislation.[42]

The thought that the organization of business along NRA principles would become a permanent feature had been expressed in December 1934 by industrialist George H. Mead in terms that further establish the NRA as the product of decades of business effort to stabilize trade practices:

> I think that the codification of industry along such lines [as the NRA] as it has been conducted is going to be continued for many years. I think that the experiment is not really a new experiment, but is the culmination of thirty years of thinking, and I think that the development is here to stay. . . .

Mead, who had served as chairman of the NRA's Industrial Advisory Board, acknowledged that this program had not been particularly revolutionary, and that if in it there was any fault to be found, it was that "too much was tried in an entirely too short a time."[43]

The campaign by business leaders to persuade Congress to extend the NRA was rendered moot when, on the eve of the statutory expiration date, the Supreme Court handed down its landmark decision, *Schechter v. United States*.[44] The case involved a small poultry-slaughtering business in Brooklyn that was charged with violating the minimum wage, maximum hours, and sales practice provisions of the NRA "Live Poultry Code." The conviction, affirmed by the circuit court of appeals, was overturned when the Supreme Court declared the NRA unconstitutional. The crux of the decision was that the act unlawfully delegated legislative power to the executive branch of the government, as well as extended federal authority beyond matters directly affecting commerce by controlling practices of a purely local nature. With the Court having earlier decided, in the *Panama Refining Company* case,[45] that the oil control section of the act had extended too much discretionary authority to the president to prohibit the transportation of "hot oil," the *Schechter* decision could not have been totally unexpected.

Though the *Schechter* case brought an end to the industry-wide system of government-enforced codes, it did not diminish the efforts of business leaders to stabilize competitive conditions and practices. In the words of Theodore Lowi, "[T]he practice of government controls in cooperation with trade associations did not end; it simply became less formal and explicit."[46] The commonly accepted notion that American business breathed a collective sigh of relief over the demise of the NRA is inaccurate. The business opposition that did develop tended to focus more upon *administrative* difficulties than upon the principle of government enforcement of industry-determined trade standards.

The board of directors of the NAM issued a statement declaring that, as a result of the *Schechter* decision, "the opportunity is again afforded for industry to go forward on a basis of voluntary self-government." They went on to "urge every trade and industrial association to take immediate steps within its sphere to stabilize wages, hours, working conditions and competitive practices on a voluntary basis."[47] Their statement seemed to reflect the attitudes of the membership, a canvass of which showed an intention to voluntarily maintain wage, hour, and fair-practice regulations.[48] The president of the U.S. Chamber of Commerce, Harper Sibley, echoed this sentiment in his call for the employment of trade associations to carry out the fair practice codes on a voluntary basis, while the Chamber's board of directors proposed the use of interstate compacts to accomplish industrial stabilization.[49] The president of the New York State Chamber of Commerce asserted that problems in industry had always been caused by a "10 percent" minority of businessmen.[50]

One industry after another met through their trade associations and, with few exceptions, proposed to continue adherence to standards and practices as set forth under the NRA codes.[51] Among the other more influential trade groups urging a continuation of existing code practices were the Cement

Institute, the National Electrical Manufacturers Association, the National Automobile Dealers Association, the Toy Manufacturers of the U.S.A., the International Association of Garment Manufacturers, the Institute of Carpet Manufacturers of America, the Associated Grocery Manufacturers of America, the National Association of Retail Grocers, the American Iron and Steel Institute, the National Association of Wool Manufacturers, and the Investment Bankers Association.[52] The degree to which the business community had come to identify government regulatory agencies with their own objectives was seen in the initial reaction of securities dealers, who looked for a transfer of NRA code principles to the Securities and Exchange Commission.[53] Even though the NRA had been swept into history, it had taught business how to achieve a political structuring of competitive practices while at the same time subjecting the controlling agency to industry influence and direction. Commenting editorially, *Business Week* declared:

> Thousands of business men have gained experience in a new kind of cooperation. Trade associations have been strengthened and trained in the business of eliminating evil trade practices and avoiding destructive competition. There would seem to be an opportunity now for a determined drive in the direction of voluntary cooperation in many industries.[54]

A subsequent *Business Week* editorial favored continuation of NRA standards and urged the passage of legislation permitting cooperation in industries suited to the code-making process.[55] Business attitudes were such that, by January 1937 Harper Sibley was able to assert: "American business recognizes the advisability and feasibility of proper regulation by government in many fields of business, as in the Interstate Commerce Commission, where the regulatory body acts as an impartial umpire among conflicting interests."[56]

With the NRA laid to rest by the Supreme Court, business interests had a revived interest in the trade practice conferences, a procedure all but forgotten in the preceding two years. Only a small number of these conferences had been held during 1934 and 1935, and those involved either conferences that had been undertaken before the NRA was in full operation or, as in the case of the wholesale drug trade, an industry that refused to adopt an NRA code. In 1936, however, the FTC held conferences for some sixteen industries, while receiving additional post-NRA voluntary codes from twenty-two other industries. More conferences were held the next three years. Gilbert H. Montague went so far as to suggest a reconsideration of the Nye bill, under which the controversial Group II rules could, if approved by the majority of firms within an industry, be made legally binding upon the minority as well.[57]

Having seen the advantages to be derived from a business-government partnership in the structuring of the marketplace, various trades and industries began—even before the *Schechter* decision—to propose legislative programs to control specific industries or regulate specific trade practices.

The sugar industry, for example, which had long felt the need to "harmonize conditions"[58] between buyers and sellers (a euphemism for promoting price stability), succeeded in getting legislation enacted in 1934 establishing a sugar quota system. This law afforded the industry the means of controlling the most important factor affecting prices, namely, production. Under it, the secretary of agriculture was empowered to establish both foreign and domestic supplies of raw sugar and to allocate this quantity among existing producers. This quota system led to a situation in which government divination of such factors as supplies and future demand replaced impersonal market influences. With production thus artificially stabilized, the sugar industry was able to realize—at the expense of consumers—a less competitive pricing structure.[59] Likewise, the Food, Drug, and Cosmetic Act— enacted in 1938 with the support of food processors—was designed to force the minority of processors to adhere to production standards advocated by the more numerous firms.[60] Further, the Agricultural Marketing Agreement Act of 1937 provided for the establishment of "marketing agreements" among producers of agricultural commodities. Upon receiving the support of two-thirds of the handlers of such products, these agreements became legally binding upon *all* handlers whether they had agreed to such terms or not. Reflecting their NRA ancestry, these agreements "provided for a three-cornered determination of price policy and the manipulation of supplies which would achieve the price objectives agreed upon by processors and distributors . . . counselled by representatives of the Secretary of Agriculture, to whom was reserved the right to approve or disapprove their proposed action."[61]

The Motor Carrier Act of 1935 was the outgrowth of support from many quarters in the field of transportation, including the railroad industry, which, since the railroads had long dominated the ICC, was desirous of bringing other transportation systems under the control of this agency.[62] The railroads were characterized by one observer as desirous of promoting "any legislation which might hinder the growth of commercial motor transportation."[63] The larger motor carriers, in a display of intraspecies aggression common to legislative campaigns, joined in supporting expanded ICC control over other facets of transportation. While the smaller operators tended to oppose the measure, the American Trucking Association backed it.[64] In recognition of the effect that free competition in the transportation industry would likely have on freight rates, backing for the concept of an expanded ICC came from the more dominant and influential trade organizations.[65]

Meanwhile, the air transport industry had been promoting federal regulation as a means of protecting the interests of existing firms from the encroachment of competition. The Civil Aeronautics Act of 1938 was fostered by industry members seeking to limit the entry of new competitors and to control trade practices in order to protect their investments. The attitude of airline industry members was well-represented in the testimony of Edgar S. Gorrell, president of the Air Transport Association, who favored such regulation in order to provide a reasonable assurance of permanence to the air carriers. Alleging that 50 percent of the investments in the industry had already been lost, Gorrell maintained that a number of airlines would face serious financial difficulties unless they were protected from so-called cutthroat competition.[66] As one scholar has described industry efforts on behalf of such legislation:

> The hearings, reports, and debates on a regulatory measure are replete with condemnations of "unbridled," "cut-throat," "disastrous," "destructive," "wasteful," "unregulated" competition and of "chaotic conditions," "unsound ventures," "haphazard growth," "blind economic chaos," and industry sowing of "wild oats." What was favored was "orderly and sound growth," "orderly planning," "a measure of stability," and "financial stability."[67]

IN RETROSPECT

The NRA was a culmination of long-sought business objectives of reducing the uncertainties and fluctuations brought on by lively and aggressive competition. It had been fathered, midwifed, and eventually mourned by commercial and industrial interests seeking the most effective machinery for cartelizing American industry. Hugh Johnson, in responding to the charge that the NRA involved business regimentation, stated that "there was not one single code that industry did not propose and beg to have applied."[68] While the business community had neither a monopoly on wanting to coerce others into group-serving behavior nor a universal and monolithic disposition for doing so, it is quite difficult to find—either before or after 1933— examples of regulatory schemes that did not arise from the efforts of some business interests to secure advantages over their competitors that were unattainable in an unrestrained market.

Gardiner Means has identified four different groups that were instrumental in helping to create the NRA: (1) business groups who had been interested in getting the antitrust laws set aside in order to allow firms in an industry to get together to eliminate "destructive price cutting or price chiseling"; (2) the "industrial self-governors" who were interested in a "more comprehensive industrial self-government" for industry; (3) organized labor; and, (4) various persons—such as Rexford Tugwell—who had more of a philosophical interest in industrial planning. Means went on to identify three principal benefits that were provided by the NRA: (1) the "therapeutic value" of ending the "state of shock" in which business found itself as a result of the depression; (2) establishing organized labor as a source of "countervailing power" within the business sector; and, (3) getting "the idea of industrial self-government"—which he acknowledged as being influenced by the "fascist experience" of earlier years—"out of our system."[69] In words that reflect the sense of "cooperation" that the business community had labored so hard to institutionalize during the postwar years, Thurman Arnold observed that the NRA "expressed the change which had come over men's thinking," adding that "[t]he profit motive, which at one time was a respectable justification for any sort of price-cutting, had become a somewhat immoral thing because of the competing symbol of cooperation."[70]

Some might wish to argue that the 1930s began in the business-dominated spirit of the Swope Plan and NRA codes of fair competition, but ended in the anti-big-business rhetoric of Thurman Arnold and the Temporary National Economic Committee. Indeed, as head of the Antitrust Division, Arnold's "trust-busting" activities gave the outward appearance of a fundamental shift in governmental policy. But while his efforts had some limited impact on business behavior,[71] there is little evidence of any business disenchantment with the general principle of a politically backed industrial "self-regulation." Quite the contrary. Arnold himself declared in July 1939 that "[i]t is business men and business men alone who file practically all the complaints with my division, and it is for business men that the anti-trust laws must be enforced."[72] One searches in vain during the post-*Schechter* years for any widespread expression of business sentiment for an economic system premised upon laissez-faire principles, or for the impersonal order implicit in Adam Smith's "invisible hand."

The New Deal is often equated, in both popular and scholarly literature, with the demise of laissez-faire brought about by a discreditation of its self-regulatory mechanisms. As a polemic on behalf of corporate-state policies, such a view is understandable. As a statement reflecting historical fact or economic analysis, it is woefully inaccurate. Legislative inroads into economic life were occasioned *not* by the failure of the market to provide order and discipline but by the market's general immunity to being corrupted for the benefit of special interests. The purpose of such legislation, including the NRA legislation, was to repress and stabilize competitive conditions—to ossify industries and restrain those influences that represented the threat of change. Although the policy arguments offered on behalf of such political programs emphasized socially conscious motives, their real purpose was to provide the coercion essential for holding together a collectivized industrial order. The partnership between business and government that continued to unfold during the 1930s was much more than a simple marriage of convenience. It represented, instead, a response made necessary by the inherent weakness in every form of collectivism (including cartels), namely, the tensions between private and group interests.

The motives of self-interest that living systems have in acting to overcome entropy spontaneously generate that intense expression of energy we call a "competitive marketplace." Perhaps, as we develop a more integrated and holistic view of our biological, economic, and psychological natures, we will begin to understand the importance of maintaining social systems and practices that maximize the opportunities for autonomous and resilient behavior. As historians remind us, there is always the danger that social organizations—created as tools to coordinate our creative, negentropic efforts—will seek to *institutionalize* themselves and to regard their organizational permanence as their raison d'être. They will then undertake—whether through voluntary or political means—to structure the environments in which they operate, so as to reduce the intensity of such negentropic efforts. When this occurs, as Quigley and others have pointed out, the processes by which we act to resist entropy and sustain ourselves become thwarted. Furthermore, because our own needs to generate negative entropy continue to express themselves, institutional efforts to maintain these structured environments become intensified. In time, unless such institutionalizing practices are reversed—thus restoring the unhindered processes by which we (individually and societally) act to resist entropy—we may experience the collapse of the civilization itself. It is upon the consideration of such broader consequences that we ought to focus our attentions in evaluating business efforts on behalf of politically enforced stability.

5

The Steel Industry

The essential purpose of a cartel is to keep competitors from cutting each others' prices. . . . The goal is to restrain disturbing influences, to stabilize prices, and to assure those in the business the comfortable feeling that their position is secure.

—Harold Fleming

The years following World War I found the steel industry actively involved in the trade association movement in an effort to harmonize and moderate trade practices. Through not only association "codes of ethics" but, more importantly, the rhetoric of "cooperation" expressed by its leading spokesmen, the steel industry sought to tranquilize competitive pressures. No industry made greater use of its trade association in seeking to promote a spirit of "cooperative competition" than did the steel industry in its employment of the American Iron and Steel Institute (AISI).

Though this study is focused upon the post–World War I years, it would be misleading to assume that only then did steel industry efforts begin to establish a more cooperative form of competition. Actually, the tone for the spirit of "cooperation" had been expressed at least as early as 1913 by two of its abler spokesmen: George W. Perkins, the right-hand man of J. P. Morgan and a director both of U.S. Steel and International Harvester, and Elbert Gary. Perkins declared:

I do not believe that competition is any longer the life of trade. . . . I have long believed that cooperation through large industrial units properly supervised and regulated by the Federal Government, is the only method of eliminating the abuses from which labor has suffered under the competitive method. I believe in *cooperation and organization* in industry. I believe in this for both *labor and capital. . . under strict regulation and control of the Federal Government* in order that they may give the public the maximum amount of good and the minimum amount of evil.[1]

123

Gary added:

> We have taken a new departure; we have left the old lanes; we have abandoned
> the old practices; we are dealing in confidence one with the other; we are look-
> ing further ahead than we used to. When prices go off one per cent, we do not
> immediately run out into the market and put our prices down ten per cent in
> order to see if we cannot get ahead of our neighbor and make five or six cents
> for ourselves, by securing business that legitimately belongs to him, even though
> we may lose five or six dollars within a week by doing it.[2]

The following year Gary added these words of advice to his colleagues:

> [L]et us have courage and let us be patient, taking care of our interests, and . . .
> trying in every way to help one another. Let us remember we cannot make
> anything for our individual selves by injuring any other person, and we cannot
> assist and benefit any of our neighbors or competitors in business without at
> the same time benefiting and assisting ourselves.[3]

There were few business leaders who devoted more of their time and
energies to moderating competitive trade practices than Elbert Gary. Employing the meetings of the AISI as his customary forum, Gary came to be
recognized as the chief missionary of the new gospel of "cooperation," a
role he carried out with the fervor and eloquence of a faith healer. "Cooperation" for the steel industry became one of the catchphrases of the day,
one of those harmless-sounding bromides guaranteed to bring convention
delegates to their feet in thunderous applause. Much of the progress that the
steel industry was able to make toward the realization of a more passive
form of competition can be traced to the efforts of Gary, whose message can
be summarized by the phrase, "destructive competition must give way to
humane competition."[4] Because of the significant impact that Gary's views
had as a catalyst for industry attitudes, rather close attention should be given
to his estimates of the quality of competitive life in American business and
his proposals for improving it.

One must preface an examination of the statements of steel industry
spokesmen by looking at conditions within the industry itself. Contrary to
the protestations of steel producers, who sought to create the impression
that World War I was a tremendous hardship on the industry, steel production and prices hit all-time highs during the war. As table 1 demonstrates,[5]
annual steel ingot production increased sharply—both in terms of tonnage
and percentage of total industry capacity—between 1914 and 1918, and
then dropped off just as dramatically following the end of the war. By 1923,
production returned to the general level of the war years 1916–18.

Table 5.1

Year	Annual Tonnage (millions of tons)	Percentage of capacity
1914	22.8	57.8
1915	31.3	71.5
1916	41.4	87.0
1917	43.6	86.5
1918	43.0	82.3
1919	33.7	63.5
1920	40.9	74.9
1921	19.2	34.5
1922	34.6	61.6
1923	43.5	76.6

The general price level rose sharply in 1916, climbed even higher in 1917, dropped off a bit in 1918 and 1919, reasserted itself in 1920, and dropped off further in 1921. In spite of the price decline following the war, the 1921 price level was significantly above the ten-year prewar average—in a range from 33 percent to 57 percent above those levels. Steel is a classic example of an industry characterized by economies of large-scale production, and the sharp changes in quantities of steel produced from year to year put tremendous pressures on firms seeking to align their respective volumes of output with their most efficient scale of production. The combination of decreased prices and production with increased plant capacity provided an environment after the war in which steel manufacturers dealt with business conditions and competitive practices within the industry.

U.S. Steel's market position at the start of the 1920s reflected the intensity of competition within the industry. Following the 1901 merger that gave it the predominant position in the industry, U.S. Steel experienced a steadily declining share of the steel market. Beginning with a 61.6 percent share of the nation's steel production in 1901, U.S. Steel found itself entering the postwar decade with only 39.9 percent of the industry's output. This pattern is not unlike that of the International Harvester Company, which, following the 1902 merger creating that firm, saw its share of the harvester market fall from 85 percent in 1902, to 80 percent in 1911, and 64 percent in 1918, while its market share for other implements also declined.[6] Since this was the era in which the courts applied the "rule of reason" to antitrust cases, and both U.S. Steel and International Harvester had been found not to have violated the Sherman Act, their respective declines in market shares cannot be attributed to a vigorous antitrust policy. Though the argument has been made that U.S. Steel's drop is explainable as the attempt of a monopolist to reduce its output in order to counter the decline in prices occasioned by the entry of new firms,[7] the phenomenon demonstrates the extent to which the company had to respond to the pressures of competition.

The postwar conditions within the steel industry helped foster a continuing criticism, by many steel producers, of the ethical standards of their competitors. Gary, for example, observed that persons engaged in competition are "naturally selfish" and "often inconsiderate and indifferent." He later explained, "[W]e seek to secure a little more of business when business is dull, because we think our stockholders or those who are depending upon us would be better satisfied if we made a little more money." He admonished his competitors to be more "reasonable and generous" with one another, and to seek "only our fair share of business, on the basis of fair profits." Noting that competition in the steel industry was "carried too far," Gary also expressed what some others had only implied, namely, that unrestricted competition was undesirable because of its effects on firms' profits, *not* because of any adverse consequences for customers:

> I do think that sometimes competition, which I have said is a great thing for all the people, has been carried too far, and from motives of selfishness we sometimes secure business for ourselves that really, justly and naturally belongs to some of our competitors.
>
> I think we fail to realize that in the long run, year by year, month by month, we will get more business, and certainly will get fairer prices, if we act more unselfishly, if all the time we consider the rights and interests of our neighbors.[8]

Gary then pointed out that it is oftentimes the newcomers to the industry who resort to the methods of "destructive competition" in order to gain a share of the market. To such persons, he suggested a policy of fairness and later declared, "We believe in competition, in vigorous, energetic, unyielding competition. . . . But we do not believe, or certainly most of us do not believe, in unfair, destructive, unrighteous competition, which is calculated to ruin the competitor. We believe . . . that stability and just dealing are desirable and beneficial to all who are interested."[9] Such statements reflect the view that the promotion of increased profits to the firm should be eschewed when the methods necessary to accomplish such ends conflict with the purpose of preserving the value of existing firms.

In an optimistic tone, Gary noted the change that had been taking place in the steel industry, a change nurtured by a spirit of "friendship" among competitors. He then quoted an industry member to the effect that "the real test of friendship is in adversity," but that such friendship had permitted business to change many of the "undesirable" business methods of prior years. "It is true," he concluded, "that the law of supply and demand still governs the output, and that we still have competition, but it is reasonable competition."[10]

Gary was later to elaborate upon his views with respect to the proper limits of competitive behavior. He said, "[E]very one of us should get out of this position of trying to get away our neighbor's business unfairly. And by that I mean the business that naturally comes to him." He then advised his colleagues to

> always take into account the rights and interests of your neighbor to the extent that you take into consideration your own. . . . [Y]ou know about what business you ought to have and how much your neighbor ought to have; and if you exercise your business rights and interests only as you ought, with decent concern for your neighbor, there will be a better maintenance of fair prices, there will be a more equitable division of business, and in the long run you will find you did a good thing, because you have been active or silent, as the case may be, in the restoration of business to its natural and proper equilibrium.[11]

As indicated earlier, any inquiry into the subject of "fair competition" by businessmen reveals that such a concept was intended as more than simply a discourse on abstract principles of ethics. The "fairness" of one firm's competitive methods was something that could be translated into another firm's profit and loss statement. The subject of "prices," then, was a continuing consideration, and Gary took occasion to outline his attitudes regarding "fair" pricing policies for business. While acknowledging that the customer has the right to seek the lowest possible price, he warned both customers and producers not to be so selfish as to end up "bringing about conditions which benefit one and prejudice the other." Then, as an expression of the concern about low prices and their effect on producers in the industry, Gary added a warning both to his competitors and to customers seeking lower prices that "there are others who are involved in the consideration of this question."[12]

Gary, in effect, rejected the role of market pricing as a regulator of economic activity. He once declared, "Prices should always be reasonable. The mere fact that the demand is greater than the supply does not justify an increase in price, nor does the fact that the demand is less than the supply justify lowering prices. What we want is stability—the avoidance of violent fluctuations."[13] The tendency of prices to seek equilibrium in response to fluctuations in supply and demand was ignored by Gary. What he was desirous of maintaining, of course, was not market responsiveness, but a stabilized level of profits that would be insulated from the consequences of managerial decisions in response to changes in market conditions.

Gary was so fervent in his hopes for greater industrial solidarity that he called for the steel manufacturers to begin holding regular meetings again, much like the old "Gary dinners." This proposal caused the industry's leading trade journal, *Iron Age*, to comment editorially upon the low prices that had resulted from intense competition and to add: "There is abundant evidence that the great problem of the steel industry, under present competitive conditions, is that of securing a reasonable profit for investors in its securities."[14] The views of Gary, then, were consistent with the sentiment that competition ought not be engaged in to the point where the existing positions of any firms were threatened. A much more restricted form of competition was envisioned, in which each firm acted with full consideration of the right of others not to be threatened with any serious invasions of their markets. It is in this sense that one must evaluate what was intended by the phrase "fair competition."

Anticipating the objection that a system of "cooperation" among members of the industry might simply be a euphemism for "restraint of trade," Gary sought to draw a distinction between competition that is "honest, fair and decent" and that which is "ruthless" and "destructive." In his opinion, "There can be perfect competition and, at the same time, perfect cooperation."[15] It is rather evident that, to Gary, "perfect competition" meant something less than a condition in which buyers and sellers would each be free to seek to maximize their well-being without having their efforts restricted by a claimed right of other sellers to be free from such a condition. "*Perfect* competition," in other words, was not to be identified with "*unrestricted* competition." The fact that "cooperation" was being resorted to as a means of moderating the influence of "unrestrained competition" makes Gary's statement but a further contribution to the already existing confusion regarding the nature of competition.

So successful was Gary in helping to mold opinion in the steel industry toward a greater degree of "friendly cooperation" and away from "destructive competition" that he was able to comment, in 1926:

Everyone present will remember the days when the steelmasters of this country were engaged in industrial war; when the hand of the steelmaker was raised against his brother; when practically, in the steel business, might made right; when the Golden Rule was subordinated to the supposed pecuniary, if temporary, success of might and strength; when jealousy, discord and brutal antagonism prevailed; and all this to the ultimate loss of all who were engaged in the strife. . . .[16]

As pointed out earlier, there were few—if any—business leaders who matched Elbert Gary's enthusiasm and influence in helping to generate an attitude receptive to bringing the dynamics of competition to within limits acceptable to most firms in an industry. There is a frankness in his views that contrasts with the sanitized pap generated by modern-day public relations technicians. His words leave us with little doubt as to the direction he felt business and governmental policy should take regarding the control of trade practices. In a visionary spirit, Gary went so far as to suggest that the principle of business cooperation be extended to the entire world.[17]

The profound influence of Gary's views upon the thinking of other members of the steel industry can be seen in the statements of men like Eugene G. Grace and Charles Schwab, both of Bethlehem Steel. Schwab, who became president of the AISI late in 1927 upon the death of Gary, offered one of the most blunt appraisals ever given by a businessman of the need for greater cooperation among producers:

> [D]estructive competition in an industry as large as ours, for the sole purpose of gaining a position in the industry, is ill-advised and costly to the people who have their money in the industry. Think of the fact that eight or nine billions of dollars are invested in the steel industry, and on the average we are not earning as much on our investment as we would if we had put our money in gilt-edged bonds. That is a wrong condition. What we want in this industry is the sincere and hearty cooperation of everybody in it. As Judge Gary has so often expressed it, live and let live. *These works are here and we have our customers and we have our trade and we have our position, and therefore we must try and respect our relative positions and see if we cannot do something toward the betterment of our returns, profits and business. That is the real purpose of the cooperative spirit that is necessary for the betterment of our business and the industry.*[18]

There is no other passage that so succinctly captures the spirit of cooperative competition. Schwab's words reflect an underlying business purpose to redefine competition as a less dynamic and flexible process, in order to maintain equilibrium conditions within industries.

Schwab, who was to succeed to Gary's position as chief spokesman for the steel industry, expressed his concern for stabilizing competition at a price level that would insure an adequate return on invested capital. He then launched an attack upon the perennial nemesis of most businessman: the "price cutter." Noting that "[t]here are always individuals who are shortsighted enough to believe that they can, by price cutting, secure an advantage peculiar to themselves," Schwab outlined what, in his estimation, were the three ways of stabilizing industry: namely, by increasing the demand for steel, by discouraging the construction of new productive capacity, and by the avoidance of "uneconomic price cutting."[19]

In an address to the AISI in October 1928, Schwab elaborated his views about the necessary conditions for prosperity in the industry. He placed heavy emphasis on limiting production through a moratorium on increased plant expansion. This would, he believed, "insure fair and reasonable profits in the industry for many years to come." Schwab again attacked price cutting, noting that the practice of charging different prices to different customers, instead of a "single price open to all," had resulted in harm to the industry "by inviting our customers to haggle over prices, and tempting them even to misrepresent the prices charged by our competitors in the hope of coaxing lower prices from us." Schwab also observed that the practice of a manufacturer from a different part of the country underbidding "the fair price" offered by the local plant would lead to "indiscriminate price cutting and to cross-hauling." He concluded that such a practice, along with the general policy of one producer lowering its price for a product would, in the long run, reduce the profit margin of each producer. An open-price policy would, in his estimation, lead to a stabilization of prices and a more prosperous condition for the industry.[20]

The similarity of thought among Gary, Schwab, and other members of the steel industry is reflected in the pronouncements of other executives and trade associations. Among those praising the importance of the spirit of cooperation for the steel industry were James A. Farrell, president of United States Steel; Willis L. King, vice-president of Jones & Laughlin Steel Corporation; James A. Campbell, president of Youngstown Sheet and Tube Company; and John F. Hazen, of Pittsburgh Steel Company. King appeared to sum up the hopes of many that this sense of cooperation would make the steel industry "what we would want and what we deserve in view of our investment."[21]

Fears of unrestrained competition were expressed elsewhere. In a message to the 1921 meeting of the AISI, one of its directors, Joseph G. Butler Jr., enunciated a typical industry reaction against "the evils of competition" that had been "directed only by a narrow and selfish policy" on the part of firms. "We all regret to observe signs of a revival of the old and disastrous idea of 'everyone for himself and the devil take the hindmost,'" he declared, and went on to urge a rededication to the "splendid policy of the last twenty years."[22] George M. Verity, president of the American Rolling Mill Company, spoke of the need for a legal way to control production in order to stabilize conditions in the industry,[23] while another industrialist, Thomas J. Foster, chairman of National Bridge Works, called for crystallizing "the best thought regarding proper relationships among competitors on the one hand and between mills and buyers on the other." Foster, concluding that business was still in a "state of barbarism," remarked that "[s]ociety cannot exist without proper controls."[24] Horace S. Wilkinson, of Crucible Steel Company of America, believed that "cooperation," rather than "attempting to do a one hundred per cent business against your competitors," would help promote prosperity for the industry.[25] Sharing these views was W. S. Horner, president of the National Association of Sheet and Tin Plate Manufacturers, who expressed his interpretation of the efforts to restrain the influence of what he termed the "killing pace of competition" from which American business had suffered an "overdose." Referring to "price cutting" as a "contagious disease" against which all of business must be "inoculated," Horner added:

> [T]here is only so much business to be placed, and each company usually obtains its due proportion, trading facilities and other manufacturing conditions considered. If more business is wanted, it is better to unite effort toward increasing the markets and uses of the manufactured product, whatever it may be, than to compete for a larger proportion on a purely price basis, at the expense of someone else, and in the end, at the sacrifice of sufficient profits necessary to the continued production of good quality material.[26]

Endorsing the same need for greater "cooperation" among members of industry, John L. Carter of Barlow Foundry told a convention of the National Founders Association in 1928: "The trend of the times is away from individualism and toward cooperative action. The foundryman who insists on running his business with a total disregard of the interests of his industry is out of date."[27] Charles N. Fitts, a steel-company executive and president of the American Institute of Steel Construction (AISC), stated: "Business individualism invites outside competition. Better organized industries from other sections of the country come in and take away from local firms the business that belongs to them by right of territorial location." Fitts urged a greater degree of cooperation "to fight for that business which is rightfully ours."[28]

Charles F. Abbott, executive director of the AISC, expressed the same desire for moderating individual decision-making in order to promote collective interests. Abbott, an active champion of industrial self-rule, stated his concern for the effects that unrestricted competition would have on one's competitors. He declared that "a manufacturer has as much right to legal protection as the consumer. He should be accorded as much protection from the vicious acts of his competitors as are consumers."[29] These statements necessarily lead to the conclusion that the major concern of the advocates of business "cooperation" was to structure the market in such a way as to eliminate competitive practices that would have an adverse effect upon established firms.

Abbott provided additional insight into his thinking when he declared that "short-sighted selfishness" was the root of most selling problems in industry. The answer to such selfishness lay in the development of a "spirit of justice and fairness and a sense of duty to one's industry," which could be achieved "through sincere cooperation and fair play." According to Abbott:

> The individual who refuses to cooperate with his competitors, and who insists upon ruthless price cutting as a means of obtaining business, is worse than a criminal. He is a fool. He not only pulls down the standing of his company; he not only pulls down his competitors; he pulls down himself and his whole trade. He scuttles the ship in which he himself is afloat.[30]

Abbott proceeded to outline what he believed were some of the more glaring unethical trade practices. These included a seller submitting "a second and lower price when the order rightfully belongs to a competitor"; a manufacturer selling to a jobber's customer at the same or lower prices than he had charged the jobber; a failure to adhere to a one-price policy; "commercial bribery"; and submitting a price to a customer that is not the lowest price the seller is willing to offer.[31]

It is rather clear that Abbott was primarily concerned with eliminating trade practices that were too competitive. Commercial bribery is nothing more than a rebate, a way of reducing the effective price to a buyer. The other practices complained of involve the outbidding of a competitor and the haggling process associated with bargaining and negotiation. Abbott believed that these practices subjected firms to a too severe competitive strain. In other words, as long as the competition did not become so aggressive as to cause other firms to have to abandon their traditional marketing practices, or did not pose a threat to established market positions, the practices would fall within the scope of "fairness." Seeking to provide stability in marketing procedures was consistent with Abbott's concern for establishing a condition of "stabilized production."[32] Much the same attitude was expressed by James Farrell in asserting that "we must get into our minds that all the customers do not belong to the man who wants to cut the price to get the business."[33]

The same sentiment was voiced by E. J. Frost, president of the American Gear Manufacturers Association, who, quoting Charles Schwab, declared: "The day of the individualist, when personal interest overshadowed all other motives, has passed. It has been forcibly demonstrated that individual prosperity depends absolutely upon the success of the industry; that no individual can permanently prosper at his industry's expense."[34] Though it may only appear that Frost was asserting that a firm could not prosper long if the product line of its industry were to disappear, closer examination reveals a concern that goes to the essence of the business community's problem in aggressively competitive behavior. Frost and other business leaders recognized that it is indeed possible for business firms to promote their individual interests and, at the same time, work against the industry's collective interests. Contrary to the literal meaning of Frost's words, individual firms *were* prospering at their industry's expense. As Mancur Olson's analysis suggests, it *was* true that individual firms were acting in furtherance of their own rational self-interest, even though their collective interests as members of an industry were being thwarted by these very actions.

Some steel-industry representatives voiced their support of the principle of amending the antitrust laws to permit businesses to cooperate more openly to stabilize competitive conditions. The Southern Metal Trades Association adopted a resolution opposing the Sherman and Clayton Acts, while the Metal Branch of the National Hardware Association voted to seek methods of modifying the antitrust laws to allow for greater cooperation. George H. Charls, president of the National Flat Rolled Steel Products Association, warned against "mindless, senseless, destructive competition" and sought to place the responsibility for adverse economic conditions upon the firm that "flagrantly slashes prices." The business community, Charls added, needed a "collective effort" to overcome "uneconomic" trade practices.[35]

The failure of the voluntary methods—whether in the form of codes of ethics or appeals to business "cooperation"—to effectively restrain such competitive conditions as price reduction, aggressive sales promotions, and challenges to a competitor's existing markets and clientele caused business leaders to turn to political methods to accomplish their objectives. Recalling Mancur Olson's analysis, where large groups are involved, "coercion" or some other "special device" is necessary to cause individuals to conform their behavior to what is in the interests of the group. It was recognized that the lack of effective means for enforcing restrictive agreements in the marketplace could be overcome by having trade practice standards enforced by political agencies that possessed the requisite coercive machinery.

In support of the proposition that the pursuit of individual interests ought to be moderated in favor of the promotion of collective interests, a number of business leaders sought to popularize the idea that entrepreneurs and managers should be regarded as stewards acting for the benefit of the general public and should be subject to the same degree of political oversight as the management of a charitable trust. Myron C. Taylor, chairman of United States Steel, asserted that "wealth is . . . a stewardship which must be exercised for the benefit of mankind at large."[36] George Perkins had made similar observations as early as 1908: "If the managers of the giant corporations feel themselves to be semi-public servants, and desire to be so considered, they must, of course, welcome supervision by the public, exercised through its chosen representatives who compose the government." Perkins was also of the opinion that "when an industrial corporation wishes to reach beyond the state in which it is created, it should be obliged to do so under Federal regulation," because, as he had often stated, the justification for government regulation of a business increased with the size of that business.[37]

In a hearing before the Senate Committee on Interstate Commerce, Perkins and Elbert Gary argued on behalf of a federal commission that would not only license but would have the authority to approve in advance, when asked to do so, the actions of corporations operating in interstate commerce.[38] Perkins envisioned a commission that would, in addition to licensing corporations, collect and publish data concerning business methods and organizational structures.[39] Whether Perkins was naive, disingenuous, or simply lacking in historical perspective is not evident from his view that government supervision of industries by agencies composed of former industry insiders posed no real threat of a conflict of interest. In his opinion, "the business man would merge into the public official, no longer controlled by the mere business view, and would act the part of a statesman." Perkins added that the business community did not fear government regulation itself—in fact, it welcomed it; it feared only "unintelligent, inexperienced administration," a condition that could be obviated by "a law requiring that those who supervise should be practical men, thoroughly versed in the calling."[40] That such "practical men" were conveniently to be found almost exclusively within the industries to be regulated attests to the cartelizing sentiments underlying a great deal of business thinking at this time. Gary reflected this view when, in 1919, he reiterated his support for a system of federal incorporation and licensing to be administered by a "disinterested commission" that would have the authority to "determine when and how and under what conditions a corporation should receive its charter or its license, and should have supervision over the management of the corporation."[41]

Like a number of other business spokesmen, Elbert Gary realized that any system for bringing competitive conditions under control would require enforcement by political institutions. His endorsement of such government regulation had been voiced in 1911 at the Stanley Committee hearings in the House of Representatives:

Martin Littleton: Your idea then is that cooperation is bound to take the place of competition and that cooperation requires strict governmental supervision?

Elbert Gary: That is a very good statement.[42]

Ten years later, he reiterated this position: "If it should be deemed necessary and wise to have governmental supervision over organized industry in order to protect the public interest, I personally would not object, provided the laws and rules shall apply alike to organized capital and organized labor."[43] He repeated this sentiment the following year when, in an address to the AISI, he noted that "the majority of individuals or associations, if they themselves are exempt and unmolested, are quite willing and even anxious to have all others subjected to the most rigid governmental investigation and exposure to the public." He then added that, while most might argue that American business would fare better without such supervision, "it seem[ed] to [him] to be fair and reasonable that big business, with all its advantages and power, should be subjected to governmental inquiry and supervision."[44] While Gary articulated such proposals as necessary for the protection of the "public interest," it is evident that the protection of much narrower *industry* interests was foremost in his thinking.

When one considers the relentless efforts of various industry leaders to create an environment immunized against aggressive methods of competition that threatened the stability and even the permanency of established firms, little imagination is required to depict the advantages anticipated from such a commission. An agency that is able not only to approve the content of business decisions but also, by implication, to withdraw the licenses of firms unwilling to adhere to prescribed standards of conduct would possess the element of enforcement necessary to make effective that which voluntary compliance failed to realize. Government, in other words, would supply the coercion that Olson's analysis tells us is essential to the enforcement of group interests.

A much bolder argument for government regulation of business was made in early 1928 by Julius Kahn, president of Truscon Steel Company. Kahn referred to the government as "the guardian of the nation's industry," declaring that "the Government must assume the trusteeship of our welfare." He then went on to state, "Every solution to the problems of bad business I feel must emanate from a guiding, central authority—namely, our Government." He then concluded by calling for "government regulation in industry . . . to prevent the abuse of good business and to establish sound business principles." In what was to prove a poor piece of prophecy, Kahn saw in such government direction of business practices the opportunity to achieve greater industrial stability, "just as it has been made possible to regulate against financial depressions and panics through a central body, our Federal Reserve Board."[45]

Thus, by the late 1920s, as a result of the failure of voluntary efforts to effectively restrain the magnitude of competitive practices, some steel industry leaders began advocating a closer relationship with the political sector in order to resolve their own internal trade problems. What they sought was not a government determination of business standards, but a means for the enforcement of proscriptions as decreed by business representatives. This step was a logical progression from the proposed system of self-regulation by business. Hence, business representatives sought to amend the antitrust laws to permit business to establish its own rules of conduct and make the

machinery of government available to enforce those rules. It would be totally erroneous to conclude that the attraction of industry leaders to the use
of political means for stabilizing internal competitive conditions reflected a
predisposition of business toward a socialized economy or a desire to turn
industrial decision-making over to forces outside their own sphere of control. What they did seek was an effective means of employing the coercive
machinery of the state against the minority of firms that would not adhere to
the restricted standards of competition sought by the majority. Implicit in all
these efforts, however, was the premise that such business interests—and not
interests outside of business—would establish the standards. This distinction was clearly drawn by Charles Schwab, who declared, "[T]he best and
most economic results will not be obtained in America by government ownership or direct control; that there should be national supervision of all great
enterprises, supervision such as will prevent destruction, but will preserve in
business, as elsewhere, our priceless gift of national freedom."[46] Elbert Gary
echoed this same thought when he stated: "I do not believe in socialism; in
Governmental management or operation; but I do advocate publicity, regulation and reasonable control through Government agencies."[47]

The steel industry, in other words, had realized the truth of Mancur
Olson's subsequent proposition: the maximization of collective well-being
required the introduction of coercion to compel firms to temper the pursuit
of their individual interests.

In the months following the stock-market crash in October 1929, members of the steel industry, along with their counterparts in other industries,
reemphasized their concern for trade stabilization. While the impact of the
Great Depression injected a new sense of urgency into their appeals, it did
not appear that leading industry spokesmen made any significant deviation
from their efforts for a system of industrial self-rule under federal supervision. The trade journal *Iron Age* renewed the call for the "rationalization"
of industry, which it was quick to point out did not mean "abolishing the
law of supply and demand," but only providing for its "adjusted operation."[48] Charles F. Abbott complained in 1930 that unfair, unethical practices had been responsible for the lack of profits in business and called for
the establishment of a governmental agency to coordinate industrial activity.[49]

Abbott expressed a widely held business sentiment in declaring that "iron
and steel products should command prices more in keeping with their intrinsic values" in order to insure the future development of remaining ore deposits. Abbott then lamented the problems associated with price declines:

> It is easy to cut a price, but it is difficult to reconstruct the price structure after
> it has once been pulled down. The constant lowering of prices is an endless
> process. In this downward trend of prices there comes a time when the selling

prices are below the cost of production, profits are dissipated, and the business is being transacted at a loss. In this wild scramble for volume, industry must learn that distress lurks just ahead and the only remedy lies in the rationalization of output.

Abbott saw this "rationalization of output" as leading to "a uniformity of success" brought about through an improvement in "prices and profits" and the elimination of "destructive forms of competition." "We have," he continued, "awakened to the necessity of putting a curb on selfishness and of ridding industry generally of the tremendous wastes in marketing produce."[50]

As one might expect, Abbott was attracted to the Swope Plan and supported the proposition that it be made obligatory for recalcitrant firms. In his words, "[W]hen all parties, through duly conducted hearings and organized expert study of the needs of public interest and safety, agree to the traffic rules, they become binding even upon the blustering individual who claims his right to do as he pleases."[51] Abbott was more vociferous in his criticism of the "irresponsible, non-cooperating, self-delusive actions" of firms that "act short-sightedly in what they suppose is their own interest," adding: "We cannot have in this country much longer irresponsible, ill-informed, stubborn and non-cooperating individualism. . . . It makes a ridiculous and tragic spectacle when industry has no effective means of coordinating itself and must look on while a part of itself is acting irresponsibly and destructively."[52] The steel industry took further steps toward trade stabilization and greater industrial cooperation when, in August 1932, Robert Lamont took over the presidency of the AISI. His role was seen, by some, as that of a "czar" or "dictator" of the industry.[53]

The steel industry, having long championed the principles of industrial self-regulation, was naturally outspoken in its support of Roosevelt's recovery bill. Following a meeting of the AISI, top industry executives voted unanimously to support FDR's efforts toward industrial recovery and, while the bill was still in the Senate, began drafting a trade practice code for the industry. Robert Lamont, president of the Institute, summarized the attitude of the steel men when he declared:

> The lip service which we have been so ready to render to the ideal of cooperation and the maintenance of ethical standards will now be supplemented by a very real cooperation and standards enforced by law. The selfish and often ruthless minority will now be compelled to conform to a code of fair and ethical practices. . . .[54]

Looking forward to a "governmental partnership," under which "ruinous trade practices and price cutting" would be replaced by "cooperation," Charles Schwab concluded: "The President offers to the business world the facilities and prestige of the government in eliminating unfair competitive practices with all of their ruinous effects upon prices, wages and profits."[55] Schwab went on to attack the "selfish interests" who engage in "unfair practices" that are "ruinous to industry," and he observed that the industry was in need of "price stability."[56]

Iron Age looked forward to the industrial self-regulation anticipated in the recovery bill, concluding that "action must be had":

> History has shown clearly that the price cutter has no respect for costs, whether they be his own or his competitors'. Unless there be teeth provided to bite him when he does so, he will continue to sell below the cost indicated by whatever wage rates and working hours that may be fixed, in order to gain for himself the personal advantages of an increased share of business. . . . We suggest that the simplest approach to steel industry control will be found in the establishment, under government approval, of an enforced price base for the more common products, established in accordance with a reasonable return to capital on the average cost of production. . . .[57]

Stripped of all excess verbiage, this proposal amounted to little more than advocating the right of the industry to engage in enforceable price fixing at levels that would not pose a competitive threat to the principal members of the industry. While regretting having to call upon government to solve the problem of enforcing the will of the "90 per cent" upon the "unfair 10 per cent," the trade journal *Steel* editorialized that since "no force, other than moral suasion" had been available to businesses to deal with the "destructive minority," the majority of industry leaders would welcome this new "partnership" with government.[58] An earlier *Steel* editorial stated: "Industry should welcome the opportunity to participate in the shaping of the national industry recovery act. . . . The majority of industrial executives will be willing to sacrifice certain rights and privileges temporarily for the benefits to be derived from sanely coordinated activity."[59]

Other trade association representatives offered their support for the objectives of the recovery bill. The president of the American Machinery and Tools Institute praised efforts to end the "unfair tactics of the sweat-shop owner and the price-cutter demoralizer" and looked forward to the "rational regulation of production."[60] The managing director of the Steel Founders Society of America hailed the bill as an "advanced step in social evolution" that was both "workable and inevitable." To his thinking, "the question has not been whether industrial control and a planned economy were wise or sound, but to determine by whom the regulation would be administered." He felt that each industry knew best its own problems, including "what fair prices for its products should be."[61]

With the bit in their teeth, some industry representatives proposed addi-

tional measures that, it was hoped, would lead to greater stability. Recognizing that an "artificially controlled price system" could invite new competition into the industry, one man suggested the development of a plan "whereby
further capacity can be discouraged." A similar statement was made by another industrialist who recommended that entry of new firms be restricted
by requiring prospective firms to obtain a "certificate of necessity," as required
in the regulation of public utilities, with trade associations advising the government as to the "necessity" for any new competitors. Yet another steel spokesman called for "a still more drastic law" that would require firms to adhere
to price schedules established by trade associations, with violators, whether
buyers or sellers, subject to criminal penalties, including imprisonment.[62]

Another industry executive suggested amending the antitrust laws, which,
in his opinion, foster "limitless cut-throat competition,"[63] a position also
taken by an industrialist who declared that "the time has come when all
manufacturers must get together and get a fair profit."[64] Support also came
from T. M. Girdler of Republic Steel, H. G. Batcheller of Ludlum Steel, and
Albert C. Lehman of Blaw-Knox Company. Lehman stated that Roosevelt's
program to eliminate "unfair competition" and "to give industry a chance
to associate itself with its competitors, under government control, as to wages,
hours and prices" would restore order to the industry.[65]

Other steel manufacturers declared that "uncontrolled competition is
causing industrial suicide" with "destructive price cutters gnawing away" at
industry. Response was virtually unanimous that "some method of avoiding
cut-throat competition must be devised," with government being looked upon
as a medium for disciplining "the recalcitrant individual who refuses to belong to any organization, and who believed that his success or money making
ability could only be maintained by an orgy of self-destructive competition."
One executive urged industry members to "work together with their competitors . . . with the help of our General Manager in Washington."[66]

Support came from other industry members as well. One declared:

We may condemn the vileness of the few in our industry who through feeble-
minded instinct and perverted judgment have dealt in policies of ruinous price
cutting, wage slashing and quality sacrifice, to the point of absolute corruption
of all reason, but there must be some effective and drastic action that will
absolutely assure an end to the source of these destructive policies.[67]

An executive of Republic Steel added:

We are not afraid of government intervention in business. If it corrects some of
the long-standing evils in the steel business it will be doing something we have
for years been trying unsuccessfully to accomplish for ourselves. We welcome
this chance to put the entire industry on an equitable and ethical basis.[68]

One of the most severe proposals for industrial regimentation was made by George Torrence, president of Link-Belt Company, who suggested the establishment of an "industry dictator" for steel, coal, oil, lumber, and agriculture. The basic role of these dictators would be to control supply within each industry in order to keep up prices. The rules established for the respective industries would be subject to approval by the FTC and, thereupon, would be binding upon all members of the industry, subject to enforcement through a system of penalties and/or licensing. In Torrence's view, these "dictators" would have authority to control production, set prices, terms of sales, and wage rates, and pass upon business consolidations and the closing of facilities.[69] His proposal is evidence of the degree to which various business leaders were willing to evoke political intervention to restrain the effectiveness of such factors as pricing and the entry of new competitors, factors traditionally thought of as the principal source of competitive discipline. It is further evidence of the lengths to which business institutions were prepared to go to maintain the status quo.

One company president not only voiced approval of the idea of amending the antitrust laws to permit firms to enter into contracts with competitors but also advocated making these arrangements binding on other firms as well! He stressed that this system would provide "a necessary means of controlling those who do not wish to be controlled," adding that he had held to this position for the previous twenty years. One means he recommended for the enforcement of this type of law would be to deny recalcitrants the use of the U.S. Mail.[70] Other executives openly called for "more restriction and more control" and praised efforts "to stabilize production, wages or prices." "Efforts . . . should not be hampered that tend to restrain a vicious, unintelligent, and uneconomic breaking down of a normal and fair price level," said one industrialist, while another argued that "industry should not be required to meet the prices of the unintelligent or price cutting producer." Still another urged his colleagues not to destroy the spirit of cooperation in industry "by attempting to obtain any selfish advantage." Steel industry representatives lined up in support of this new piece of legislation that promised to bring forth an industry-controlled condition of stabilized production and prices and to put an end to "unfair trading" practices that one spokesman openly equated with "below cost" pricing.[71]

As we have seen, the great concern of steel manufacturers in early 1933 was, as it had been for a number of decades, to find an effective, enforceable means of restricting aggressive sales practices that had the effect of lowering steel prices. In an effort to stimulate business, some manufacturers offered special inducements, such as long-term, low-price requirements contracts, which the dominant members of the industry considered to be unfair. The criticism of these practices was not founded on any contention that they constituted dishonest or fraudulent behavior. The real objection was directed to the efforts of some companies to secure orders by resorting to that most competitive element—offering to undersell one's competitors.[72]

COMPETITION AND THE "STEEL CODE"

Steel industry spokesmen responded favorably to the NRA code system. Praise for this "new sort of helpful partnership between government and business" was expressed by George M. Verity. Asserting that "we have accepted an entirely new philosophy," Verity added, "We are in the midst of a new deal and we seem to like it," suggesting that the old laws requiring unrestricted competition should be replaced by the new system of cooperative competition. Reflecting upon the "destructive competition" that had hitherto existed in the industry, he saw in the NRA a program containing "almost unlimited power for good or ill" that provided "a means for the elimination of the ills, weaknesses and withering effect of conflicting effort."[73] Like other industry leaders, Verity called for an "improvement" (i.e., increase) in prices, making the anomalous argument that "[i]t is not in the interest of the public to buy these splendid products of industry at ruinously low prices."[74] Verity rejoiced at the economic improvements he believed had been realized during the early months of the New Deal and sought to preserve these gains.[75] He expressed the belief that business would continue to embrace this new philosophy "as long as we feel it is sound."[76]

James W. Hook of Geometric Tool Company praised the NRA as a system for stamping out "bad competitive practices" such as "selling below cost" and the granting of "trade-in allowances, secret rebates, [and] unreasonably free servicing." He also praised it for requiring "uniform accounting systems." Hook embraced a widely held sentiment when he stated: "The old notions of unbridled competition, wild and baseless expansion of producing capacities . . . are rapidly giving way to a belief in rationalized regulation as a means of saving us from our own selves." Then, in a gross example of contradictory reasoning, Hook proceeded to criticize that portion of the NRA giving the government authority over matters involving labor-management relations. He saw this provision as a "usurpation" of management prerogatives and expressed a fear that "the Government agency may not decide correctly or in line with our own judgment."[77] That the entire NRA was, in fact, created for the purpose of usurping business decision-making and that members of the "recalcitrant minority" might also object to having decisions imposed upon them that were not in line with their own judgments apparently did not trouble Hook. His position also has the self-serving weakness of favoring industry determined trade practice standards, while discouraging the regulation of employment practices in which labor organizations might exert substantial influence.

Thomas J. Foster recounted the history of voluntary efforts to deal with unfair practices in the steel industry dating back to the year 1907. Observing that these practices were "as old as industry," he added that "no method of voluntary control ha[d] been successful" because of the lack of enforcement powers, a condition that the NRA would correct. This system could not succeed, in Foster's view, "unless selfish interests [were] overruled" and unless industry came to realize that "the right of each individual is made secure only by circumscribing the rights of all."[78]

Eugene Grace concluded that as a result of the NRA "a sounder basis has been developed for industry out of these hard times than it has enjoyed at any time during the postwar period." Grace added that one of the major contributions of the legislation "has been the banishing of speculation in industrial prices." He asked, "Why should any company be confronted with the disturbing situation of having its entire financial structure continually at the mercy of negotiations between customer and salesman?"[79] To anyone who has confronted an analysis of the law of supply and demand, it may seem a little strange that companies should believe themselves imperiled by the presence of customer free choice in the negotiation of prices. Clearly, this attitude reflected a compelling desire to secure business organizations from the elements of risk and speculation associated with a system of private capitalism.

This speculation in prices had been curbed, Grace thought, through an open-price system within the steel industry. Open pricing, which many business leaders had long advocated, required (as we have observed) each firm to publicly announce its price lists and to make that price available to all buyers without deviation therefrom. A firm could ordinarily change its prices (provided, as Grace pointed out, it did not attempt to charge prices that did not cover all costs of production), but only after filing a new schedule. While this system may seem rather innocuous and appear to have little effect upon competition, its intended consequence was to prevent a particular firm from deviating from its standard price in order to consummate a sale with a buyer who might otherwise be attracted to another supplier. Furthermore, the open-price system took the guesswork out of determining a competitor's effective prices. Both factors combined to stabilize the price structure, a situation sought by producers since the memory of man runneth not to the contrary. Grace acknowledged that this open-price policy had led to a uniformity of most prices throughout the steel industry, a condition that could contribute to "purging business of vicious activities and policies to the end that there might be a fair return on investment and a satisfactory compensation for labor."[80]

Open pricing, coupled with a prohibition of "below cost" prices, had another not-so-obvious, anticompetitive effect: if the prices of a given firm had been attacked on the grounds they did not permit the firm to recover its costs, which included not only variable costs but a pro rata share of fixed costs as well as a reasonable return on investment, the respondent firm could successfully defend itself by showing that the lower prices were the product of improved efficiency. This, in effect, would require the more efficient firms that were able to lower the unit costs of production to publicize the techniques that gave them a competitive advantage, thus serving to benefit their competitors.

Grace's approval of the NRA and his hope for making its basic concept a permanent fixture in American economic life were clearly expressed in rhetorical fashion:

> What shall we do if the period of the emergency is over at the end of the two-year limit indicated in the Act? . . . [A]re we willing to throw overboard the benefits which have been derived from this experience? I think not. I think that we have learned a great deal which can be and must be preserved for the benefit of the future. . . . We should watch [the NRA's] progress constructively with the object of preserving its best features for the years to come.[81]

The *Schechter* case dashed any industry hopes that the "best features" of the NRA would become permanent. The initial response of the steel industry to the decision was to seek to continue the stabilizing influences that had been realized under the NRA, with some company spokesmen advocating legislation to permit cooperative efforts to regularize trade practices. There was a concern within the industry that abandonment of the open-price system that existed under the code, along with the dropping of provisions relating to labor, might tend to a general reduction in prices.[82] Frank Purnell, president of Youngstown Sheet and Tube Company, seemed to sum up the sentiments of most industry members when he expressed a hope that "a way will be found so that the cooperative experience of the last two years will be continued for the benefit of labor, business and the public."[83] Similar ideas were expressed by executives of other major steel producing firms including United States Steel, National Steel, Republic Steel, Jones & Laughlin Steel, and American Rolling Mill Company. Eugene Grace was emphatic in urging a continuation of existing code provisions; he declared that "nothing in the *[Schechter]* decision requires the industry to go back to chiseling of wages, secret rebates or any discriminatory methods of competition" and that the industry should exert "every possible effort to prevent a recurrence of the evils, abuses and unfair business methods of the past" in order to protect the positions of both employees and investors. When asked if he had seen any indications of price cutting following the Court's decision, Grace responded, "Not one, thank God! Not one." Meanwhile, at a special meeting of the AISI, some two hundred executives representing over 90 percent of the productive capacity of the industry unanimously resolved to continue following the NRA code provisions on a voluntary basis.[84]

It would be unrealistic to suppose that the experience with the NRA had, in any significant way, soured steel-industry leaders on the idea of government interventionist programs for the stabilization of trade, pricing, and production practices. Though there were gradations of opinion and lack of universality of support for particular proposals, one searches fruitlessly for any evidence of advocacy, within the steel industry, of laissez-faire policies. The illusions of efficiency and profitability associated with so-called economies of scale had been the major contributor to the highly structured nature of this industry. But the apparent advantages of massive organizational size concealed an Achilles' heel: such firms found themselves vulnerable to the loss of competitive resiliency, a loss occasioned by the enervating nature of size itself. Such were the harsh realities that contributed to steel-industry efforts to restrain the constant inconstancies of vigorous competitive practices.

6
The Natural-Resource
Industries

Now *here*, you see, it takes all the running *you* can do, to keep in the same place. If you want to get somewhere else, you must run at least twice as fast as that.
—The Red Queen, in *Through the Looking Glass*

The campaign to instill a spirit of intraindustrial cooperation and self-regulation in business was quite intense in the so-called natural-resource industries, particularly petroleum and coal. Because of the significance of these industries to American economic life, the fundamental changes occurring within these industries and the similar problems shared by them, they shall be considered together in this chapter. Because of the inconstancy associated with vigorous and dynamic economic conditions, pressures were exerted by industry members for a more stabilized, equilibrium-based form of competition.

One of the most successful arguments employed by the natural-resource industries for gaining public acceptance of efforts to preserve existing market positions and stabilize prices was that free competition permitted the employment of greater quantities of natural resources that, it was argued, led to "waste." The solution proposed was a simple one: enact legislation to "conserve" such natural resources in order to assure that future generations would not suffer from the prodigality of today. Conservation became a cause in which its advocates, wrapped in self-approbation, were able to polarize the issue as a choice between planned, intelligent use of scarce resources, on the one hand, and their wanton, reckless, and wasteful squandering, on the other. In popular sentiments toward thrift, many business organizations had a ready-made platform from which to gain support for objectives having to do more with reducing the impact of competition than preserving resources.[1] Conservation served, quite well, the broader business purposes of controlling those aggressive competitive practices having the effect of creating lower and unstable prices.

145

Conservation was, because of its tendencies for controlling production, popular among businessmen. In early 1917, for instance, the U.S. Chamber of Commerce announced the results of a referendum in which 90 percent of the voting commercial organizations favored a proposition to allow firms in the natural-resource industries to enter into FTC-supervised cooperative agreements.[2] Such a proposition reflected not only the cartelizing mood of the general business community but the compatibility of such attitudes as conservation and the restraint of competition. Whatever may have been the motives of others who were active in the conservation movement, it cannot be denied that certain business interests found the conservation arguments consistent with their objectives of restricting—and, hence, stabilizing—the quantities of production within various industries. This was especially true in many of the basic natural-resource industries—such as petroleum, coal, and lumber—where the relative ease of turning existing stands of timber into finished lumber, or the unpredictable discovery of large new oil fields, served to make production levels somewhat erratic.[3] This irregularity had the effect of causing price levels to fluctuate as well, which prompted industry members to seek methods of bringing production, and with it the general price structure, within more stable and predictable parameters.

THE PETROLEUM INDUSTRY

The condition that characterized the petroleum industry throughout the 1920s and on into the New Deal years was that of a highly competitive and rapidly expanding market that, at the same time, was experiencing a development of production exceeding the new demand. While, as figure 1 demonstrates,[4] the industry was enjoying an increased demand for its products, it was enduring an even greater supply, resulting in a decline in prices. Annual national crude oil production totals of 442.9 million barrels in 1920 had risen to 713.9 million barrels in 1924, then to 770.9 million barrels in 1926, and then to 901.1 million barrels in 1927. The consequence was a general decline in the price level, further accentuated by the disruptive influences of newly discovered fields. Average prices for crude oil declined from just over $3.00 a barrel in 1920 to $1.25 a barrel by 1929.[5]

Because of such unstable conditions, no industry devoted more energy to seeking to stabilize trade conditions than the petroleum industry. The same rhetoric of "cooperative competition" that rang throughout other industries was present in the oil industry. The principal trade publication, the *Oil and Gas Journal,* editorialized that the same "spirit of co-operation, of fair play among rivals" was being evidenced in that industry. After attacking "radical price cutting"—which was but a reflection of the erratic production

**Figure 1. Supply, Demand, and Prices of
Crude Oil: 1920-1929**

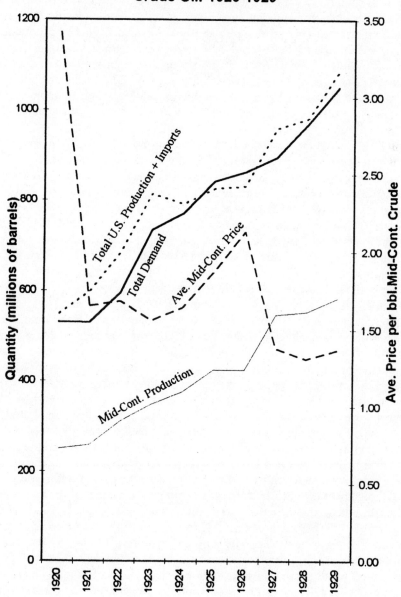

patterns occasioned by the discovery of new fields and the profit-maximizing efforts of individual firms—the editorial concluded: "[T]he new trend in American business methods is not going to be defeated. The education of business opinion . . . is bound to continue until selfishness in business is as universally condemned by public opinion as selfishness is socially."[6]

By the end of 1924, the combination of increased annual oil production and the aftermath of the Teapot Dome scandal exerted a strong influence for the adoption of a federal conservation program. Industry leaders, such as Henry L. Doherty of Cities Service Company, worked on behalf of political solutions to the problems of overproduction. In Doherty's opinion, "only through the efforts of our Federal Government, can the oil problem be solved."[7] Doherty's energies were not wasted, for in December 1924, Calvin Coolidge created the Federal Oil Conservation Board (FOCB), the function of which was largely investigatory and advisory in nature. The general reaction of industry representatives to the creation of the board was favorable; the hope was expressed that it could aid in bringing the production problem under control.[8] Walter C. Teagle of Standard Oil (New Jersey) and William S. Farish of Humble Oil encouraged the industry to cooperate with the FOCB. Consistent with the spirit of "cooperative competition" that had permeated much of the business community, they recommended that the American Petroleum Institute (API) develop a "code of business ethics" covering each stage in the production and sale of petroleum.[9]

In April 1925, the so-called Committee of Eleven of the API issued a report that concluded that American oil reserves were not in any immediate danger of being depleted and that new production methods made the prospect of oil shortages highly unlikely. The report, which was prepared to counteract the anticipated support by the FOCB for conservation legislation, suggested that a free market, regulated by competitive prices, would best serve the industry. J. Howard Pew, himself an advocate of a free market for the petroleum industry, made good use of this report in challenging Doherty's proposals for federal regulation. But by the time of its annual meeting in December 1926, the board of directors of the API opted for a compromise position between Pew and Doherty, which it found in a report by the FOCB that year recommending the control of production by the states and state encouragement of uniform state laws or interstate compacts. In the interest of harmonizing the differences of opinion within the industry, the FOCB's report received the backing of the API, which then appointed a committee of its members to draft recommendations to be submitted to its board of directors for a legislative program that would allow producers to cooperate to restrict oil production. It is quite apparent that, while a few individuals like Pew and Gulf Oil's G. S. Davison wanted a free market for oil and were content to allow competition to flourish, most members of the industry desired some sort of restriction in production, with the primary debate center-ing on federal control versus state control versus voluntary restrictions by the producers themselves.[10]

Beginning in 1926, the discovery of major new fields added to the pro-duction that was sending oil prices downward.[11] The discovery of the fertile Seminole field in Oklahoma on 26 July 1926, introduced one of the most destabilizing influences that the American petroleum industry ever experi-enced and prompted new efforts by oilmen to obtain a workable system to limit oil production. The influence of Seminole is readily seen from produc-tion records that showed a daily output from that field of 192,500 barrels in January 1926 and 275,000 barrels in February, increasing steadily to 490,700 barrels by July. As new wells were brought into production, the sharp in-crease in supply led to a corresponding drop in prices in the Seminole area, with declines ranging from $2.69 to $2.10 a barrel on 17 November 1926, and a further drop to $1.28 a barrel by 12 March 1927. When one contrasts daily Seminole production with national figures, and then relates this total production to demand, a greater appreciation is had of the intensely com-petitive nature of the industry. The daily average total production of oil in March 1927, was 2,610,000 barrels, compared with 2,239,000 barrels for March 1926, while total demand was 2,350,000 barrels per day in March, 1927, compared with a daily average of 2,172,000 barrels in March 1926. Thus, while daily production was up by 16.5 percent over a comparable period a year earlier, demand was up by only 8 percent.[12] By May 1927, with daily production at Seminole averaging some 350,000 barrels per day, crude oil prices in the midcontinent area dropped to a range of $1.10 to $1.15 per barrel.[13]

The additional production problem from Seminole, combined with the discovery of other highly productive fields, helped to create a condition that led to unstable patterns of production. Erich Zimmerman seems to accu-rately summarize the condition within the petroleum industry during the period of this study:

[I]t appears that the decade 1920–29 was one of increasing pressure build-up through rising stocks. The pressure rose further when the market crash of 1929 and the depression that followed brought on a sharp decline of demand. Pres-sure "blew the top" when in 1930 discovery of the largest domestic field, the East Texas Field, led to further large increases in production.[14]

A factor that contributed to efforts by many producers to maximize production within various fields was the failure of the legal system to pro-vide identifiable property concepts for underground oil. Under the so-called law of capture, *possession* became the means for acquiring ownership in subsurface oil, thus providing an incentive for producers to maximize production, lest other producers in the same field recover the oil first. The common law courts—which had long regarded possession as an important element in establishing ownership over previously unowned property—failed to identify exclusive property interests in underground oil that would protect an owner's pool from trespass by other producers. Had such property interests been recognized by the courts, producers would have been more inclined to make production decisions in accordance with market conditions, rather than seeking to acquire possession of petroleum before their competitors did. As a consequence, many industry members directed their attentions to the so-called common-pool problem, a condition created not so much by the market as by the failure of the legal system to adequately define and protect subsurface property rights.

Conditions such as these led to renewals of debates within the industry over the most desirable means of restricting petroleum output, with Henry Doherty repeatedly urging federally enforced unit operation of oil fields along with "voluntary" cooperation—with legal sanctions to be provided by the federal government—by members of the industry to restrict production. "Unit production" has been defined as "developing and operating an oil field as an entity under one management."[15] There was a basic split of opinion within the industry over this question of government compulsion, with officials of Standard Oil (New Jersey) and Humble Oil, and such men as G. S. Davison and J. Howard Pew voicing opposition, while Doherty and others—such as Mark Requa, a mining engineer who had served in the U.S. Fuel Administration during World War I—urged federal enforcement to solve the problem. Humble Oil took a position supporting "any character of legislation which will permit the orderly production of oil and gas from a pool," whether through industry agreements or state regulatory bodies. Doherty's devotion to a mandatory unit plan of operation was premised on his having "always believed that the majority should rule," while opponents of the idea believed that unitization should be *permitted* but not *required*.[16]

In an effort to get at the immediate Seminole problem, a number of oil producers requested the State Corporation Commission of Oklahoma to intervene directly to regulate production.[17] The commission had the power, since the enactment of prorationing legislation in 1915,[18] to regulate the production of petroleum in order to eliminate what the statute defined as "waste." While appearing to address itself to the waste of oil through seepage from storage tanks as well as the lateral movement of oil within pools, a closer reading of the statute evidences a concern more for the *economic* consequences to the industry than for the physical *conservation* of natural resources. The statute prohibited, for example, the taking of oil from the ground "at a time when there is not a market demand therefor at the well at a price equivalent to the actual value of the oil." It went on to define "actual value" as "the average value as near as may be ascertained in the United States at retail of the by-products of such crude oil or petroleum when refined less the cost and a reasonable profit in the business of transporting, refining and marketing the same." In order to eliminate the "waste" engendered by the low prices, the commission was authorized to issue orders prorating the quantity of allowable production (i.e., the maximum amount of production that would not lead to "waste") among the existing producers. It seems rather clear that such "conservation" legislation was, in fact, directed toward the elimination of those conditions that lead to unstable prices in the industry. On 9 August 1927, the commission issued a prorationing order covering the Seminole field.[19]

Oil producers were greatly attracted to methods of control that combined industry-determined standards with adequate government enforcement. This was evident when a group of the nation's largest operators selected Ray M. Collins to serve as a referee to enforce the production restrictions that had been agreed to by operators within the Seminole field. Collins was more than simply a peacemaker seeking voluntary resolutions of disputes among oil producers. He was, in fact, an appointee of the Oklahoma Corporation Commission who, along with an advisory committee of operators, was given the task of enforcing prorationing orders of the commission. His salary and expenses were paid by voluntary contributions from the producers within the area he was to supervise, an arrangement that could scarcely be considered free of any conflict of interest and identified the real beneficiaries of prorationing. In time, Collins's authority was extended to cover new pools that opened up within the Seminole field, and he was empowered as a virtual "dictator" over Seminole, having final authority to establish production restrictions therein.

There may well be a seductiveness associated with the idea of conservation that fosters a benign neglect of the inherently cartelistic nature of the practices employed in the Seminole field. It would be difficult to imagine the same degree of public indifference to the creation of an industry-selected, government-backed "dictator" to control the production of shoes, foodstuffs, or consumer appliances in order to maintain a price level acceptable to the manufacturers of such goods. To be able to enjoy the benefits of a state-enforced monopoly and to have such a system popularly accepted as an example of "socially responsible" business behavior must surely stand as a high-water mark in industrial public-relations campaigns.

It was the opinion of leading executives within the industry that the program of control operating in the Seminole field would ultimately lead to the "unit pool-operation" long sought by Doherty, under which a government license had to be obtained before new drilling for oil could begin. In any event, the oil producers selected a committee to try to develop a permanent plan to limit production in "all producing areas in which there is a prospect of large new development."[20] The proration system that had begun at Seminole was later extended to the Yates Pool (1927) and Hendricks Pool (1928), both in Texas, and the Hobbs field (1930) in New Mexico and served as a foundation for conservation laws in various states.[21]

Due largely to their failure to work out a plan for the voluntary curtailment of production, operators in the midcontinent area directed their attentions to securing the assistance of the federal government to help establish a cooperative program to stabilize production. A meeting was held in New York City, attended by officials of the leading oil companies having operations in the midcontinent area, the purpose of which was to seek the most rigid method possible under the law for limiting production. One of those attending, William H. Gray, president of the National Association of Independent Oil Producers, outlined what, to his thinking, were the only two possible ways of solving the problems of the industry: "one of them is honest cooperation of the leaders of twelve large companies controlling 80 percent of the production of North and South America, and the other Federal regulation and control of this basic industry."[22] On 23 May 1927, a committee of leading oil representatives, headed by Walter Teagle, met with federal officials in Washington with a view to developing plans for restricting production. Two days later, another meeting was held in Teagle's offices among representatives of the leading oil producers operating in the Seminole area in an effort to bring about an agreement curtailing production.[23]

During this same period, the Oil and Gas Association of Okmulgee, Oklahoma, an association of over two hundred independent producers in eastern Oklahoma, passed a resolution seeking to lay the blame for overproduction on, among other causes, useless rivalry and cutthroat competition among the various producers. The resolution went on to state that any efforts toward conservation should give first consideration to the small, independent producers, and declared that what the industry needed most was "an honest and sincere effort toward permanent stabilization."[24] Out of a fear that the larger oil companies would have greater influence with a federal agency, many independent oil producers looked upon state regulation as a preferable solution to the problems of the industry. Thus, the question that split most of the petroleum producers was not that of a free market versus governmental regulation, but rather the question of which *level* of government— state or federal—would be most beneficial to their respective interests.[25]

The desire for a legal environment that would allow intraindustrial agreements in order to stabilize the industry found its most vocal and persistent expression in the petroleum industry. One of the more prominent attorneys representing the oil industry, F. C. Proctor, attacked the antitrust laws for creating a hindrance to cooperative action on the part of oil companies to limit production. In his view, the "anti-trust laws must be so amended at once as to permit the oil industry through agreements to restrict production of oil, and . . . this is essential in the interests of the public."[26]

As suggested earlier, there is no apparent danger to the public in producers joining together—provided it is done voluntarily and not as a matter of legal compulsion—in an effort to maintain certain levels of production and prices. In the first place, as Mancur Olson's analysis demonstrates, such arrangements will tend to collapse due to the inherent conflicts between individual and collective interests in the industry. But even if such problems could be overcome, to the degree the agreed-upon price or production levels deviated from what would prevail in a more highly competitive environment, other existing firms (or new ones) would be motivated to take advantage of the extra-competitive profit margins that result from artificially higher prices. Not only is this *theoretically* true, it reflects the historic experiences with private efforts to circumvent competitive disciplines. Even within the petroleum industry—contrary to the expectations of many business critics who view any industry as a single-minded monolith—one of the major hindrances to trade and price stabilization through industry agreements came from those producers whose preferences for even greater profits made their cooperation with the moderating objectives of their competitors unlikely. While the antitrust laws interfered with the freedom of producers to enter into such agreements, such laws did not assure the existence of competition. The market—which, by definition, is void of legal restrictions upon entry, trade, and pricing practices—*itself* guarantees competition. On the other hand, the history of the antitrust laws has been one of *interference* with competition, not its *encouragement*.[27]

That government regulation has served to *diminish* rather than *promote* competition is nowhere more evident than in the petroleum industry. In 1927, for example, the industry was able to secure the enactment of legislation in California prohibiting the "unreasonable waste of natural gas." The new law, steeped in the semantics of the conservation movement, was to be administered by the state oil and gas supervisor within the Department of Natural Resources. Upon a complaint filed by other operators, or on the initiative of the supervisor himself, a hearing would be conducted for the purpose of determining whether or not an unreasonable waste of gas exists within a given field and, if so, to issue an order restraining such waste. Enforcement of the law was provided for in the form of injunctions, fines, and, if necessary, imprisonment. As an assurance of industry control over the regulatory process, the statute provided for a review of the decisions of the supervisor by a district board of commissioners made up of petroleum operators elected from within the various producing districts.

An important section of this statute—one that reflected the perennial interests of most oil producers—provided for agreements by producers, enforceable within the courts as an exemption from the state antitrust laws, for the unit development of oil and gas fields. Such agreements, made binding by statute upon the "successors and assigns of the parties" entering into them, could also provide for operators agreeing upon "the time, location and manner of drilling and operating wells."[28]

On the surface, there might appear to be nothing coercive in a statute that simply *permits* producers to enter into such agreements with one another, leaving nonsigners free to continue operating their own businesses as they see fit. However, a nonindustry supporter of the legislation considered this very possibility and concluded that due to "the inter-relation of the various provisions of the law," pressure might easily be brought to bear to penalize the recalcitrant minority "on the grounds of gas wastage and abnormally high gas-oil ratios" and "to compel them to cooperate with the majority."[29] In other words, those producers who did not "voluntarily" agree with their competitors to the unit development of petroleum fields might well find themselves subject to a formal charge of engaging in "waste," with the agreement providing a prima facie standard by which to judge "waste" and with the decision in such a case subject to the review of, presumably, these same competitors! It hardly needs suggesting that such an arrangement would be lacking in the impartiality normally attendant to the principles of judicial review and procedural due process.

As already indicated, efforts to deal with "waste" invariably confused *physical* with *economic* "waste." It is true, of course, that a great deal of natural gas was allowed to escape in the production of petroleum. In the *physical* sense of the word, one could characterize this as "waste," but to do so is only to substitute one's personal preferences for those of other market participants. It is not uncommon for a person to be accused of wasting his or her time, money, or other resources when engaged in an activity that does not comport with the accuser's sense of values. It is also to ignore the principle of the conservation of energy, which informs us that matter and energy can be neither created nor destroyed, but only *transformed*. As the study of chaos might suggest, what our limited understanding may perceive as "wasteful" conduct might only represent processes by which resources are being transformed into more orderly and complex systems.

In the *economic* sense, furthermore, there can be no such thing as a volitional act of "waste." The value of any resource is reflected in its market price, and if owners of the resource make an inadequate effort to capture or retain it, it is because the *costs* of doing so are greater than the *benefits* to be derived by being able to sell it at the prevailing market price. Contrary to the views of many conservationists, it would constitute economic "waste" to compel a producer to expend more valuable resources in order to protect less valuable ones. In the same way that we are inclined to judge the behavior of others as "altruistic" or "selfish" depending upon the identity of our purposes with theirs, labeling another's use of resources as "wasteful" reflects only the projection of our preferences onto the conduct of that other person.

That the conservation movement in the oil industry was motivated principally by economic considerations is further attested to in a report, to the governor of Kansas, written by an expert in the field of petroleum. In his view, the major producers, desirous of eliminating the smaller independent refiners and retailers, enlisted the backing of the FOCB "on the false plea that 'over-production' constituted 'waste.'" The ensuing restrictions on production helped to limit the independents' sources of oil and, eventually, led many of the smaller firms into bankruptcy.[30]

There is a fine line between the stated objective of conserving scarce resources and the real objective of stabilizing production at a level that will maintain prices desired by the industry. After all, if production increases at a greater rate than demand, there is—to the person unknowledgeable about economics—the appearance that the amount produced in excess of demand at a given price has been "wasted," and that regulation of production is necessary to prevent such an "inefficient" use of resources. In point of fact, such production is not "wasted" at all, but is absorbed by buyers in the market through the mechanism of lowered prices that have the effect of increasing demand to clear the market. As Edward G. Seubert, president of Standard Oil (Indiana) testified before a congressional hearing in 1934:

> *Mr. Cole* – You say there is an excessive supply of crude oil today. Where does it go?
> *Mr. Seubert* – Well, speaking for my company, it is going in storage, both crude oil and refined products.
> *Mr. Cole* – Then, speaking of the man who does not have storage facilities, where does it go?
> *Mr. Seubert* – Well, it finds its way to the market.
> *Mr. Cole* – None of it is wasted?
> *Mr. Seubert* – Well, it is wasted in the fact it is put in the market at demoralizing prices and is wasting to the extent of demoralizing the general industry. . . .[31]

That Seubert's advocacy of government regulation of production was motivated principally by a desire to regularize competitive conditions within the industry was further borne out by his response to the question:

> *Mr. Wolverton* – Is your suggestion for federal control based upon the necessity for conservation or stabilization of the industry?

Mr. Seubert – Well, primarily for stabilization of the industry and obviously the conservation element is coming along with it. I think that they are hand-in-hand.[32]

The so-called waste and demoralization in the petroleum industry were, in effect, a reaction of industry members to the fact of declining prices, a response hardly unique to petroleum. Similar efforts in other industries to seek stabilization of conditions through legislative programs have been documented, with the desire for the regularization of prices one of the main considerations.[33] Stripped of its overtones of "social responsibility," the conservation movement in petroleum can be seen for its self-serving motivations. As economist Fritz Machlup has observed with regard to proration regulations: "The chief purpose of production restriction is price maintenance, which is called 'stabilization' of the industry. It is made possible by large-scale collusive activity between oil companies and governmental authorities." Former API president Amos Beaty echoed this same thought: "[M]uch that has been done in the oil and gas industry in the name of conservation is really stabilization."[34]

The arguments on behalf of such gas waste laws often took strange turns. A consulting geologist, for instance, suggested that "higher prices reduce waste" and, therefore, that a higher protective tariff would help reduce waste, not only within the nations whose oil exports were reduced but in the United States as well. While it is true that there is a greater incentive to economize the use of a resource as its market value increases—such as by reduced consumption of the resource or *increased* use of substitutes—there is an apparent contradiction in the contention that an *increased* demand for domestic oil would tend to reduce waste *and* that a consequent *decline* in demand for foreign oil would also reduce waste in the foreign countries. Such statements were similar to the arguments offered, in later years, in defense of restricting the importation of foreign oil in order to encourage domestic exploration. That would, so the argument went, *enhance* U.S. oil supplies.[35] The suggestion that reducing oil imports would help protect American reserves (that would now have a higher demand placed upon them) is rather specious, although it certainly received warm support from the industry. Actually, a *decline* in prices would tend to reduce oil production by the refiners until such time as prices rose to approach market equilibrium. An *increase* in tariffs with a consequent rise in prices would tend to encourage greater domestic production, and how such a state of affairs could *preserve* oil supplies is difficult to comprehend. On the other hand, one would have to be somewhat credulous to believe that petroleum interests were truly concerned about the depletion of reserves. What was uppermost in their minds was not the "waste" of the natural resource itself, but the decline in prices that led to the so-called economic waste that this same consultant described as "the effort of time, work and money by operators without profits proportionate to the hazards of the industry."[36] That the petroleum industry's interest in conservation was basically opportunistic and directed toward the stabilization of prices can hardly be questioned. But again, there is nothing particularly sinister in members of an industry seeking to get as high a price as they can for their product, just as buyers desire to get the product at as low a price as possible. Rather than being critical of the self-interested motivation itself, it would be more fruitful to get a clear understanding of the manner in which political intervention, this time under the guise of "conservation," was utilized to help promote such self-interest. Competition between sellers and between buyers tends to discipline the self-seeking behavior of all market participants, moderating their demands and expectations in anticipation of the responses of their respective competitors. Where such competitive influences are restrained by law, however, the capacity of the market to provide such discipline is diminished. When such restraints are sought by producers, the result is a reduction in those market influences that would tend to a lowering of prices.

It should be emphasized that, while industry members were desirous of maximizing profits, their immediate concern was to stabilize prices. Even though they would have preferred prices to stabilize at a *high* rather than a *low* level, oilmen wanted to be rid of the sharp fluctuations in price that, when high, encouraged more price-reducing production from the wildcatters. The advantage of a high price for their own production was, to the established firms, offset by the disadvantages of a subsequent lower price occasioned by the increased production. Price fluctuations tended to interfere with business decision-making by lessening the capacity to predict prices. It should also be noted that high prices for crude oil were a problem to companies that bought their crude from others (e.g., the independents).

The petroleum industry continued its efforts on behalf of achieving some form of control on production. Consistent with the response of so many other industries, "cooperation" and "self-regulation" became convenient slogans to rally industry on behalf of "rationalized production." Such purposes, spiced with the emotional issue of "conservation," helped to rally industry members during the 1920s and 1930s. As with other industries, one should not interpret appeals for "cooperation" among oil producers as evidencing any reluctance to invoke political power to achieve production and price stability. When, in 1927, James A. Veasey of the Carter Oil Company declared that compulsory legislation should be resorted to if the industry's own conservation endeavors were unsuccessful, he doubtless expressed a common sentiment among members of his industry.[37]

The role that "business cooperation" was designed to play in regularizing prices and production was often-stated by industry leaders. In petroleum, as in other industries, there had developed a collective spirit that one oil executive was later to describe in these words: "We are living in the age of cooperation, not only as the man of the street thinks of it, but in the sense of a very much higher cooperative vein—an aim based on the fact that all industries are becoming visibly . . . interdependent."[38] The *Oil and Gas Journal,* speaking editorially in April 1928 of the efforts on behalf of "co-operation for conservation," declared: "Many of the problems which have been considered impossible of solution under selfish competitive conditions will be found easy of solution when tackled in a co-operative spirit. . . . Competition that leads only to losses must eventually be succeeded by cooperation for the benefit of all."[39] This same journal had, earlier in the year, demonstrated that its real concern was not for such "conservation" purposes as the depletion of reserves, but the effect that increased production and intense competition had on the industry price structure: "Excessive competition begets excessive competition which sooner or later takes the form of price cutting. Then everybody in that area suffers."[40]

Similar sentiment was expressed by E. P. Salisbury of Standard Oil (New Jersey), who foresaw a "fair return" to the industry "through the avoidance of wasteful production." In his estimation,

> Competition in the oil business, as in every other industry, will regulate itself, but as it is at present organized, its earnings cannot be sufficient without a larger measure of cooperative effort in the balancing of production and demand. . . . It seems inconceivable, and it certainly is undesirable, that an industry of such magnitude, concerned with the manufacture and distribution of products so essential to public welfare, should go through a period of intense uneconomic competition.[41]

As new oil fields were brought into production during the 1920s, the petroleum industry sought to cope with the ever-increasing sources of supply in a variety of ways. In 1928, for example, a number of oil companies established the "Long pool," a cooperative effort under which its manager would purchase "distress gasoline" from the smaller independent refineries. The "Long pool" later came under attack by the U.S. Department of Justice, which alleged, among other charges, agreements on prices and the boycotting of those retailers who refused to adhere to a system of fixed prices in sales to their customers. In 1930, a consent decree enjoining such activities was agreed to by the defendants.[42]

Other proposals on behalf of the industry included one by Axtell T. Byles, president of the Tidewater Associated Oil Company and vice-president of the API, who recommended the establishment of a small committee—or even one person—to carry out a program of "rationalization" of production. Citing the need for cooperation in combating overproduction,

Byles pointed out that the industry would not be able to maintain its profits unless stabilized production was achieved through some "central coordinating influence." He observed that either cooperation from within the industry or control from outside it was needed to solve the problem—that "sound economics" must replace "destructive competition" in order "to conserve an indispensable and irreplaceable raw material for those who come after us."[43] William Farish looked to government and industry cooperation "to balance production with consumption." Farish later declared, "We are interested in conservation; we are interested in proration or other forms of cooperative development and production whether voluntary or compulsory. . . ." To accomplish this stability required, in Farish's view, "additional power" being given to "conservation authorities."[44]

Support for such proposals came from outside the industry as well. Craig B. Hazlewood, president of the American Bankers Association and vice-president of the Union Trust Company of Chicago, declared that some effective system for the positive control of production and distribution through a legal method of cooperation was needed in the petroleum industry.[45] Voicing a similar proposal was J. S. Cullinan, former president of the Texas Company and retired chairman of the American Republics Corporation, who declared that the petroleum industry was in need of a "czar," similar to those in existence in other industries, to resolve conditions within the industry. Among the recommended candidates for such a position, Cullinan named Herbert Hoover, General John J. Pershing, Edward N. Hurley (a man who had been a manufacturer, a president of the Illinois Manufacturers Association, and, during World War I, chairman of the FTC), and Julius H. Barnes.[46] Cullinan later drafted a proposal to set up a coordinated program to curtail oil production through a nationwide system of cooperation. Cullinan proposed a minimum of a 20 percent reduction in production and stated that he would seek the aid of the president and other federal officials, as well as governors and other officials of the principal oil-producing states.[47]

The price-stabilization purposes of conservation programs were further evidenced by Sir Henry Deterding, managing director of Royal Dutch Shell Companies, who stated that conservation was "the only way to eliminate the evils of overproduction." "Without conservation," he went on, "the industry will continue to bring in new producing fields before they are needed; *price wars will continue; oil profits will disappear.*"[48] Deterding went on to praise efforts by those within the industry—and the cooperation of state and federal agencies—to work out agreements and programs to control the production of petroleum, but noted that such efforts had run up against the antitrust laws. Like so many other industrialists, Deterding saw the solution as lying in a modification of the antitrust laws in order to bring them "into conformity with a program of conservation," a program that, he maintained, "would apply to all industries because the oil industry is not alone subject to overproduction." Deterding added that *"[p]ossibly all industries and all nations are faced with the task of reinterpreting the term 'conservation.'"*[49]

Expressing the same sentiment was Charles E. Bowles, statistician and publicity director for the Independent Petroleum Association of America, who declared that the petroleum industry faced a menace from "super-efficiency and super-capacity" in the production and marketing of oil products. He added that "the super-capacity to produce crude oil far beyond the needs of refineries, and the super-capacity to produce refined products far beyond the needs of the public—absolutely demands control of that super-capacity." Such control, he felt, should come from within the industry.[50] The marketplace does, of course, provide a means for controlling the supply of a product to conform to consumer demand. That means, as we have seen, is the pricing mechanism. Any industry that found it had made a collective miscalculation of consumer demand would experience—if production exceeded demand—a decline in prices that would discourage additional production until such time as the market was cleared of any surpluses. However, as has been shown, the petroleum industry was faced not so much with the problem of anticipating consumer demand as with the presence of many producers who were willing to continue producing and selling petroleum at prices lower than what many others found acceptable. Mancur Olson's observations illustrate the difficulties associated with getting industry members to make a collective effort to withhold petroleum from the market until the price level rose.

While industry representatives such as Walter Teagle were declaring that "[t]he oil industry is faced with financial chaos unless the government can help to extricate it from overproduction,"[51] a few others, such as Treasury Secretary Andrew Mellon, were of the view that the market itself would make the necessary adjustments to relieve the problems of overproduction.[52] To anyone unfamiliar with the incestuous relationship between industry and the political state, it might seem paradoxical that some businessmen would be arguing for government restraints on the market, at the same time some government officials were advocating market solutions to problems. It is the failure to understand the benefits, to the business system, of political structuring of the marketplace that accounts for so wide an acceptance of the notion that legislation regulating the production of petroleum was fostered by a social concern for the efficient management and use of natural resources.

Petroleum Marketing

Let us shift our attention from the production to the marketing of petroleum. The executive committee of the API endorsed the idea of a workable code of ethics for oil marketers. While distributors in some states opted for establishing codes through the FTC's trade-practice conference procedures, others turned to the more direct political means of state statutes. Mississippi distributors were successful in getting a statute enacted in that state making it unlawful "to give or allow a rebate, bonus or concession of any kind . . . for the purpose of hindering, preventing or destroying competition." While it might at first appear that not all rebates, bonuses, or concessions would violate the statute—but only those that interfered with competition—the statute went on to provide that the granting of such a price reduction was itself "prima facie evidence of the purpose to hinder, prevent or destroy competition." The statute provided not only for injunctions, fines, and/or imprisonment for its enforcement, but for a forfeiture to the state of all sums received for sales at less than the prices listed by the seller, as well as a sum representing the amount of the bonus or gratuity. Then, in a section with obvious due-process ramifications, this state-enforced price-fixing scheme declared that the retention or reemployment of any person convicted under the statute was "prima facie evidence of notice and knowledge" of these violations, and the firm employing such person would be liable for penalties for any subsequent violations of the statute by that person.[53] The severity of this statute attests to the vigor of the oil marketers' reaction against trade practices utilizing price cutting as a tool of aggressive competition.

This response to price-cutting practices was made one year later in a code of marketing practices worked out by petroleum-industry members and the FTC at a trade-practice conference. The code was riddled with provisions attacking various practices, including lotteries, selling of products below cost, giveaways as sales inducements, and leasing and subleasing arrangements that had the effect of creating rebates. Each of these practices would result in a lower effective delivered price to the consumer, and many industry members desired to put an end to them. This conclusion is further confirmed in a section of the code prohibiting "any deviation from . . . posted prices . . . by means . . . which may directly or indirectly permit the buyer to obtain gasoline or kerosene at a lower net cost to him."[54]

The reaction of independent marketers to the code was mixed, but most seemed to favor it, provided their competitors went along with it. One man voiced the frustration associated with the enforcement of code provisions when he declared: "I signed one code of ethics and on the day it went into effect I changed my price to conform to it, only to lose a lot of gallonage to another company who would not change their price." The concern for a too-rigorous form of competition was expressed by a number of distributors who spoke of the business that had been leaving them because of the practice of other dealers in offering lower prices. As one stated, "[W]e are merely holding our accounts against invasion, pending adoption of more constructive policies by our competition." More than one said, "[W]e are ready and more than willing to stop the practice on the assurance from [our competitors] that they will not pirate on our business." That not all distributors were enthusiastic about such a code is evident from one man who regarded the enforcement of "association made laws" as "repugnant to free born Americans."[55]

The Depression Years

As if the Great Depression had not been enough, efforts of the petroleum industry to realize a desideratum of stability were shaken when, in late 1930, the East Texas oil fields were discovered. Increasing from a production level of some 105.7 million barrels in 1931 to 171.8 million barrels by 1933, the East Texas fields accounted for almost 19 percent of the total domestic production by the first year of the New Deal, a situation that only served to accentuate the production-control problems of the industry. As one might expect, crude oil prices plummeted.[56] Comparing December crude oil prices in a few fields, one begins to feel the impact that unregularized production and the depression itself were having on the industry. In the Bradford-Allegheny fields of Pennsylvania, for example, crude oil prices averaged about $3.40 per barrel during the 1920s, but fell to $1.85 and $1.72 per barrel during 1931 and 1932, respectively. Likewise, in the Oklahoma-Kansas fields, prices during the 1920s averaged around $1.69 per barrel, but declined to $.77 and $.69 per barrel in 1931 and 1932; by early 1933, they had fallen to as low as $.25 a barrel. Within the Gulf Coast region, 1920–29 averages of $1.45 per barrel had slumped to $.80 and $.88 per barrel during 1931 and 1932, with 1931 summer prices in the East Texas fields dropping to as low as $.10 per barrel.[57]

Conditions in East Texas became so serious that in August 1931 the Texas legislature passed legislation for the "conservation" of oil.[58] The governor of Texas responded to the situation by declaring the East Texas oil fields to be in "a state of insurrection, tumult, riot, and a breach of the peace" and placed these fields under martial law. While no evidence was adduced to show any actual or threatened violence, or any violations of state laws that could not have been handled through the judicial system, the governor sent some four thousand troops in to enforce the shutdown of existing wells. The governor had claimed that martial law was a necessary expedient to give the Texas Railroad Commission adequate time to conduct hearings and issue appropriate orders under the new law. The commission held such hearings on the question of establishing production controls, at which the oil producers seemed to be in agreement that a maximum production level of four hundred thousand barrels per day would be satisfactory for their purposes. The commission considered the evidence and, not surprisingly, issued an order restricting daily production to four hundred thousand barrels. By midsummer of 1932, crude oil prices had climbed to $.85 per barrel.

Early in 1932, the U.S. Supreme Court handed down a decision that declared Oklahoma's prorationing statute to be a constitutional exercise of state power.[59] The Court ruled that the right of oil producers "to take and thus to acquire ownership is subject to the reasonable exertion of the power of the State to prevent unnecessary loss, destruction or waste," and that the limitation of production to conform to market demand was a valid exercise of such power.[60] Heartened by this decision, the Texas legislature enacted, in November 1932, a statute similar to the Oklahoma statute and consistent with the long-sought objectives of the petroleum industry: rationalizing production to demand. Titled, appropriately, the "Market Demand Act," the legislation expanded the authority of the Railroad Commission. It was brought into being a month before the U.S. Supreme Court handed down another decision, this one declaring the actions of the Texas governor in establishing martial law to be, under the facts of the case, a violation of due process.[61] Consistent with the earlier *Champlin* case, however, the Court did declare that the right to the ownership of oil properties was "subject to reasonable regulation by the State" in the prevention of waste, a ruling that, although pleasing to leading oil spokesmen, provided yet another inroad on the private decision-making authority that is the essence of market activity. Such interference with the market came at the expense of providing the industry with a mechanism that could be used to stabilize production and, consequently, prices.

On the surface, it appeared that the East Texas problem had been resolved. However, by the spring of 1933, it was estimated by some producers that, in spite of the Railroad Commission establishing a four hundred thousand-barrels-per-day maximum on those fields, as many as eight hundred thousand barrels were coming in daily from East Texas, an amount comprising over 25 percent of the production totals for the entire United States. Such increased production, coupled with an approximate 5.6 percent decline in motor fuel consumption over the previous year, and a 2.5 percent decline in total demand for crude oil, led industry members to renew their pressures for political solutions to the problems. Amos L. Beaty, president of the API, responded to conditions in these words: "I cannot accept the theory of unrestrained production, and I believe the industry is well set against it. I believe not only in the curtailment of production by voluntary action of the industry, but in curtailment by statutory enforcement. . . ."[62]

One of the more prominent oil men, C. B. Ames of the Texas Company, proposed as a solution to industry problems the establishment of a governmental agency that could approve or disapprove agreements among producers in order to promote greater stability. In his view,

> Our individualistic competitive system has resulted in rapid, scientific progress. Much of this is entirely commendable, but much of it has resulted in excessive additions to fixed investment, and plant capacity has overrun the consumptive ability of the country. . . . The producer is unable to find a satisfactory market for his crude oil at a satisfactory price.

Ames then added that "[t]he unwise expansion of many producing companies into the marketing business, the outrageous multiplication of marketing outlets and the inordinate desire for volume regardless of profit have caused many unfair methods of competition."[63]

This view is but a restatement of the position long held by many businessmen: that the unregulated entry of competing suppliers resulting in the unrestrained introduction of additional supplies of a given product was the principal cause of the intense competition that usually took the form of lowered prices. In other words, many business leaders believed that competition could be made more "workable" if only it were not so effective! To an existing supplier, content with his relative position in the market, nothing was more disturbing than to find himself confronted by new competitors who threatened to realign market relationships through "unfair methods of competition" (i.e., through methods that were *effective* in getting customers to shift their purchases from one supplier to another).

Ames was later to advocate a compact among the oil producing states whose purpose, of course, would be "to prevent waste and to protect the natural resources from premature exhaustion," the same "conservation" stratagem examined earlier. Under such a plan, a centralized agency would have the task of forecasting demand for oil and then allocating production quotas to each of the oil-producing states. Within each state, this quota would be apportioned among the various producers. The consequence would be a tightly regulated cartel arrangement, made effective by the enforcement powers of the courts. In Ames's view, this plan would not only prevent the waste of petroleum but would protect "the consumer against premature exhaustion of the supply."[64] As we have seen, those who have sought political means of promoting their own interests have often attempted to rationalize such efforts in terms of satisfying "altruistic" or "socially conscious" objectives. Ames's contention that unrestricted competition—with its attendant low prices—had to be brought under control in order to protect *consumers* is all the more remarkable for its suggestion that consumers would benefit from a measure designed to *raise* prices.

By 1932, then, most oil industry representatives would probably have subscribed to William Farish's appeal to "conservation" sentiments in describing business conditions: "[T]he greatest burden which the petroleum industry has brought upon itself through its inability to control its production of crude oil is, undoubtedly, the economic waste that has arisen through the over-expansion of manufacturing and distributing facilities. . . . The costs of marketing have pyramided and multiplied until they have become fantastic."[65]

Oil and the New Deal

When FDR took office in 1933, he found the petroleum industry not unlike other industries that sought a workable method for stabilizing production and prices. The prorationing system, which relied upon voluntary cooperation for most of its effectiveness, was weakened by the general business decline of the preceding three and one-half years and, as in other voluntary systems that have sought to short-circuit normal marketplace functions, enforcement was found wanting. To a large extent, the struggle continued to be one between the major producers and the independents. Employing the economies-of-scale argument, the majors had always considered the oil business to be like the steel industry in that it required large, well-financed organizations in order to operate efficiently, and they looked upon the independents as meddlesome interlopers. As one might expect, the larger companies were the most faithful to the prorationing agreements. Defense of the system was made by one official of Humble Oil who declared: "Proration, properly understood, . . . does prevent the collapse of price due to inordinate over-supply, but it does not lead to an artificial price by the limitation of price below the reasonable demand for oil."[66]

Even Harry Sinclair, who had long opposed prorationing, was brought around to the position of the other majors, and the prorationing advocates began a campaign to get the federal government to aid their cause by restricting from interstate commerce all oil produced in violation of state laws. Consistent with the tendency of other trade groups to label the more aggressive competitive practices as criminal, loathsome, and morally unwholesome, this oil was tagged "hot oil" by industry members. R. C. Holmes of the Texas Company picked up on this theme in a telegram to FDR in which he said that a "lawless element" threatened to "complete the destruction of the industry here and abroad," while *Business Week* correctly summarized the thinking of the oil industry when it declared, "What it needs is more self control and enough governmental aid to enforce it."[67]

An appreciation of the plight of the oil industry can be gleaned from a study of the wholesale price index for crude petroleum and petroleum products. Using 1913 as the base period (100.0), pricing patterns were as in table 6.1.[68]

Table 6.1. Pricing Patterns for Petroleum

Year	Crude Petroleum	Petroleum Products
1920	358.3	222.1
1921	212.8	120.9
1922	193.9	123.3
1923	153.3	102.6
1924	172.4	99.3
1925	199.6	109.4
1926	210.5	114.3
1927	154.9	85.6
1928	147.2	86.6
1929	153.1	84.1
1930	136.8	71.4
1931	85.7	47.8
1932	101.9	52.0
1933	83.8	50.5

It is little wonder, then, that the oil industry faced the New Deal and Roosevelt's recovery measure with a sense of optimism.

In May 1933, a bill providing for joint federal-state regulation of the petroleum industry was introduced into Congress. Known as the Marland bill and drafted by a group of oilmen, the measure proposed to give the secretary of the interior almost total control over petroleum (should the oil states fail to enact effective legislation), including not only the power to regulate production (including imports) but the authority to establish prices, determine wage rates, and fix the hours of labor. In addition, criminal sanctions and a tax on "hot oil" were provided to help deter violations of the regulated standards.[69]

Inasmuch as the Marland bill had come under consideration at the same time that Congress was dealing with the industrial recovery bill, the decision was made to incorporate the oil bill as a special provision in the more general recovery legislation. Thus, for purposes of assessing industry support of the concept of a government-enforced system of stabilized production and pricing, reaction to these two measures can be treated simultaneously. While there was some limited opposition from oilmen to injecting as much political supervision into the industry as was envisioned in these measures, it is nevertheless the case that most producers favored such an approach. Economic conditions had reached the point where some industry members were willing to try about anything rather than endure much more of the inconstancy that had characterized the depression years. This should not, however, cloud the fact that the principal firms in the petroleum industry had—since long before the depression—favored the establishment of effective machinery that would make pricing and production factors much more predictable and controllable by the industry itself. As was true with other industries, oilmen saw in the New Deal legislation more than just a response to the momentary problems caused by the depression. For them, it was an opportunity to realize long-sought anticompetitive objectives.

Support for such federal regulation of the industry was voiced by representatives of various petroleum trade associations and producers, including Wirt Franklin, president of the Independent Petroleum Association (IPA), who declared that the industry backed such proposed legislation "with practical unanimity."[70] Harry Sinclair added his support, saying: "While personally I share in the general aversion of business men to government control, I am willing to surrender my feelings at a time like this and to join in any effort which promises to hasten the end of the deplorable conditions that have existed in the past few years."[71] This bill was also endorsed by the Pennsylvania Grade Crude Oil Association, as well as by officials of the North Texas Oil and Gas Association, the Oklahoma Stripper Wells Association, and a number of other Texas oil associations. At the same time that Walter Teagle had been active in the preparation of the industrial recovery measure, James A. Moffett—also of Standard Oil (New Jersey)—had been working energetically on behalf of legislation to control the oil industry.[72]

Declaring that "over 90 per cent" of the oil industry strongly favored the Marland measure, Franklin assessed the attitude of other petroleum men as exhibiting a "willingness to get behind the President and the present administration, even though this means surrender of their liberty of action, in order to promote the common good." Only a few individualists, according to Franklin, were opposing the bill.[73]

After many years of frustrating efforts to eliminate competitive instability, it was not surprising to find the petroleum industry's proposals being directed toward the regularization of production and prices. Industry members supported measures under which the president of the United States would be permitted to establish maximum levels of petroleum production, with many going on to advocate the establishment of minimum and maximum prices for petroleum. There was a split of industry opinion on the latter point. Some, including most officials of Standard Oil (New Jersey), felt that if production controls were maintained, prices would stabilize automatically. Other industry people also believed in a system of code price-fixing at each level in the market. It was further proposed that the production, sale, or purchase of oil in excess of the maximums established by the president (i.e., "hot oil") would constitute "unfair competition"; and, further, it was proposed that no new drillings could be undertaken without first obtaining the permission of the president.[74] While all of these recommendations were defended on the traditional grounds of promoting the "conservation" of natural resources, it is quite evident that considerations of profitability were of foremost importance to members of the industry and constituted the raison d'être of such proposals. It would be difficult to imagine a more thorough politicization of economic activity—short of outright nationalization—than what was offered by the petroleum industry as an apparent solution to the "uncertainties" associated with free competition.

So influential was the petroleum industry in helping to draft the recovery bill that one section of the act[75] authorized the president to prohibit the shipment in interstate commerce of "hot oil." This section of the act was designed to augment the state laws by providing enforcement beyond the individual state boundaries. With this long-sought power to enforce limitations on production and the opportunity to put together a workable code of "fair competition," the petroleum industry was hopeful of achieving a greater degree of trade stability.

The general attitude of petroleum industry members in embarking upon the NRA was, perhaps, most succinctly stated by *Business Week:* "Big interests believe they will fare best under the general industry control; little fellows are afraid of just that."[76] The *Oil and Gas Journal* was able to observe, however, that both the majors and independents were agreed that "no time should elapse before the police power should be applied to correct evils in the industry."[77]

The hearings on the proposed NRA "code of fair competition" for the petroleum industry elicited countless replays of the "evils" of unrestricted competition that had plagued the oil producers for the past dozen years, and of the corresponding need for a government-enforced system to control production and, consequently, stabilize prices. Resurrecting the previous problems of enforcing prorationing laws, Axtell J. Byles, president of the API, referred to oil produced in excess of state quotas as "stolen oil" and said it had contributed to the demoralization of the industry. Wirt Franklin also observed that past failures to stabilize conditions were due to the lack of "cooperation" of the federal government. As the *Oil and Gas Journal* editorially queried: "There are obvious dangers and disadvantages in government intervention, but could . . . a federal partnership be worse than dictatorship by bootleggers and price cutters?"[78]

The debate within the industry over the content of the proposed Oil Code reflected the diverse competitive interests—interests that would ordinarily have been resolved by the impersonal machinations of the market's pricing system, but which were now to be the subject of political maneuvering and manipulation. Proposals were offered for the establishment of production quotas, but the major argument that split the industry had to do with the setting of minimum prices. It was actively sought by the API, Wirt

Franklin, and a number of oil company executives, such as Union Oil's L. P. St. Clair. It was opposed by such industry leaders as J. Howard Pew, C. B. Ames, and Shell Oil's Van Derwoude. The question of federal regulation of prices caused divisions not only within the industry but among officials of the same company. The small independents tended to favor both production controls and price-fixing, a position shared by Harry Sinclair and Standard Oil (California).[79] After much politicking, a code was approved giving the code administrator the authority to establish production quotas and, if necessary, to regulate prices.[80]

The immediate effect of Oil Code controls on production and pricing— including restrictions on the creation of new productive capacity and controls on the amounts of additional inventories that could be stockpiled—was seen in the price structure of crude oil, which rose from a level of $.25 per barrel in May 1933, to $1.08 per barrel in October 1933.[81] By 1934, conditions in the industry had so improved that R. L. Blaffer, president of Humble Oil, could declare: "We have emerged from a condition of chaos and threatened collapse of all conservation efforts . . . to a fair degree toward orderly production and termination of the wasteful and ruinous practices of the past."[82] Walter Teagle, meanwhile, continued expressing his support for the NRA.[83]

In spite of the so-called hot-oil provision of the Recovery Act, unstable prices (at least in the East Texas field) and "hot oil" continued to plague the industry. Then, in January 1935, the U.S. Supreme Court, in *Panama Refining Company v. Ryan*,[84] declared this section of the act unconstitutional for having delegated legislative power to the executive branch without setting forth a "primary standard" for determining the scope of executive authority. This case was, as indicated earlier, but a prelude to *Schechter*, which brought the NRA to an end. Consistent with the responses from other industries, the directors of the API responded to the *Schechter* decision with a call to its members to continue a voluntary observance of the Oil Code labor provisions and, in order to cover the marketing as well as the production phases, urged a revision of the trade practice conference rules that had been approved in 1931.[85]

The oil industry was not as disappointed as other industries over the death of the NRA, since efforts to legislate solutions to production problems had long been under way within the industry. That the oil companies continued to favor such legislation not out of a desire to promote the conservation of resources per se but to control the production of petroleum in order to stabilize prices was reiterated in 1934 by API president Amos L. Beaty.[86] This continuing sentiment for the stabilization of the industry via legislation was also confirmed late in 1934 by a resolution of the IPA endorsing the Thomas-Disney bill for the federal regulation of petroleum production. This association went on record favoring a limitation on the imports of foreign oil; the establishment of federal oil production quotas; the limitation of withdrawal of oil from storage; a "provision for planned orderly development of new pools by agreement of a majority of operators"; and the establishment of a federal agency to administer this law. Such an agency would have been comprised, in the view of the IPA, of the secretary of the interior plus either four or six other members who were "experienced in the oil industry," an arrangement that would leave little doubt as to whose interests were to be served by this legislation. All in all, the IPA saw such a proposal as providing an opportunity to eliminate the "excessive production," "economic waste," and "demoralization of the industry" and to promote "stabilized conditions" for the petroleum industry.[87]

The IPA further supported the inclusion of a provision in such legislation allowing for the creation of compacts between oil-producing states to control production within federally established quotas. By the time the *Panama Refining* case had been decided, there had already been a growing amount of industry support—led by the API—for the idea of interstate oil compacts. By mid-1935, six states had, indeed, ratified the Interstate Compact to Conserve Oil and Gas.[88]

Following the *Panama Refining* decision, Congress wasted little time in passing the Connally Act,[89] which prohibited the interstate shipment of "hot oil." With this act augmenting, through federal enforcement, state efforts to control production through industry-dominated state regulatory bodies, the oil producers had no fear of a return to the highly competitive atmosphere of the 1920s. The combination of state controls over production and federal "hot oil" legislation assured to the industry the enforceability of the will of its dominant members over those who had not been disposed to "playing the game." Walter Teagle seemed to sum up the feelings of most petroleum men in praising the effects of the NRA upon the industry and then voicing his confidence in the combined efforts of state authorities and oil producers to curtail production.[90]

THE COAL INDUSTRY

Like the petroleum industry, the coal industry experienced a great deal of instability in the years following World War I. As figure 2 demonstrates,[91] the development of petroleum and natural gas as alternative fuel sources triggered the general decline of conditions within the bituminous coal industry. This factor, coupled with a World War I–generated increase in productive capacity, resulted in a marked increase in idle capacity during the period

Figure 2. Percentage of U.S. Energy Consumption Supplied by Alternative Fuels: 1900-1935 (percentage on B.T.U. basis).

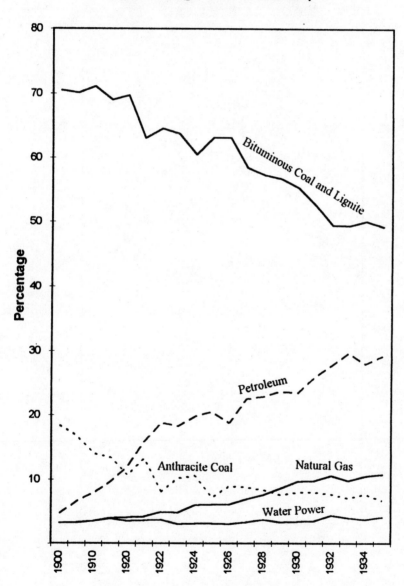

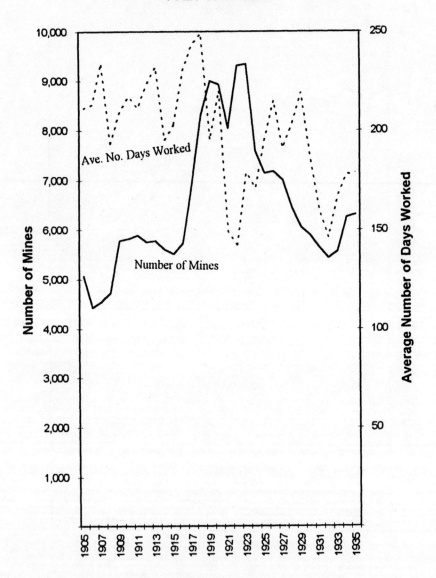

Figure 3. Number of Bituminous Coal Mines and Average Number of Days Worked Per Year: 1905-1935

Figure 4. Production and Prices of Bituminous
Coal: 1900-1935

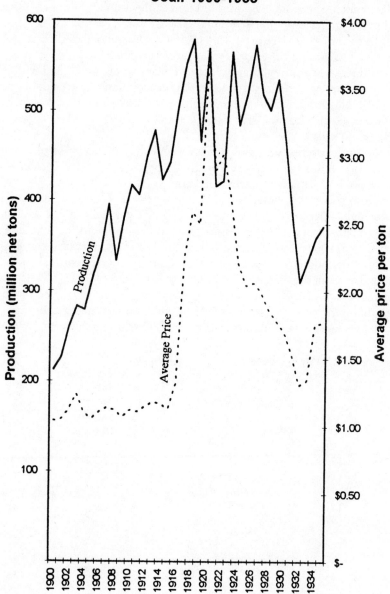

1920–35. Prior to World War I, the coal industry operated, on the average, at 75 percent of capacity. This increased to 81 percent during the years 1916–20, but then began to fall off significantly. The wartime demand that led to coal prices rising from $1.13 per ton in 1915 to $3.75 per ton by 1920 understandably encouraged a proliferation in the number of mines. While, as figure 3 indicates,[92] fifty-five hundred coal mines existed in 1915, just under nine thousand were producing by 1919. The end of a coal-consuming war that had fostered a 63 percent increase in mining capacity and a 27 percent increase in production over the prewar average combined with the rise of competing fuels to drive operating capacity and coal prices downward. As illustrated by the average number of days worked (see figure 3), average productive capacity fell to 67 percent in the 1920s and to 63 percent during the 1930s.[93]

Coal prices reflected these changes. Following the lifting of price controls at the end of the war and a nearly 20 percent cutback in production occasioned by a lengthy strike by coal miners, 1920 prices rose to $3.75 per ton. From that point, however, as shown by figure 4,[94] there followed an almost steady decline in prices to a low of $1.31 per ton in 1932. Industry profits mirrored these conditions. As Edward Devine, a member of the U.S. Coal Commission, demonstrated in his study of the profits of eighty-eight identical coal operators, net income and return on investment figures were unusually high in the years 1917, 1918, and 1920 (see table 6.2).[95] The economist Jacob Schmookler has suggested that the high prices enjoyed by coal operators during these years invited the development of new mines that, in ensuing years, contributed to the problem of idle capacity.[96]

Table 6.2. Profits of 88 Coal Operators, 1913–1922

	Cents of net income per net ton produced	Percent return on total investment in coal operations
1913	.17	5.7
1914	.13	3.8
1915	.13	4.0
1916	.21	7.2
1917	.72	21.5
1918	.61	16.3
1919	.34	7.5
1920	.89	20.3
1921	.30	5.4
1922	.36	7.1

There was another factor that added, to some extent, to increased capacity within the industry: the policies of the United Mine Workers union. The hard-line insistence by the UMW on maintaining high wage rates in the North, coupled with successful opposition by Southern operators to unionization, led to the growth of many new coal mines in the South. Schmookler suggests that the effect of such policies was to redistribute idle capacity from one region to another more than it was to increase the net amount of increased idleness.[97] Schmookler's subsequent findings suggest that union policies may be more causally related to the problem of increased idle capacity than he is prepared to admit. In his words, "This low-cost labor, in the main, made development of southern mines profitable. *As these mines came into existence* they inevitably captured markets of older, higher labor-cost operators, *and made old capacity idle.*"[98]

Whatever the relative influence of the various factors, there is little disagreement that the bituminous coal industry was plagued, in the 1920s, by competition from alternative fuel sources and by problems of overcapacity generated by the demands of World War I and, to some extent at least, the UMW. Prices and profits were depressed and many firms were eliminated. While business voices were understandably quick to attribute these depressed conditions to "the ruthlessness of the competitive struggle in recent years,"[99] it seems more reasonable to treat falling prices and the demise of some companies as a reflection of the readjustment the industry had to make to the decline of coal relative to other fuels, and to government and union policies that exacerbated industry problems. When conditions become severe, there is a tendency to regard problems as the products of the malevolence of one's competitors. It is well to remember, however, that even during the trying years 1929–33, the average annual production of coal was nearly 405.6 million tons, and the number of mines in operation averaged 5,714 per year. Coal prices during this same period averaged $1.53 per ton. This compares well with the pre-World War I years of 1910–16, in which average annual production was just over 445.6 million tons, the number of mines averaged 5,721 per year, and prices averaged $1.17 per ton.[100] Put in its proper perspective, the coal industry is an example of a trade suffering less from "ruthless competition" than from the disruptive influences of governmental and union policies that worked opposite to changes taking place in the energy field and thus fostered miscalculation. As figure 2 indicates, many of the problems faced by the coal industry during these years were the consequence of increased competition from petroleum, natural gas, and electricity as energy sources. As these alternative forms of energy developed and brought with them new product lines that were dependent upon these new energy systems, coal experienced a concomitant decline in significance as a fuel source.

It was the dynamics of change and growth rather than market failures that accounted for industry difficulties.

The "New Competition" and "Conservation" in the Coal Industry

Coal industry spokesmen joined leaders from other industries in attacks upon "selfish" and "unrestricted" competition. John C. Brydon, president of the National Coal Association (NCA) declared in 1923 that

> Individual ideas regarding fundamental matters, when opposed to a majority idea in the interest of the general good, should be submerged. In matters which affect the industry as a whole, the minority should willingly subject themselves to the settled experience and convictions of the majority. . . . Selfishness and distrust must be forgotten.[101]

Mergers and consolidations had been employed in other industries in efforts to stabilize trade conditions. Alluding to the success of such practices in the coal industry, E. C. Mahan, who had succeeded to the presidency of the NCA, observed that while such a movement offered the only means of escape for the "victims of cut-throat competition," it had failed to attract a wider acceptance due to the "strong spirit of individualism in the industry." Mahan added: "When the operators of this country decide to discard a go-it-alone policy, the day of profit taking, in contrast to price cutting will have dawned."[102] Another industry executive, H. A. Glover of Knox Consolidated Coal Company, echoed the same thought, declaring that "we must relinquish our individuality in the interest of the common good." Meanwhile, another president of the NCA, M. L. Gould, called for greater "co-operative effort" among competitors in working toward greater efficiency. According to Melvin A. Traylor, president of the First National Bank of Chicago, such efforts could lead to greater stability within the coal industry. Traylor was of the view that competition between coalfields with a "fixed labor cost" and those with a "flexible labor cost" tended to encourage "overdevelopment" (i.e., "overproduction") and, inferentially, price declines among producers. Traylor called for a "uniformity of labor standards" to alleviate such a problem, a recommendation that again suggests a rather apparent competitive advantage to higher-cost producers in increasing the costs of their more efficient, lower-cost competitors.[103] The price stabilization tendencies of labor cost standardization would, in later years, lead many business interests to actively promote the enactment of minimum wage legislation, the Wagner Act, and other employment practice laws.

One also finds the previously discussed "conservation" arguments used as a rationale for price stabilization efforts in the coal industry. As with the petroleum industry, "conservation" was seen as a vehicle for regularizing the production that led to the fluctuation of prices. As Fritz Machlup has concluded: "In the coal industry, too, price maintenance has been the chief purpose of government regulation although the necessity of regulation has frequently been justified as a 'conservation' measure."[104]

Industry "codes of ethics" were looked upon by coal producers as tools, along with "conservation" programs, for realizing stabilized production. In the words of C. E. Bockus, president of the NCA, such codes could supply "some restraint . . . upon the cut-throat competitive practices" in the industry.[105] The related purposes of codes of ethics, trade practice conferences, and conservation efforts in the fuels industries can be seen in a code adopted through a trade-practice conference by the Southern Appalachian Coal Operators' Association. The salient features of this code were provisions banning the shipment of coal on consignment and the sale of coal below cost when done to injure a competitor or control competition. The code contained an "open-price" section requiring the filing of minimum price schedules—along with any changes thereto—with the administering body. This code went into effect at a time when profits in the bituminous coal industry had declined to just over $2.545 million, down from $7.570 million for the preceding six-month period. The profit figure for the six-month period subsequent to the establishment of the code was over $8.385 million. No suggestion is being made that there was necessarily a causal relationship between this code of ethics and the general profit level for an entire industry. What is being pointed out, however, is the greater tendency of industries to be concerned about the ethical standards in their trades during periods of declining profits or the threat thereof than during periods of expansion, growth, and increasing profits.[106] Firms that enjoyed increased profits during nonequilibrium periods were not heard to decry the market instabilities that produced such benefits. It was only when those same processes worked to their *dis*advantage—as when such firms lacked resiliency to respond to changes—that the inconstancies of trade were regarded as a problem!

Tying the "conservation" movement in with efforts on behalf of business "cooperation" and "self-regulation," Bockus noted the advantages the European cartel system offered in allocating markets and setting prices for members of the cartel. He added that such practices were, unfortunately, prohibited by the Sherman and Clayton Acts. He commented upon the efforts of members of the industry, through trade practice submittals to the FTC, to improve trade conditions, but then observed:

[S]o long as the anti-trust laws remain unchanged, nothing can be embodied in those [trade practice conference] codes which provides for either the cooperative regulation of production or prices, or for any division of territory. And as it has been stated, these are the very practices on which the success of the European cartels is based.

Bockus then concluded by calling for a modification of the antitrust laws in order to permit members of the industry "the right to secure, by cooperative action, the continuous adjustment of the production of bituminous coal to the existing demand for it," a procedure he felt would help insure "the prosperity of its operating companies."[107]

In December 1931, some 137 coal producers operating in the Appalachian region created an exclusive selling agency for the collective marketing of their coal. Created in response to conditions in the industry, including severe price-cutting practices in the Southern states, the sales agency helped to moderate competition among the member firms through price-fixing. The U.S. Supreme Court was already on record, in the *Trenton Potteries* case,[108] that price-fixing arrangements could not be defended as "reasonable" restraints of commerce under the Court's previously enunciated "rule of reason." Price-fixing, in other words, had been considered unreasonable per se. Nevertheless, the Court stepped aside from this doctrine in the *Appalachian Coals* case,[109] upholding the coal operators' sales agency system. Taking into account the depressed condition of the entire coal industry, the relatively small impact of this system, and the otherwise valid intentions of the producers "to remove abuses, [and] to make competition fairer," the Court found the practice unobjectionable. The Court elaborated: "The fact that the correction of abuses may tend to stabilize a business, or to produce fairer price levels, does not mean that the abuses should go uncorrected or that cooperative endeavor to correct them necessarily constitutes an unreasonable restraint of trade."[110]

The conflicting economic interests in the coal industry were evident in efforts to put together an NRA code. Over thirty proposed codes were submitted to NRA administrator Hugh Johnson before the Bituminous Coal Code was approved on 18 September 1933. Comprised of a national code authority and five geographical code authorities, the Bituminous Coal Code reflected the conditions that had long been an annoyance to industry members. Code sections regulated hours (by setting a forty-hour-per-week maximum), wages, the right of employees to engage in collective bargaining, and the elimination of unfair trade practices. Among the unfair trade practices detailed in the code were prohibitions against sales below a "fair market price," with such prices determined by industry marketing agencies or code authorities. Also prohibited were allowances, discounts, credits, refunds, rebates, use of brokerage commissions, or prepayment of freight charges when the purpose or effect was to create price discrimination. Commercial bribery and sales to agencies representing industrial buyers were also proscribed, as were consignments of unordered coal. As in other industries, the bituminous coal industry took advantage of the NRA code system to attempt to reduce the intensity of competition.[111]

The NRA experience did little to dissuade the coal industry from advocating political intervention as a means of tempering competitive relationships among firms. By the end of 1934, *Coal Age* was able to comment that the fears of returning to the pre-NRA conditions had "triumphed over deepseated predilections for untrammeled freedom of action." The *New York Times* reported, on the eve of the *Schechter* decision, that there was "virtually unanimous opposition" within the bituminous coal industry to terminating the NRA. The *Schechter* decision resurrected industry fears of a return to prior practices, prompting *Coal Age* to observe that "[t]he drift back to pre-code profitless prices and practices which began some months ago had become too pronounced for comfort."[112]

Industry satisfaction with political direction was such that, following *Schechter*, the National Conference of Bituminous Coal Producers proposed new legislation that, among other things, sought to create a National Bituminous Coal Commission; to reestablish a code of fair competition containing the same unfair trade practices as condemned under the NRA code; to impose a 25 percent sales tax on the mine price of all coal, with 99 percent of such tax being refunded to any coal producer agreeing to abide by the code; and to create some twenty regional coal boards with the *mandatory* power to fix minimum prices and the *permissive* authority to set maximum prices for coal. The commission would also have the power to enforce industry-determined wage and hour standards, and to control and allocate coal production. With John L. Lewis providing the backing of the UMW, the legislation was rushed through Congress. Bearing the name "Guffey-Snyder Coal Act of 1935," the new law was referred to as the "Bituminous Coal Conservation Act," evidencing the popular tendency within the natural resources industries to identify practices designed for the regulation of prices, production, and trade practices as being synonymous with the efficient management of resources. As Machlup has pointed out, the fact that the measure had virtually nothing to do with conservation did not slow industry enthusiasm for its enactment. After the U.S. Supreme Court declared the law unconstitutional in the 1936 *Carter Coal* case, support was quickly mustered for the enactment of legislation that would permit price-fixing and yet avoid the practices found objectionable by the Court. The consequence was the Guffey-Vinson Act (Bituminous Coal Act of 1937), a legislative creation whose price-fixing provisions were later upheld by the Supreme Court.[113]

CONCLUSION

Since, by definition, the supplies of natural resources are limited to what is discovered in nature, efforts to control production (and thus prices) within such industries as petroleum and coal had to take the form of controlling the development of existing reserves. To this end, industry members found the "conservation" arguments an effective tool for gaining popular support for their cartelizing programs. Of course, economic analysis would suggest that the pricing mechanism of the market is itself the most efficient regulator of resource use. The price of any resource will rise or fall depending upon the relationship of the supply of that resource to its demand. Assuming a steady demand for a resource, if its availability should suddenly decrease, the users will allocate the shortage by bidding the price upwards. This, in turn, will decrease the demand for the resource and encourage exploration for more of the resource. Assuming a long-term or even permanent shortage of a resource, the increased price will cause users to better economize its use and/or to shift to substitute resources (for instance, by changing over from coal to natural gas for power). In either event, the market will respond to the relative scarcity of a resource by increasing its price; this, in itself, provides a natural and informal system for the "conservation" of resources.[114] To suggest that extramarket practices must be resorted to in order to reduce "waste" totally misconceives the nature of resource use. In a market in which resource owners make decisions regarding the uses to be made as well as the prices and terms of such uses, there is no way that resources can be intentionally "wasted": they can only be *transformed*. Their use is converted according to the demands made upon them in the market, with resource owners having an incentive to employ them in the satisfaction of those demands that promise the greatest return to the owner.

Every resource—which, by definition, is in "scarce" supply—is subject to the conservation argument. One could seek to control the employment of any resource, including human labor, by contending that private decision-making threatens supplies for future generations.[115] The entire argument is especially suspect when one notes the popularity of conservation measures rising and falling within the various industries in a manner correlating, quite well, with economic conditions therein. One becomes even more suspicious when the arguments are advanced not by resource owners seeking to protect *their* assets from destruction, but by nonowners and owners of competitive resources seeking to interfere with the resource pricing decisions of others. That the sentiments for "conservation" within the natural resources industries amounted to little more than rationalizations of economic self-interest is evident from the behavior and the rhetoric of industry members during the years under study.

The dynamic changes occurring in the energy-producing industries afford an opportunity to examine public policy responses to nonequilibrium conditions. The preference of firms for competitive stability might be superficially understandable: the specter of extinction would seem threatening. But, as the study of entropy and chaos remind us, the survival of any system depends, in the long run, not only upon a *resiliency* to change, but a willingness to *seek* such changes. The seductiveness of a sense of permanence and equilibrium clouds the entropic nature of all orderly systems. Entropy—not some ideological bias in favor of free competition—dictates that we either remain vibrant and creative, or perish. Discoveries from the study of chaos are helping us to understand how the dynamical processes of nonequilibrium are essential to life-sustaining efforts to overcome entropy. By institutionalizing stability and rigidifying resiliency, the natural resource industries were threatening not only their own survival, but that of other firms and the economic system itself.

7

Retailing and
Textiles

Merchants and master manufacturers . . . draw to themselves the
greatest share of the public consideration. . . . As their thoughts,
however, are commonly exercised rather about the interest of their
own particular branch of business, than about that of the society,
their judgment, even when given with the greatest candor . . . is
much more to be depended upon with regard to the former of
those two objects, than with regard to the latter.
                                                    —Adam Smith

THE RETAILING TRADES

Nowhere was the revolution in business more disruptive of the positions
of existing firms than in retailing. Almost overnight, the independently owned
retail establishments found themselves confronted by well-organized and
financed department stores, chain stores, and mail-order businesses, a development previously discussed in connection with Carl Taeusch's analysis of
the changes taking place in twentieth-century American life. Such changes
also had a profound impact on the wholesaling trades. In his analysis of the
evolution of managerial systems within larger firms, Alfred Chandler observed that "these new managerial hierarchies replaced the wholesalers with
their own salaried employees and managers." These developments were erod-
ing the business done by wholesalers. Between 1889 and 1929, Chandler
informs us, "the proportion of goods distributed by wholesalers . . . was cut
in half."[1]

The popular image of retailing has been that of a confrontation between
the locally owned, family-operated grocery, drug, or department store, and
the impersonal, nationally managed corporate giants, whose trademarked
names provided the substitute for personal "reliability" that local buyers
had previously attributed to the neighborhood retailer. The "mom and pop"

store was giving way to the A & P, and those whose interests were threatened by such changes became vocal champions of the "ethical" trade practices that were synonymous with the methods of the old order.

There prevails a highly romanticized view of the small, independent retailer as the paladin for a system of free and open competition. An examination of the evidence, however, reveals few trades with a better track record than independent retailers at getting to the political arena with programs for depriving somebody of a competitive advantage. Virtually every innovation in retailing has met with the organized and vocal opposition of retailers who were unwilling to adjust their own selling methods to meet the competition, and who responded with legislative proposals to preserve the status quo. The targets of the old order were any organizations or sales practices that offered a substantial threat to existing retailing methods. The suggested legislation—whether in the nature of a Green River ordinance, a Sunday closing law, anti-street-peddlers ordinances, fair-trade laws, anti-price-discrimination laws, or tax proposals to confiscate chain stores out of existence—attested to the eagerness of some retailers to use the coercive powers of the political state to weaken or destroy their competitors. As one writer has observed:

> The history of retailing reveals that every innovation in distribution methods has been opposed by those fearful of its impact on the existing order. Department stores, mail-order houses, house-to-house sellers and, most recently, the supermarkets, each in turn ran into more or less organized opposition. Almost invariably the State legislatures were appealed to for special taxes or other restrictive measures designed to check the new method of distribution or to stop it altogether.[2]

One of the early—and more blatant—anticompetitive efforts of independent retailers involved the use of the taxing powers of government at both the state and federal levels to put an end to the chain store movement by the simple process of confiscation of property through taxation. At the convention of the National Association of Retail Grocers (NARG) in 1922, legislation was urged limiting the number of chain stores allowed in any community. This proposal was followed the next year by the introduction of a bill—at the behest of independent retailers—in the Missouri legislature to impose a progressive tax on chain stores. While the bill did not pass, independent retailing interests began descending upon state legislatures with various proposals to limit—or prohibit—the operation of chain stores. During the period from 1923 to 1933, some 689 anti-chain store tax bills were introduced in state legislatures across the nation, with 28 of them being enacted into law in twenty states.[3] Such legislation was actively promoted by independent retailers and their trade associations, including such groups as the NARG which, in 1928, was successful in getting a United States Senate resolution passed calling for, among other matters, an inquiry into "[w]hat legislation, if any, should be enacted for the purpose of regulating and controlling chain store distribution."[4]

Characteristic of the political efforts to interfere with the emerging trade practices was a Grocery Trade Conference of over five hundred representatives of retail and wholesale grocers, as well as grocery manufacturers. Its purpose was to adopt resolutions to be submitted to the FTC for approval as trade practices to govern the grocery trade. One-third of the resolutions dealt with pricing policies and included, among others, condemnation of "secret rebates" or "secret allowances"; "free deals, operating to induce merchants to purchase beyond their economic sales requirements"; "premiums, gifts or prizes"; selling products at or below cost; and deviations from agreements regarding discounts for cash. At the instigation of the American Wholesale Grocers' Association (AWGA), the conference went on to adopt a resolution "that commercial bribery, whatever the bribe, however it is given, and whether given with or without the consent of the employer, is an unfair method of business."[5] The condemnation of so-called bribery, even when done with the consent of the employer, strips away the argument that the practice is "unfair" because it induces an employee's breach of trust with his employer. The real objection related to the fact that "commercial bribery" increased the cost of obtaining a customer's business or, stated another way, reduced the effective price of a competitor's good or service to the customer.

The degree of animosity that independent retailers had developed against aggressive competitive activities in general—and the chain stores in particular—can be seen in the statements of some of the more prominent industry spokesmen. One of the foremost champions of self-styled "ethical" trade practices was Edward A. Filene, president of William Filene's Sons Company of Boston and an ardent advocate of industrial self-regulation. Lashing out at what he considered unfair trade practices, Filene offered a rather emotional characterization of businessmen who, under the custom of trade practices, charge as high a price for their merchandise as they can induce their customers to pay. He drew an analogy between such businessmen and the "thief," "robber," and "cheat" who obtains money by force or fraud. In his view,

> The merchant who buys a pair of shoes and sells them for more than a fair advance over cost, performs no adequate service to the community and is ethically no more entitled to a profit than is the man who steals an automobile and sells it to some unsuspecting purchaser, or the man who makes adulterated goods and sells them for genuine.[6]

As a perusal of trade journals will verify, the condemnation of competitive business practices was often accomplished by associating price cutting, invasion of another firm's territory, and other aggressive trade practices with acts of a violently or fraudulently criminal nature. This approach, typified by Filene's observations, is subject to two fundamental criticisms. In the first place, statements such as Filene's attack the firm that charges too *high* a price for its merchandise but, as the evidence demonstrates, the real concern was for those firms that were *undercutting* the prices of competitors. Thus, it would appear that Filene was setting up a straw man; he was seeking to take advantage of popular sentiments against high prices by identifying the practices of the price cutter as being opposed to the interests of the consumer.

Second, to equate the practice of charging as high a price as a customer is willing to pay with open theft is an aggravated abuse of poetic license and a corruption of the meaning of words. It demonstrates the underlying premise of many businessmen that competitive trade practices can be as objectively defined "honest" or "dishonest" as can an act of robbery. By identifying a criminal act—in which force is used to deprive a victim of a property interest he or she does not choose to part with—with trade practices that are consummated voluntarily and without the use of force, one can then proceed to construct a seemingly "objective" system of "fair" prices, "fair" profits, and "fair" sales practices. The effort by many members of the business community to construct "codes of ethics," criteria of "unfair trade practices" and, ultimately, "codes of fair competition" under the NRA all attest to the support given to the notion that subjective economic values can be evaluated in objective terms, and that some members of the business community are as justified in imposing their preferences upon an entire economy as police are in the effort to rid society of thieves, robbers, and burglars! As we saw earlier, retailing interests took a back seat to no one in employing trade association "codes" in just such an effort to specify acceptable and unacceptable trade practices.

Filene confirmed that the movement toward "cooperation" and "ethical trade practices" was really directed against self-seeking business firms employing energetic competitive methods to maximize their profits: "The coming war on waste will force us out of that extreme individualism that has been a heavy handicap to business. . . . We will come to know that the independent individualistic production by thousands of manufacturers of even the right thing will result in a wasteful surplus."[7] Once again, business rhetoric treats aggressive competitive practices as synonymous with "waste."

In an effort to stimulate a greater degree of stability in retailing, the U.S. Chamber of Commerce sponsored a National Distribution Conference in 1925. The basic purpose of this conference was to help develop an environment in which both "unethical" and "uneconomical" trade practices could be brought under control. One of the leaders of this effort was another Filene—A. Lincoln Filene—who chaired a committee that considered such problems as price fluctuations, the disrupting influence of "fly-by-night" businesses, and lack of standardization in products and trade practices. Noting that "the practices of the least progressive should be brought up to a higher standard," Filene's committee recommended the establishment of a Joint Trade Relations Committee, the function of which would be to receive complaints of trade abuses and take action to eliminate these and other unethical practices. It would also encourage the development of codes of ethics and methods for dealing with trade disputes; such an organization would then become a repository for the "common law of business."[8] The term "progressive" applied, in this case, not to those innovators who, in Schumpeterian terms, were introducing radically new distribution methods, but to business firms that had accepted the gospel of "business cooperation" and conformed their activities to the object of maintaining a competitive detente. Indeed, the "progressives" were those doing their best to *resist* innovative changes and to preserve the status quo.

Lincoln Filene continued his efforts when, in June 1926, his committee proposed the establishment of trade relations committees among manufacturers, wholesalers, and retailers, with the ultimate purpose of organizing a regulating committee comprised of all sectors involved in the production and distribution of goods. The function of this committee would, in the opinion of Edward L. Greene, managing director of the National Better Business Bureau, be akin to organizations such as bar associations, which dealt with the unethical practices of lawyers.[9] The Better Business Bureau had itself been created by existing business interests principally to discourage the entry—especially at the local level—of new business firms. Legislative proposals, coupled with public relations campaigns to convince consumers to trust only the "established" firms in their communities and to be skeptical of the fledgling and out-of-state enterprises, were resorted to in efforts to inhibit the growth of competitive alternatives.

Along related lines, the National Retail Dry Goods Association (NRDGA) set up, in 1927, a Bureau of Trade Relations, the purpose of which was to study unfair trade practices. It was further contemplated that a clearing house for complaints would be established, through which alleged code violations would be reported. Lincoln Filene interpreted the attitude of supporters of this bureau as favoring it as only a "first step" in a longer-range effort to solve economic problems of the industry. Future concerns of the bureau might, in his view, include agreements on "popular price levels for different types of merchandise."[10]

In looking back upon the idea of a Joint Trade Relations Committee, Lincoln Filene observed that, while such experiments had, prior to 1925, taken place in such industries as hardware, men's clothing, and women's garments, this committee's contribution to progress had been to extend the trade-practice control idea to both industry-wide and tradewide organizations. That such efforts ultimately failed was due, Filene felt, "to the fact that there was no compelling economic pressure on business nationally to induce it to spend time on reforms which then seemed unimportant. Self-interest was not sufficiently endangered." Further, according to Filene, the failure of the FTC to determine which unfair trade practices could be legally controlled had contributed to the failure to reform unfair trade practices.[11]

Consistent with Lincoln Filene's efforts, George L. Plant, director of the NRDGA's Trade Relations Bureau, outlined in 1928 a program to be proposed to the trade relations committee of his association. Part of the proposal envisioned, according to Plant, a "really workable code of ethics" for each segment of the industry, as well as the establishment of cooperative efforts with other trade associations to better coordinate production and distribution as well as to collect and disseminate information on undesirable business practices. Plant added that "there are many practices, which while not in themselves illegal, are nevertheless regarded as undesirable and unethical." It was hoped, he went on, that a trade practices code could provide effective enforcement for approved business standards. After such a code was set up, Plant foresaw a program in which a "central clearing house" could be established among the participating associations to collect information and maintain files on complaints involving members of the association.[12]

Such proposals were the outward manifestation of a pervasive change in the attitudes of businessmen toward each other, a change that was brought about by a desire to reduce the threat of free, unrestricted competition. The rallying point for such a change was the "spirit of cooperation," through which the businessman sought to convince his competitor of the evils of "greed," with the "greedy" being defined as those whose interests were in substantial conflict with his own.

As we saw earlier, many business leaders used the Great Depression to intensify their prior appeals for a more cooperative, less aggressive form of competition. Lincoln Filene exemplified this attitude when he stated:

> [A]long with the innumerable lessons learned from the depression came the realization that the age-old and illegal abuses of good faith in the dealings of business men with one another must in some fashion be done away with. The depression has, I believe, laid a solid groundwork for constructive progress in this field over the years to come.[13]

By the start of 1933, the retail trades were heavily involved in efforts to seek legal restraints against those retailers—especially the supermarkets—

who engaged in loss-leader selling. Retail trade associations, composed largely of independent retailers, mounted campaigns to convince consumers—and legislators—that there was something almost fraudulent about a retailer offering to sell certain items below their actual costs as an inducement for customers to shop at that store. The Associated Grocery Manufacturers of America prepared a model state law that, it was hoped, would be used by retailers within their respective states in seeking legislative solutions. Some disagreement arose within the industry not as to the *principle* of such legislation, but of the *form* it should take. As a result, the AWGA also prepared a model bill for use against the chains. This alternate bill defined "loss leader" selling as selling below *cost,* whereas the manufacturers' bill addressed itself to sales below *purchase cost.* The wholesalers felt that the manufacturers' bill could benefit the chain stores at the expense of the independents by permitting the manufacturers to sell grocery products to the chains at quantity discounts, thus allowing the chains to sell such items at a legally lower price than the independents could do.[14] This debate continued up into 1936 and helped spark interest in securing passage of state fair-trade laws, the Robinson-Patman Act (1936), and the Miller-Tydings Act (1937).

Nowhere was the attraction to political solutions more evident than in the New Deal–era responses of independent retailers to the bogey of chain stores. The initial reaction of this group to the NRA was to devise a marketing code that would effectively strip the chains of any competitive advantages they enjoyed—a move the chains, understandably, sought to counter. The NARG, for example, supported a measure limiting the number of hours of employment for stores, a proposal that would have had less impact on the independent retailers, who could operate above the maximum hours level by having themselves or members of their immediate family working.[15] The National Wholesale Grocers Association supported the maximum-hours concept and also offered recommendations for the prohibition of sales below cost, secret rebates, and "free deals." At the same time, a group of New York City retailers—with the improbable name of the Business Independence League—called for a federal investigation of chain-store ethics and urged the enactment of a city tax on chain stores.[16]

In spite of opposition from R. H. Macy's Percy Straus, other retailing interests were able to prevail on behalf of an anti-price-cutting provision in a code proposed by the NRDGA. The language in question prohibited sales at prices below cost (based on invoice) plus 10 percent.[17] Other retailers anticipated code provisions dealing with minimum wages, the elimination of overproduction and unfair competition, and the restraint of unfair advertising, style changes, and house-to-house selling. One retailer suggested the creation of local, state, and national retail boards empowered to license retailers.[18]

Picking up the pace established by other retailers, the retail tobacco dealers met to put together an NRA code for their industry. A debate ensued over a proposal to require a minimum profit of 20 percent on the sale of cigarettes. This proposal was favored by 80 percent of the participating tobacco organizations, with the opponents objecting that a 20 percent minimum was not high enough. There was little question, however, that the tobacco retailers were generally pleased with the NRA concept. Nor was there any question as to the anticompetitive, price-raising consequences of the NRA code. For example, Macy's department store in New York City had, for some time, conducted a very profitable business selling cigarettes at cut-rate prices. As soon as the tobacco retailers' code was approved, however, Macy's was forced to stop selling lower-priced cigarettes. It reopened this department the day following the U.S. Supreme Court's decision striking down the NRA.[19]

The drug industry greeted the NRA with code-enforcement machinery already provided for in the Drug Institute. Patterned after the AISI and receiving its inspiration through such men as Charles Walgreen, the Drug Institute had sought to stabilize competitive conditions within the industry and found the NRA to be quite consistent with its objectives. By the time the legislation had been signed into law, drug retailers had let it be known that they wanted code provisions that would maintain "fair" profits and "fair" wages, as well as product standards, and would seek to prevent overproduction, the demoralization of prices, and "unfair" methods of competition. They also sought code language that would eliminate such competitive advantages as the advertising of fixed prices for prescriptions or listing one's business as a "cut-price drug store"; the dispensing of medicines by physicians, or the granting of professional discounts to physicians on merchandise; and the practice of department stores in absorbing sales taxes in the price of merchandise. Drug manufacturers, likewise desirous of taking a crack at distressing sales practices, sought to prohibit retail clerks from trying to persuade customers to shift their preferences from one brand to another.[20]

The impact that the NRA would have on sales practices in general—one of the major facets of competition—was considered by a number of executives familiar with the advertising industry. One called it an "encouraging development" that business would "be required to cease selling below cost," adding that this "should eliminate the most vicious and destructive of the price cutting." Another executive looked forward to "the elimination of piratical tactics by the destructive minority," while yet another characterized the pre–New Deal era as

one grand throat-cutting contest. Manufacturers were simply interested in finding out how many sub-cellars there were in the price structure. They found that every time they took a couple of steps down they ran into more competitors, and that giving things away was not the solution. Now the Government is making them be good to themselves. That is, they can't give things away, and so will be forced to rely on other appeals than price.[21]

In contrast to these highly competitive practices, Dudley Cates looked upon many of the retailing codes with these sentiments: "They tend to discourage enterprise, to check the trading instinct which makes a merchant, and to crystallize forms and practices for all time or until the dam bursts from the pressure within."[22]

Retailing interests had expressed general satisfaction with the NRA and approved its retention. Writing in 1934, Edward Filene described the "new relations between business and government" as "a new world, . . . a new era." He then added that the NRA had not changed the preexisting social order, but had simply recognized "the fundamental laws of that order." Prior generations had, according to Filene, simply been too myopic in their outlook, and had they exercised the proper degree of responsibility, they "would have taken much the same attitude and much the same course that we are taking now."[23] Lincoln Filene, meanwhile, asserted his support for the permanency of a government-enforced system of trade practices, declaring: "[T]here is no turning back to the days when business was a law unto itself, and . . . both progressive business leaders and the public will in the future demand some method by which the federal government will permanently have something final to say in matters affecting the daily functioning of business. . . ."[24] Calling for a "revised, enlarged, and strengthened Federal Trade Commission" that would serve to enforce codes established within the various industries, Lincoln Filene detailed a program that, he hoped, would "make permanent the gains which the initial impulses of the NRA have made it possible to expect."[25]

Other retailing spokesmen voiced their support for the NRA. The pre-*Schechter* efforts to secure a renewal of the NRA system were endorsed by the board of directors of the NRDGA; and in a poll of automobile dealers, some 77 percent favored retention of the NRA code "if properly enforced." At the same time, the Retailers National Council—which was made up of representatives of eleven national retail associations—issued a statement expressing its desire of "cooperating with the President in his further efforts to promote recovery."[26]

With the exception of a few persons such as the inveterate individualist Sewell Avery of Montgomery Ward, the retailing trades were fairly unanimous in their expressions of regret for the *Schechter* decision and urged a continuation of NRA codes on a voluntary basis.[27] The president of the National Retail Council declared: "Since all but one of the trade associations in the council asked that NRA be continued, there will be great disappointment at the decision. The code of fair practices, backed up by the law, had given thinking merchants throughout the country what they had long wanted."[28] One association executive then declared: "The unexpected has happened and the fight must be started again. This association must redouble its efforts to fight for the NRA's existence."[29] The attitude of the retailing industry toward the *Schechter* case was fairly well summed up by *Business Week:* "Wholesalers and many independent retailers everywhere will mourn the NRA. Through codes, they had gained a large degree of protection against the inroads of department, chain-store, and other types of mass-selling competition that now have them helpless again."[30] Consistent with this analysis, the National Association of Retail Druggists (NARD) expressed resentment at the end of the code system, while two national associations representing wholesale grocers began urging alternative legislation to deal with trade abuses. The National Automobile Dealers Association announced its intention to carry on the basic principle of the NRA code. Other associations representing the retail trades recommended a voluntary adherence to NRA code standards, while the board of directors of the New York Pharmaceutical Council, representing some forty-five hundred retail druggists, and the New Jersey Retail Grocers Association each called for new legislation embodying the principles of the NRA.[31]

As we have already seen, the general satisfaction business had with the NRA quickly manifested itself in the form of various efforts to superimpose political solutions upon what were perceived as intraindustrial problems. Following the *Schechter* decision, retailing interests lost little time in promoting legislation that would take a whack at the chain and discount operations. It was a matter of record that the chains were able, by virtue of their being able to engage in quantity buying, to demand—and usually obtain—price concessions that the smaller retailers were not in a position to realize. These lower costs permitted the chains to offer their merchandise to consumers at lower prices. While the independents were very critical of such "price-discrimination," these buying and selling practices of the chain stores provided for a more efficient utilization of resources, benefiting not only the chains but consumers who found themselves paying less for retail items.

The conditions of free competition are most objectionable to those firms least able to compete effectively, and in this sense the responses of the so-called independent retailers were not wholly unanticipated. While retail trade associations railed against the "price discrimination" that they saw as characterizing quantity-discount buying, and while their arsenal of rhetoric was more than capable of turning out propaganda to show such buying practices to be in conflict with egalitarian sentiments, in point of fact what these interests were resisting was not some sinister chain-store "conspiracy," but the revolution in distribution that was taking place within the economy generally.

The retailing sector of the economy, no less than any of the other areas, was undergoing fundamental revisions that, to established interests, were perceived as threats to their very existence. One of the natural consequences of free competition is change, or what is often called innovation, a condition that has been described as "the disturbance of peaceful, unchanging business routine by bold innovators who institute new methods."[32] This factor took the form, in retailing, of a restructuring of the entire distribution process. The more familiar retail outlets—most of which tended to be owned by an individual or a very small group independent of other retail, wholesale, or manufacturing firms—were suddenly confronted by the chain stores, which had integrated a number of retail outlets into a singly owned organization. In the decade 1920–30, twenty of the larger chain operations had grown from a total of 9,912 stores to 37,524, while government figures indicate that, as of 1929, 10.8 percent of all retail establishments were part of a chain organization.[33]

In addition to the threat of horizontally integrated competition—carrying with it the threat of such competitive advantages as quantity-discount buying—the independent retailers found themselves up against organizations that had begun to integrate themselves vertically as well. Innovation in retailing was beginning to take the form of companies such as A & P, which not only brought a number of retail outlets into one organization but had incorporated wholesaling, brokerage, and food processing into the system. The efficiencies already realized through horizontal integration were enlarged upon, and the independent retailer was fast finding himself at the disadvantage of offering identical products to the consumers at prices higher than those offered by the chain stores. In the face of competitive superiority, the independents increasingly turned to the political state to get legislation passed to deprive the chains of their competitive advantages.

The bargaining advantages enjoyed by the chains in being able to obtain quantity discounts in their purchase of merchandise continued to aggravate the independents. While this same quantity-buying advantage was available to the independents through retailing alliances, their attentions were drawn, instead, to the Robinson-Patman "anti-price discrimination" bill in Congress, which proposed to strip the large retailing organizations of their purchasing advantages. This bill proposed to make the giving of quantity discounts unlawful unless such discounts reflected actual cost savings to the seller. It also sought to prohibit discounts—even though based upon cost savings—that were restricted to too limited a number of buyers. The independents saw in such proposed legislation an effective means of taking from the chains the cost advantages that the less-efficient independents were unable to realize in the marketplace. That the measure was designed only to redistribute economic advantages from the *more* efficient to the *less* efficient firms (and had nothing whatever to do with fostering abstract egalitarian premises) was evident from the provision that price discrimination was unlawful *only* "where the effect of such discrimination may be substantially to lessen competition or tend to create a monopoly . . . or to injure, destroy, or prevent competition with any person who either grants or knowingly receives the benefit of such discrimination, or with customers of either of them."[34] Nor was the enthusiasm of the independents dampened by the fact that the bill would make retailing less efficient—thus increasing prices to consumers.

Support for the bill seemed to come most strongly from those retailing sectors in which the chains were most active, namely, grocery and drug stores. While such groups as the NRDGA and the National American Wholesale Grocers Association joined the chains and some wholesalers in opposing the Robinson-Patman bill, they were more than offset by such organizations as the NARG, the National Wholesale Druggists Association, the National Retail Druggists Association, the United Independent Retail Grocers and Food Dealers Association, the Associated Grocery Manufacturers of America, the National Retail Grocers Association, and the National Food Brokers Association, all of whom backed the proposal.[35] The efforts of the independent retailers to legally deprive the chain stores of their advantageous positions had assumed the proportions of a campaign to protect public morality itself. In the words of one trade association executive, the overriding objective was "to obtain legislation which will outlaw crooked and misleading trade and merchandising practices and protect small business against the wiles of the ruthless price cutter."[36]

Success in obtaining passage of the Robinson-Patman Act in 1936 whetted the appetites of retailers for further political restraints on competition. Support for the so-called fair-trade laws resulted in the passage of the Miller-Tydings Act in 1937. Such legislation, designed to enforce resale price maintenance arrangements, was actively promoted by a number of retail trade associations—most notably the NARD and the NRDGA[37]—in order to get at another branch of competitive "culprits," the discount stores. The more-established retailing interests were not prepared to acknowledge the American capitalistic system as encompassing the right of some firms to sell name-brand merchandise at prices lower than they were willing or able to charge. They were, as a result, quite active both in Congress and the state legislatures in securing laws that would allow a manufacturer not just to contract with individual retailers to establish a minimum retail price for the sale of its merchandise but, in some instances, to impose the terms of such contracts upon retailers not parties thereto.

Any analysis of resale price maintenance must distinguish, conceptually, those arrangements brought about by agreements between a manufacturer and its distributors from those imposed upon unwilling distributors by legislative fiat. It is one thing for a manufacturer to insist upon its right to freely contract with distributors and to have the terms of that contract enforced. It is another matter for distributors to seek to impose pricing standards, via legislation, upon their competitors who have not contractually agreed to such terms. In promoting resale price maintenance laws, there is no evidence that the retailing interests were simply seeking to foster the principle of freedom of contract. In California, for example, the "non-signers" provision was incorporated into the legislation at the urging of retailers.[38] Under the "non-signers" system, a price-maintenance agreement between a manufacturer and any one retailer would effectively establish a minimum price for the sale of that item upon *all* retailers within the state, even if they had not agreed with the manufacturer on such a price.[39] These provisions resulted in the imposition of pricing policies upon unwilling participants, thus giving the manufacturer benefits for which he had not contractually bargained and binding some distributors to the terms for which their competitors had bargained. When, in 1936, the U.S. Supreme Court declared state fair-trade laws to be constitutional,[40] the groundwork was laid for the federal legislation that was to follow.

At the state level, retailing interests were also actively promoting "unfair practices" and "anti-loss-leader" legislation. As with earlier trade association and NRA codes, these laws were premised on the establishment of industry-wide (within the states where they were enacted) standards for the determination of minimum prices. Generally prohibited was the selling of merchandise below such prices when done with the "intent" or "effect" of "injuring a competitor." As we saw earlier, the practice of attacking "below cost" pricing was designed not to dissuade "predatory" and "malicious" retailers from carrying out ill-motivated designs upon their competitors, but to intimidate them into not cutting prices. A retailer might have a difficult time gauging, in advance, whether his pricing practices could have the "effect" of "injuring a competitor" within the meaning of the statute, especially since the act of lowering one's prices is likely to draw customers away from a competitor. As one observer has pointed out, "state laws became mere subterfuges" for the restrictive activities of trade associations, leading—in the case of the unfair practices laws—to "significant limits upon aggressive loss-leader selling."[41]

A desire to return to the basic structure of the NRA continued to intrigue many retailing interests. By early 1937, the membership of the NRDGA had approved the principle of the establishment of a "little NRA" for retailing. The former chairman of the Dress Code Authority told the association: "The unwilling minorities of retail trade groups as well as industrial groups will not be allowed to stand in the way of progress. Legislation backing up this control will be available if we take the lead in asking for it." Later in the year, after the inability to get agreement from the membership on the form such a "little NRA" should take, the board of directors of the association approved the enactment of state laws regulating maximum hours and minimum wages in retailing.[42]

The chain stores provide a striking example of an industry serving both as a victim and an employer of political intervention for the regularization of trade practices. Many of the chains, which had been the objects of numerous legislative attacks, were nevertheless supporters of the fair-trade laws. One of the consequences of the depression was, apparently, a diminution of price cutting as an effective tool by the chain stores. Chain stores, however, continued to experience price cutting by other competitors. As early as 1932, men such as Charles Walgreen, George Gales (president of Louis K. Liggett Company), and Malcolm G. Gibbs (president of Peoples Drug Stores) led other drug chains in supporting such laws in order to stabilize *their* positions vis-à-vis "price cutters" who were competing with them, just as the independent retailers were seeking legislation to protect *themselves* from the "price-cutting" chains.[43] The situation poses an anomaly only if one makes the mistake of assuming that business supported—or opposed—various political programs out of a sense of ideological commitment. Opponents of restrictive legislation were, in the main, no more devotees of the principle of undiluted laissez-faire capitalism than the proponents were the disciples of state socialism. Most businessmen—then, as now—could be described as "pragmatists," ready to align themselves with any cause that promised either short-range or long-range benefits to their firms. In this regard, the motives of most retailers (and other businessmen) has been put forth no more clearly than by Adam Smith himself:

The interest of the dealers . . . in any particular branch of trade or manufacture, is always in some respects different from, and even opposite to, that of the public. To widen the market and to narrow the competition, is always the interest of the dealers. To widen the market may frequently be agreeable enough to the interest of the public; but to narrow the competition must always be against it, and can serve only to enable the dealers, by raising their profits above what they naturally would be, to levy, for their own benefit, an absurd tax upon the rest of their fellow-citizens. The proposal of any new law or regulation of commerce which comes from this order, ought always to be listened to with great precaution, and ought never to be adopted till after having been long and carefully examined, not only with the most scrupulous, but with the most suspicious attention. It comes from an order of men, whose interest is never exactly the same with that of the public, who have generally an interest to deceive and even to oppress the public, and who accordingly have, upon many occasions, both deceived and oppressed it.[44]

The independent retailer's use of the powers of the political state to promote intratrade interests reached its zenith in the "death sentence" bill of Congressman Wright Patman in 1938. Through the use of a progressive tax, chain stores would have literally been taxed out of existence, a prospect that tended to fill the independent retailers with delight. The proposed tax would have escalated upward from an annual rate of $50 per store for a chain of ten stores to $1,000 per store for chains with over five hundred stores. The bill was made all the more outrageous by a provision that multiplied the total amount of the tax, as computed by the above scale, by the number of states in which the particular chain was in business. The effect of such a tax on chain stores can be seen in table 7.1.[45]

Table 7.1. Impact of Patman "Death Sentence"
Bill on 24 Chains as of 1938

Company	No. of Stores	No. of States	1938 Earnings	H.R. 1 Tax
American Stores	2,416	8	$ 57,627	$ 17,652,000
A & P*	12,000	40	9,119,114	471,620,000
Bickford's	106	4	558,924	92,800
Bohack, H. C.	488	1	(179,741)	279,700
Dixie Home Stores	172	2	189,197	105,800
Edison Bros.	123	29	919,323	894,650
Fanny Farmer	237	15	904,009	1,315,500
First Nat'l Stores	2,350	7	2,705,191	14,983,500
Gamble-Skogmo	247	18	278,538	1,686,600
Grant Co., W. T.	491	38	2,766,424	10,731,200
Kinney, G. R.	328	37	151,503	5,420,500
Kresge**	679	27	8,997,051	12,676,500
Kress, S. H.	235	29	3,668,216	2,508,500
Kroger Co.	3,992	19	3,741,569	71,867,500
Lerner Stores	164	39	1,299,231	1,922,700
Liggett	552	36	518,432	12,330,000
Mangel Stores	106	27	18,674	626,400
Melville Shoe Corp.	639	40	1,484,061	17,180,000
Newberry	476	45	1,792,741	12,100,500
Penney, J. C.	1,541	48	13,739,160	63,912,000
Safeway***	2,873	22	4,206,781	58,597,000
Schiff Co.	277	28	265,180	3,127,600
Walgreen Co.	510	37	2,067,846	11,118,500
Woolworth Co.***	1,864	48	28,584,944	81,070,500

 * Estimated U.S. stores; earnings include Canadian stores.
 ** Includes Canadian stores and earnings.
 *** Includes Canadian and Cuban stores and earnings.

Had this measure been enacted into law, these twenty-four chains would have paid a total tax of just under $874 million in the first year—a figure almost *ten* times their combined earnings, and which compared to a total 1938 federal budget of $6.792 billion.[46] Stated another way, this tax would have imposed on twenty-four corporations the burden of paying almost 13 percent of the federal budget for 1938! While such a measure could not be justified as the chains' "equitable share" of the costs of government, it was not proposed for such a purpose. The measure served as an example of the ultimate power of government—reminiscent of John Marshall's classic observation that "the power to tax involves the power to destroy"—to fashion an environment suitable to the economic interests of some at the expense of others.

The bill was enthusiastically supported by the trade associations representing independent retailers, including the NARD, the NARG, the United States Wholesale-Grocers Association, the National Retail Hardware Association, and the Motor Equipment Wholesalers Association.[47] The popular image of the small, independent retailer as the champion of "free competition" is an illusion that consideration of the "death sentence" bill should help lay to rest. However one may choose to rationalize legislation that is directed at the regulation of sales and pricing practices, when one gets to the advocacy of the political state legally confiscating the businesses of competitors, the outer limits of economic authoritarianism have been reached. That retailing interests could so easily endorse such a proposal is evidence of the degree to which so many in business had, by 1938, abandoned the marketplace as the disciplinarian of economic activity and accepted the politicization of the economy.

THE TEXTILE INDUSTRIES

The textile industries, having also experienced many years of intense—and, to industry members, unstable—competition, shared the view that intraindustrial cooperation was necessary. One of the leading executives of the industry, Royal W. France, president of Salt's Textile Company, expressed a commonly held sentiment in his recognition of the need for self-regulation in his industry.[48] In a speech to the American Cotton Manufacturers Association (ACMA), George E. Roberts, vice-president of the National City Bank of New York, discussed the nature of the then-current competitive conditions, observing that "it is a common saying that business generally is overdone, that competition is excessive, [and] that profits are inadequate. . . ." While he regarded such irregularities as "inherent in the system of free and competitive business activity," Roberts went on to recommend industrial "cooperation" that could result in a "well-ordered industry."[49] At this same meeting, Walker D. Hines, president of the Cotton Textile Institute (CTI), attacked the notion of the "survival of the fittest" in the cotton industry; such a notion, he said, "seems to assume that the mills should not join in an exchange of information as to production, stocks, costs, etc., should not encourage each other to try to balance their production with demand, and should not encourage meeting together in groups to discuss their common problems."[50]

One of the more influential trade associations, the CTI was formed in 1926 in an effort to bring stability to an otherwise beleaguered industry. The cotton industry had, for a number of years, experienced a rather erratic pattern of production, brought on largely by changes in clothing styles and retailing methods, and the existence of highly autonomous units. These conditions led this industry—like the steel and oil industries—to become one of the chief advocates of a system of effective intraindustrial self-regulation of production, pricing, and "unfair trade" practices that, it was felt, resulted from and served to reinforce a general state of instability within the industry. While supply and demand balanced out on an annual basis, it was quite ordinary for production to run well ahead of sales during one time period and to lag sharply during another. The consequence of this was a sharply fluctuating employment of plant facilities from year to year. Many firms, rather than permit their machinery to stand idle, began round-the-clock production as a means of lowering unit fixed costs. The increased production, of course, helped drive industry prices downward. Understandably, the reduction of production was one of the causes to which the CTI and many of its members became firmly dedicated. The institute, which conceived its main function as being the stabilization of prices through the prevention of overproduction, undertook the solicitation of pledges from industry members to limit weekly hours of production, a campaign that included an effort to eliminate night work. It also sought agreement from firms to cease the employment of women and minors during night hours, an effort motivated *not* by humanitarian impulses but by a desire to restrict production. These campaigns resulted in compliance by over 80% of the industry.[51]

Problems of overproduction also existed in the wool industry. In 1927, this industry had the capacity to produce—at prevailing prices—some $1.75 billion in goods, while sales amounted to only $656 million for that year. Similar patterns were seen, in 1929, in the weaving and spinning divisions, with the former experiencing a 37.5 percent, and the latter a 35.8 percent, ratio of actual consumption to productive capacity. Between 1924 and 1928, wool machinery activity fell from 73.7 percent to 66.4 percent of actual capacity.[52]

Industry expectations of the CTI were undoubtedly expressed by one executive who looked for a system of cooperation with "every mill radiating from a central point, which we will call the American Cotton Textile Institute." He went on:

With every mill reporting fully to the Institute, and receiving in return full and complete data, we will have an industry pitched on broad and sound principles. This naturally is predicated upon the complete elimination of the ignorance, jealousy, and lack of confidence, that appear to thoroughly permeate the industry as a whole today. We have reached the point where something has to happen.[53]

Concern over price-cutting practices was as intense in the textile industries as any other sector of the economy. A resolution adopted in 1927 by the ACMA declared, in part, that "[c]utting of prices below a fair profit level is the greatest single menace to the industry as a whole. . . . Ethically, it is a form of dishonesty to one's self."[54] It is not really clear how one could be said to be "dishonest to one's self" in seeking to maximize his self-interest, but the statement does reflect industry fears. Along the same lines, J. H. Hartig, president of the International Association of Garment Manufacturers, declared, in 1928, that low prices were harmful to the industry, adding: "Just as lower prices cannot materially increase the available business for an industry, so unwise concessions merely produce a deadly competition within the industry."[55]

Another concern was the consolidation of various units. Walker Hines told the ACMA in 1928 that "there are far too many mills in this country," and recommended the consolidation methods that had been employed with such success in other industries. Even though all of these voluntary efforts resulted in a sizeable amount of "cooperation" from industry members, the inability to persuade all firms to participate in limiting production in order to keep prices up—for reasons explained by Mancur Olson—led many textile-industry leaders to the conclusion that government compulsion was necessary to universalize such efforts.[56]

The factors that most distressed the cotton textile industry were (1) a reduced demand for textile goods—influenced by fashion changes, lowered population growth rate, and competition from substitutes and foreign textiles; (2) productive overcapacity; and (3) regional competition existing between Northern and Southern mills. While modern, more efficient machinery accounted for much of the competitive advantage enjoyed by Southern producers, lower construction costs, the availability of lower-priced labor, and the absence of labor unions combined to attract firms into the South. The wage differential enjoyed by Southern mills—the amount of which diminished as Southern wage levels rose—gave the Southern producers a cost advantage they were able to convert to lower prices. The increased production that was coming out of the South was reflected in figures that showed the percentage of productive capacity located in the South increasing from over 50 percent in 1920 to approximately 80 percent by 1940.[57] Between 1923 and 1929 alone, the ratio of active spindle hours between Southern and New England producers increased from approximately 56:39 in 1923 to 68:28 by 1929.[58]

Representatives of the textile industry expressed their concern for what they felt were problems of overproduction and price cutting, and they proposed solutions for dealing with them in order to help provide stability between production and consumption. Among the suggestions offered was the development of a system of standardized cost-accounting procedures, mutual agreements by producers to limit working hours, the creation of a "special supreme court for industry," and the application of the principle of the Webb-Pomerene Act—which permits combinations of producers for export purposes—to domestic industries "for the purpose of controlling production."[59] One industry member declared: "Price fixing should be allowed when it is done in the public interest. This would result in increased employment and tend to stabilize legitimate industries." Walker Hines, meanwhile, urged "intelligent planning to keep production in balance with demand."[60]

The efforts on behalf of cooperation, consolidation, limitation of production, and self-government in the textile industry all served the same objectives sought by members of other industries: the voluntary alteration by industry members of pricing, production, and sales practices in order to stabilize prices and prevent the disruption of those conditions that would maximize profits for the industry. The self-interest of competing firms—each of which hoped that *others* would comply with the restrictive agreements, all the while looking for ways for itself to cut corners—ultimately provided the marketplace remedy for voluntary cartels: the collapse and abandonment of such agreements. In the meantime, many textile producers continued, along with members of other industries, to maintain the illusion that freely competitive conditions in a market could be short-circuited by agreements that were premised on the notion that men could be induced to abandon their selfish motivations.

The textile industry was not without its advocates of political intervention to restrain competitive practices. One of the most remarkable proposals for government regulation came from the executive director of the United Women's Wear League, who called for the establishment in that industry of an advisory authority invested with the licensing power to declare who was and who was not competent to enter business. This trade official drew upon earlier French legislation that provided for an officer of the government to judge the "competency and financial right" of prospective businessmen to enter a given trade. He also made reference to a law that required all businesses to keep their financial records in books supplied—and owned—by the government; erasures were considered "prima facie evidence of fraud," permitting prosecution.[61] A similar proposal was made by a member of the knitted goods industry, George Boochever, who complained that in spite of the existence of a code of ethics for his trade, there was no effective means of enforcing such codes against violators. As a solution to such a problem, he proposed that business adopt the same sort of licensing and "disbarment" procedures used to discipline members of the legal profession.[62]

There were seemingly endless proposals from business groups to use the powers of the political state to effect some advantage against a competitor. An example of the inconsistent attitudes businessmen had toward government involvement in economic affairs was colorfully sketched, in 1928, by John T. Flynn:

[M]arching legions of the trade associations descend on Congress with a "truth-in-fabric" bill. The men who make pure wool are in competition with the men who make a mixture of wool and cotton. There is nothing so shocking about mixing wool and cotton as one might suppose. It is not like mixing Scotch and wood alcohol. It may actually improve the fabric. But whether it does or not, the wool fabric men propose to have Uncle Sam on their selling staff. They demand government action: they want laws, inspections, government labels introduced into the fabric business. They may be the first to denounce the government for its officious meddling in the affairs of the railroads, but they appear to think a little meddling in the wool business would be an excellent thing. They think it is shameful interference with business to protect the citizen as he gets into his railroad coach, but it is quite proper to protect him as he steps into his morning tweeds.[63]

Industry members were becoming increasingly aware that voluntary methods of achieving competitive stability were doomed to failure. Political solutions—which offered the coercive powers of the state for enforcement purposes—began to dominate industry thinking even before the New Deal. B. B. Gossett, president of the ACMA, asserted in June 1932,

[W]e must have some form of economic control. Such a plan would involve not only the balancing of production to demand but perhaps also reasonable price regulation and the proration of business. Unfortunately, the limitations of the present laws will not permit of the setting up of such a plan of economic control. It is therefore felt that an effort should be made to have the antitrust laws amended to such an extent as will permit of the regulation of these matters in a reasonable way, possibly subject to Government supervision, alike in the interest of the manufacturers and their customers as well as the public in general.[64]

The highly competitive textile industry, which had been seeking stabilization of prices for many years, eagerly anticipated the New Deal recovery bill. The CTI voiced its support for the measure, while the leading trade journal *Textile World* observed in a May 1933 editorial, that what the industry needed most of all was industrial self-regulation, backed with the power of enforcement that the industry had heretofore lacked. It hoped to eliminate "unfair" methods of competition such as low wages, price cutting, and "[u]nlimited operation of plants." Concluding that "the imposition of the will of 85% upon the other 15% could hardly be called tyranny," the editorial asserted what, by now, had become one of the principal tenets of the new industrial order: "Those who still believe that the rights of the individual cannot be curtailed in the interests of the group are merely living in a bygone era."[65] H. P. Kendall, president of the Kendall Company, said: "Undoubtedly, the Recovery Act means that the Government has taken a long step toward state socialism, which is described as 'cooperation with business.' Will the textile industry carry on in such a way that the Government will not have to exercise further control?" Another industry member bluntly declared: "It is time that an industry incapable of intelligently managing its own affairs should be forced to accept outside control."[66] Members of the garment industry—who had longed for greater security from the vicissitudes of competition—saw the opportunity for the enforcement of trade-practice standards having "the force of law behind them."[67] Noting that "unfair competition has created demoralization in the industry," the board of directors of one industry council representing 180 clothing manufacturers adopted a resolution supporting enactment of the recovery bill.[68] G. H. Dorr, president of the CTI, added his support to the idea of government-enforced trade-association rules. He had no objection to making the coercive powers of the state available to force the minority into compliance with the wishes of the majority. In his view, "You can't have self-government in industry unless you have power to govern the minority. . . ."[69]

It is not surprising that, with the prospect of enabling legislation to permit effective industrial self-regulation, members of the textile industry began formulating plans for dealing with the perennial nemesis: overcapacity of plant facilities. A number of textile executives met with President Roosevelt to propose a plan for stabilizing the industry. Such a plan included, among other matters, provisions for regulating the hours of work for employees, the hours of plant operation, and the permanent abolition of night-shift employment for women and minors. The restriction or elimination of night employment had been actively sought by many within the industry as a means of restricting production. In testimony before the House Committee on Labor, Ernest Hood, president of the National Association of Cotton Manufacturers, renewed industry support for a provision to eliminate such employment for women and minors. Hood concluded by calling for legislation that would allow trade associations to enter into agreements for the regulation of production and prices.[70]

At the 1933 convention of the ACMA, B. B. Gossett issued a plea for "sustained cooperation" from industry members to help solve the problem of seasonal fluctuations in demand and production. Gossett said that in the cotton industry supply and demand balanced out for the year as a whole, but such seasonal fluctuations had the effect of reducing prices "below the cost of production," a level that—consistent with the prevailing view of businessmen as to what constituted "below cost" pricing—was "insufficient to meet labor cost, taxes, insurance, supplies, selling expenses and administrative overhead." Such price reductions, which Gossett strangely identified as a "burden on our customers," could be overcome, he felt, by intentional industry-wide production adjustments prior to the drop-off in demand. Warning his associates not to be motivated by "selfishness," Gossett concluded by saying: "We must put aside individualism; we must put aside unenlightened selfishness and stand together as one in a great irresistible push with stability and prosperity for all as our goal."[71]

One rather intriguing proposal for voluntarily regularizing the woolen industry came from a manufacturer who suggested establishing a bank, to be subscribed to by industry members who also agreed to do all their financing through this bank. The bank would, through its control over credit, be in a position to discipline those firms that violated industry rules. The promoter of this plan acknowledged the difficulty associated with voluntary efforts to restrain market activity. Even though he claimed that some 25 percent of the productive facilities of the woolen industry were backing his idea, he acknowledged that if a significant number of manufacturers refused to participate, the plan would not work.[72]

Members of the various textile trades entered into NRA code making with a sense of optimism. The cotton-textile industry lost little time in drafting what became the Cotton Textile Code. Provisions in the code faithfully reflected the competitive struggles within the industry. The comparative cost advantages enjoyed by Southern mills in lower wage rates were reduced by establishing a minimum wage of thirty cents per hour for Southern producers and thirty-two and one-half cents per hour for the Northern mills. In an effort to limit production, restraints were placed on adding new machinery and mills were prohibited from operating more than forty-hour work shifts each week. The failure of this latter provision to resolve the problems of overproduction led, in 1934, to a further cutback to thirty-hour maximums.[73]

As we saw previously, business leaders tended to resolve the conflict between government regulation and economic freedom by coming down on the side of regulation whenever it suited their immediate interests to do so.

This was as evident in the textile industries as elsewhere, as witness the statement of G. H. Dorr. In response to the question whether the NRA codes interfered with the rights of individual businessmen, Dorr stated:

> What is this boasted freedom that we talk about? In the absence of any self-regulation in an industry, a minority, and a small minority, can force on the industry as a whole an unduly low price, unsound trade practices and unsound and destructive competitive conduct.
>
> This is an essential characteristic of the competitive system. The unintelligent or unscrupulous minority can ordinarily make the majority dance to its tune. It is ordinarily only through the collective action of a code that the majority can get the "liberty" to conduct their business by the competitive methods and standards that they desire.[74]

When it is recalled that the pre-NRA rhetoric was also directed against the "minority" of competitors who invariably upset the restrictive and cartelizing efforts of the dominant firms in an industry, and when economic analysis demonstrates the inherent weakness of voluntary cartels to prevent the maverick firms from disrupting the competitive stability sought by other firms, it is quite evident what men like Dorr were attacking: any condition that interfered with the anticompetitive ambitions of industry members. Unrestrained competition, in other words, was unacceptable to those firms desirous of securing their positions against the effects of what, to consumers, were more attractive trade and pricing practices. The defense of the NRA on the grounds it provided the majority of industry members with "the competitive methods . . . they desire" pays lip service to competition while rejecting the unrestrained exercise of choice by market participants that is implicit in a system of free competition. The suggestion that competition can be legally stripped of its most effective operational and disciplining features and still be regarded as "competition" serves to encourage that corruption of language that has come to be associated with the political process. The notion that the "liberty" of the majority can be realized only by suppressing that of the minority has contributed to an understanding of "human freedom" as a *collective* rather than an *individual* attribute. Just as it has become popular to define the scope of "human freedom" as that conduct not otherwise prohibited by law, so business efforts to legally proscribe certain trade practices and to structure intraindustrial relationships into a less effective form of competition have undoubtedly helped to foster the belief that one who is aggressively seeking to promote his business by undercutting other firms and making his product more attractive to buyers is a threat to competition!

Following the *Schechter* decision, the hard-pressed textile industries lined up in support of a continued observance of code principles,[75] with some industry spokesmen advocating the enactment of legislation to provide for the enforcement of such codes.[76] One such proposal sought "to preserve, through industrial self-government, such stabilizing benefits as accrued to this industry under the National Industrial Recovery Act" and went on to recommend "the strongest possible bureau of fair trade practices."[77] The influential ACMA recommended conformity to existing codes for its members.[78] At about the same time, a meeting was held—under the auspices of the Industry and Business Committee for NRA Extension—among representatives of some 150 industries to discuss a proposal for legislation to create a new NRA system under which codes would be submitted to a congressional body for approval.[79] This measure, offered by Peter Van Horn, president of the National Federation of Textiles, was an obvious attempt to satisfy the Supreme Court's objection, in *Schechter,* that the NRA code-making process involved an unconstitutional delegation of legislative authority. By submitting such codes to Congress instead of to the executive branch, the approved codes would—the proponents of the measure hoped—have the effect of a validly enacted piece of legislation. A resolution favoring such a law received unanimous backing at this meeting.[80]

In spite of *Schechter,* the textile industry had not given up on seeking political solutions to competitive problems. The desire of Northern textile firms to impose higher labor costs on their Southern competitors—both to reduce the comparative advantage in pricing enjoyed by the Southerners and to reduce total production—led many in the textile industries to become some of the principal advocates of minimum-wage legislation.[81] It was the quite practical interests of some employers seeking to benefit themselves at the expense of their competitors, and not any "humanitarian" sentiments, that was responsible for the enactment of the Fair Labor Standards Act in 1938. Minimum-wage laws not only served to increase the hourly rate of pay for Southern mills but placed a premium on overtime work, factors that both added to the production costs of the Southern mills and reduced the incentives for maximizing production. Labor unions added their support to such legislation in order to help eliminate lower-priced sources of labor.[82] Any suggestion that the textile industries had soured on the use of the political state to alter market relationships and deprive competitors of their comparative advantages is hardly warranted by the evidence.

CONCLUSION

No industries were more plagued by intense and aggressive competitive practices than the retailing and textile trades. Industry efforts to develop an effective consensus on behalf of a more sedate, cooperative form of competition were frustrated by the relative ease of entry of new firms and the lack of concentration in each of these trades. In addition, revolutionary changes in retailing methods and periodic changes in clothing styles only reinforced collectivizing sentiments among industry members. The efforts of many retailers and textile manufacturers to persuade their colleagues to voluntarily restrain the pursuit of firm interests—in favor of the collective interests of the industry—met with failure. As in other industries, the ineffectiveness of such voluntary efforts led many within the retailing and textile industries to embrace political solutions to the problems associated with too freely competitive an environment. Supporting both the general trade-regulating machinery of the NRA and the more specific legislative programs designed to deal with particular conditions within the respective trades, many industry members became eager enthusiasts for an extension of political authority over the economic life of the nation.

8

In Retrospect

The aversion to change is in large part an aversion to the bother of
making the readjustment which any given change will necessitate;
. . . any innovation calls for a greater expenditure of nervous energy in making the necessary readjustment than would otherwise
be the case. It is not only that a change in established habits of
thought is distasteful. The process of readjustment of the accepted
theory of life involves a degree of mental effort—a more or less
protracted and laborious effort to find and to keep one's bearings
under the altered circumstances.

—Thorstein Veblen

The revolution that was forging institutionally structured organizational
patterns upon American society demanded fundamental reforms of the environment in which these new systems were to operate. During the years 1918–
38, notions of economic autonomy and self-regulating market behavior
confronted the forces of industrial concentration. Free competition—with
attendant low prices and aggressive trade practices—was identified with the
older, unstructured forms of organization characterized by smaller, self-governing business firms. An unrestrained marketplace brought with it the specter of incessant change, a condition that was unacceptable to those charged
with the responsibilities of managing and preserving the assets and market
positions of business organizations. In the confrontation between "individualism" and "institutionalism," competition came to be identified with the
decentralized, unstructured practices representing the past. Individual self-
interest, with its decentralizing tendencies, had to be suppressed in favor of
the emerging institutional order. The attack on autonomy was a defense of the
new order: the institutionally dominant, centrally directed, collective society.
Businessmen came to embrace the industrial theology of "responsibility,"
and learned a new set of cartelizing catechisms. The campaign to reform
trade practices and promote "fair" competition had little, if anything, to do
with business ethics, efficiency, "justice," "fairness," the elimination of waste,

or any of the other rationalizations employed on behalf of "industrial self-rule." It was, instead, part of a strategy designed to secure the political supervision indispensable to the group domination of industry members. Only in the structuring of economic behavior, it came to be thought, could the status quo be maintained against the inconstancies and uncertainties of the marketplace.

As the law of entropy, chaos theory, and history combine to remind us, however, efforts to structure and institutionalize the processes by which negative entropy is produced can be fatal to both firms and civilization as a whole. Life is defined in terms of a continuing capacity to respond to nonequilibrium conditions. Change, not stability, and uncertainty and variation, not security and the status quo, are the characteristics of any healthy, surviving system. That the increased politicization of American life, during the twentieth century, has detracted from such resilient capacities, can no longer be denied. It will be left to historical analysis to assess the contributions of such practices to the decline of the American economic system—and, perhaps, the civilization itself.

A major public policy question raised by this inquiry has to do with the role of free competition as a regulator of economic behavior in society. To what extent—if, indeed, at all—should political intervention be invoked to structure market relationships and decision-making? To what extent—if at all—should market participants be deprived of competitive advantages earned through successful responses to the demand preferences of others? If Mancur Olson is correct in concluding that—under the conditions he specified—the collective interests of a large group cannot be advanced without the use of coercion, do the collective interests of various industries in securing stable pricing and nonaggressive competitive practices, justify the abandonment of an environment of unrestrained economic decision-making? These and many other questions still await a more thorough public analysis.

An examination of such questions must be prefaced by clearly distinguishing between the *myth* and the *reality* of competition. Though our public-policy rhetoric is replete with endorsements of the abstraction "competition," it is difficult to find any consistent institutional support for the concept when translated into the functional realities of concrete decision-making. When operating as a *buyer* of raw materials, a firm may have undiluted praise for the competition that allows it to bargain among competing sellers for a lower price. But that same process becomes an "unfair method of competition" or "unethical price-cutting" when employed by buyers and sellers in the market in which that same firm is a *seller* of a finished product. Labor unions argue for the "freedom of contract" to allow unions and employers to agree to make union membership a condition of continued employment, but deny to workers with low marginal productivity the "freedom to contract" to work at a less than prescribed minimum wage. Politicians publicly extol the virtues of "free competition," but then privately devote themselves to working on behalf of special interests to enact legislation to weaken or destroy competition. About all that one can safely conclude about public responses to competition is that business firms, labor unions, consumer groups, trade associations, political agencies, or individuals will—on a case-by-case basis— either support or oppose the principle of unrestrained competition depending upon their perception of what is to their self-interest. Beyond that (except for some isolated ideological commitment to free competition) it can hardly be said that American society shares any consensus favoring a freely competitive market environment.

Within the post–World War I business community, as we have seen, any consensus—if it existed at all—was in favor of a lessening of competition. Even before the turn of this century, many business leaders were involved in efforts to eliminate or reduce competitive threats. These efforts involved a mixture of voluntary and political methods. As Gabriel Kolko has pointed out, the merger movement at the beginning of this century was just such an effort to bring competitive trends under control, an undertaking that failed and led businessmen to look to the federal government for a solution to the problems of unhindered competition.[1]

Throughout the 1920s, trade associations helped set the tone and supply the machinery for collective efforts to reduce the intensity of competition. As Robert Himmelberg has concluded, such endeavors (including proposals for revising the antitrust laws to allow for a more "cooperative" mode of competition) "originated in the enthusiasm for cooperative capitalism which businessmen felt as a result of their wartime experience."[2] Both simplistic and sophisticated attempts to persuade business firms to voluntarily restrain their self-seeking impulses were inadequate, however, to overcome the inherent conflicts between *individual* and *group* interests.

As a result of such influences, many business leaders were drawn to more formal, politically enforceable alternatives. Being dissatisfied with an economy in which decision-making was diffused among autonomous and unsupervised business firms and customers, many leaders of commerce and industry began opting for a centralized direction of economic life through business-created, government-enforced trade practice standards. By the time the Great Depression brought the decade to a close, a sizeable and influential portion of the business community had already accepted the basic premise underlying what has been termed the "corporate state." That premise is that the impersonal, voluntary influences of a market regulated by the pricing mechanism should be replaced by politically structured restraints upon the exercise of economic free choice. The trade associations helped to facilitate the emergence of an environment favoring the cartelization of American industry and, with it, the diminution of the role of free, unhindered competition as the catalyst in determining the success or failure of business firms. Such efforts played a significant role in helping to shape and direct the relationships between business and government in succeeding years.

STABILITY OR CHANGE

There is a prevailing view that government regulation serves both as a countervailing force to economic influence and a substitute for preexisting market disciplines that have been eroded through years of intense competition. According to this view, the competitive processes are truly "destructive," with unsuccessful competitors gradually being eliminated until only a few large, powerful, and efficient firms remain. The market is seen, by the adherents to this position, as a self-consuming process, with large corporate enterprises and heavily concentrated industries surviving as the natural consequence of aggressive, highly competitive market activity. This outlook is an extension of the interpretation of industrial growth and development during the so-called age of the robber barons in the late nineteenth century. It assumes that a market economy is unable to maintain internal discipline and will naturally evolve into monopolistic or oligopolistic forms.

Studies of the origins of government regulatory programs belie such interpretations of economic behavior. In the first place, it is not at all clear that large enterprises necessarily have, by virtue of their size, a commanding advantage over their smaller competitors. As Kolko and others have pointed out, the merger movement at the beginning of this century often failed to provide the stabilizing results business had desired. Far from providing increased concentration, domination, and control, mergers frequently resulted in substantial declines in market shares for the firms that had merged. Alfred Chandler Jr., of course, has identified many of the advantages associated with the organizational changes that led to the emergence of the modern "multiunit business enterprise."[3] Nevertheless, size alone did not seem to assure any firm a secure market position. It was the *efficiencies* associated with vertical integration, and not the *domination* of an industry sought by horizontal combination, that accounted for organizational success. Since the rhetoric of the regulatory process is grounded in notions of "power" and "abuses" of power, it is important to distinguish, at least conceptually, between situations in which size gives a firm nearly arbitrary power to dominate markets and competitors and those situations in which size promotes efficiency and allows a firm to put its products into the market at lower prices.

Any analysis of the nature of competitive influences within a given market must take into consideration the time frame within which such behavior is evaluated. Let us assume, hypothetically, that a firm thoroughly dominates its particular industry and, furthermore, seeks to take advantage of its position by trying to charge monopolistic prices. Let us, for purposes of this example, disregard the fact that competition might well be present in the form of industries offering substitutable goods or services (e.g., aluminum, concrete, or lumber, as a substitute for steel in construction) and consider this firm as having no direct competitors. The classic model of competition would suggest that, unless legal coercion is available to prevent the entry of new firms into that market, the monopolistic prices will quickly attract new competitors. Since it would take some period of time for one or more competitors to get into production, our hypothetical firm might enjoy a short-term noncompetitive benefit. But, as a *long*-term proposition—again, assuming the absence of any legal restraints upon entry—such practices offer little concern. Indeed, a rationally managed firm in such a position might well wish to avoid trying to take advantage of its situation in order not to attract new competitors.[4]

Any assessment of systemic change—or of unsystemic change—must keep such temporal factors in mind. Work being done in other disciplines has greatly modified our understanding of the processes of growth and change in systems generally. Earlier assumptions about the *continuous* processes of development are giving way to models of *dis*continuous, or *punctuated,* change, wherein a major nonlinear break occurs, followed by a period of relative stability.[5] If punctuation *does* more accurately describe the temporal framework within which systems evolve, it should be apparent to us that "stability" and "change" are inextricably entwined, as work in the study of "chaos" and "complexity" suggest.

It has not been the purpose of this study to thoroughly explore any general theory of organizational development. The contrasting views on this subject by such scholars as Joseph Schumpeter, Arthur Dewing, and Alfred Chandler Jr. suggest that such questions are best left to separate and more extensive inquiries. Nevertheless, it is apparent that increased size has a tendency to foster inertia, conflict, inflexibility, and general instability within organizations. It also appears that large organizations tend, as a consequence of these internal counterpressures, to become less resilient, less capable of making satisfactory responses to market changes. There is much evidence to support the contention that large organizations are increasingly less capable of sustaining their market positions in the face of competitive challenges without the use of artificial restraints to control the behavior of other firms that pose threats to their established interests.

This is not to deny that many large firms have been able to overcome these internal, countervailing influences. Chandler's research documents the

effectiveness of the organizational changes occurring throughout much of
the business system. Both before and during the twentieth century firms did,
indeed, respond to the conditions in which they found themselves, and many
became organizationally more efficient. But to what extent did the artificial
structuring of competitive relationships become an increasingly attractive
strategy to large business organizations *because* of certain dysfunctional
factors associated with firm size? At the same time, what influence did an
extended political intervention into economic decision-making have in the
fashioning of organizational structures? The organizational changes identified by Chandler were occurring within a much broader politico-economic
context in which corporate-state policies were increasingly influencing, and
defining the parameters of, economic behavior. It would be difficult to
isolate all the variables to determine how much of the organizational revolution taking place within the business system was actually fostered by anticompetitive, trade-stabilizing policies of government. It is clear, for example,
that the regulatory process tends toward greater industrial concentration by
permitting larger firms to more easily spread the costs of regulation over its
production than is the case with smaller firms. In the words of Walter
Adams:

> [I]ndustrial concentration is not the inevitable outgrowth of economic and
> technical forces, nor the product of spontaneous generation or natural selec-
> tion. In this era of big government, concentration is often the result of unwise,
> manmade, discriminatory, privilege-creating governmental action. Defense con-
> tracts, R and D support, patent policy, tax privileges, stockpiling arrangements,
> tariffs and quotas, subsidies, etc., have far from a neutral effect on our indus-
> trial structure. In all these institutional arrangements, government plays a cru-
> cial, if not decisive, role. Government, working through and in alliance with
> "private enterprise," becomes the keystone in an edifice of neomercantilism
> and industrial feudalism. In the process, the institutional fabric of society is
> transformed from economic capitalism to political capitalism.[6]

In any event, it can hardly be denied that many business leaders and trade
associations perceived that their interests would be furthered by an extension of political controls over their competitors, and that such controls have
helped to shape contemporary American commerce and industry. What may
prove to be the case is *not* that increased government intervention emerged
as some countervailing force to large business enterprises, but that the interests of large firms and the state worked, in symbiosis, to aggrandize the
power interests of *both* sectors.

Traditional interpretations of economic behavior fail for a more compelling reason: they are contrary to historical evidence. Government intervention has been invoked *not* at the behest of persons who saw the market

failing to function properly, but at the prompting of business interests who were concerned that the market was functioning all too well. None of this is to suggest that all business interests desired political intervention. The events of the 1920s and 1930s clearly demonstrate that many business firms enjoyed a comparative advantage under a system of unrestricted competition, and not only opposed political efforts to eliminate that advantage but resisted any temptation to use political means to benefit themselves. Nevertheless, while businessmen have always paid homage to the litanies of "competition," the energies of far too many of them have been devoted to establishing political controls that would make "free competition" secondary to the maintenance of an environment of *stabilized security*. Any public policy inquiry must be premised on a clear understanding of the tensions between a *stabilized* and *structured* form of economic order, on the one hand, and, on the other, the order that is associated with the continuing *processes of change* to which firms must be prepared to respond. This distinction has been made by Robert A. Dahl and Charles E. Lindblom in these terms:

> [O]rder is not the same as the absence of change. Competition is often identified with disorder—hence, by some doubtful logic, monopoly with order—because competition means losses as well as profits and because it calls for a never ending procession of bankruptcy. But preferences change; so also do technology and resources. If an economy is to economize, the first requirement is adaptability. An economic *order* provides for the systematic elimination of the obsolete and inefficient, as well as for constant experimentation. The test of genuine experimentation is that much of it fails.[7]

This view of order is finding additional confirmation in studies of "chaos," which remind us that the health of any system—be it an individual, a firm, an industry, or a society—depends *not* upon maintaining conditions of equilibrium, but upon the capacity and resolve to remain responsive to those endless processes of nonequilibrium.

The principal purpose of this inquiry has been to provide a more complete understanding of the business purposes that have helped influence public policy responses to competition. The lessons learned herein must, however, be put into perspective: the advocacy of restraints was neither new to nor unique with the American industrial system. In the final analysis, perhaps, this inquiry only serves to remind us of an observation by Adam Smith that is two centuries old. In words that seem to have anticipated both the "Gary dinners" and the NRA, Smith warned:

> People of the same trade seldom meet together, even for merriment and diversion, but the conversation ends in a conspiracy against the public, or in some contrivance to raise prices. It is impossible indeed to prevent such meetings, by

any law which either could be executed, or would be consistent with liberty and justice. *But though the law cannot hinder people of the same trade from sometimes assembling together, it ought to do nothing to facilitate such assemblies; much less to render them necessary.*[8]

Notes

INTRODUCTION

1. Clair Wilcox, *Public Policies Toward Business*, 4th ed. (Homewood, Ill.: Richard D. Irwin, 1971), 8.
2. Paul Douglas, *Controlling Depressions* (New York: W. W. Norton, 1935), 247.
3. Some of the more significant contributions have included Gabriel Kolko, *The Triumph of Conservatism* (Glencoe, Ill.: Free Press, 1963); Gabriel Kolko, *Railroads and Regulation, 1877–1916* (Princeton: Princeton University Press, 1965); James Weinstein, *The Corporate Ideal in the Liberal State, 1900–1918* (Boston: Beacon Press, 1968); G. William Domhoff, *The Higher Circles* (New York: Random House, 1970); Michael Parrish, *Securities Regulation and the New Deal* (New Haven: Yale University Press, 1970); Robert Cuff, *The War Industries Board* (Baltimore: Johns Hopkins University Press, 1973); Murray Rothbard, *America's Great Depression* (Princeton, N.J.: D. Van Nostrand Co., 1963); Ron Radosh and Murray Rothbard, eds., *A New History of Leviathan* (New York: E. P. Dutton, 1972); Melvin Urofsky, *Big Steel and the Wilson Administration* (Columbus: Ohio State University Press, 1969); James Gilbert, *Designing the Industrial State* (Chicago: Quadrangle Books, 1972); Ellis Hawley, *The New Deal and the Problem of Monopoly* (Princeton: Princeton University Press, 1966); and Robert Himmelberg, *The Origins of the National Recovery Administration* (New York: Fordham University Press, 1976).
4. Kolko, *Triumph*, 57–58.
5. Myron Watkins, *Public Regulation of Competitive Practices in Business Enterprise*, 3d ed. (New York: National Industrial Conference Board, 1940), 38.
6. Robert Wiebe, *The Search for Order, 1877–1920* (New York: Hill and Wang, 1967), 297.
7. Carl Taeusch, *Policy and Ethics in Business* (New York: Arno Press, 1931), 258.
8. Ibid., 258–59.
9. Joseph Schumpeter, *Capitalism, Socialism, and Democracy*, 3d ed. (New York: Harper & Bros., 1950), 156. It should be noted that a contemporary economist of the Austrian school, Israel Kirzner, minimizes the distinction Schumpeter draws between "price competition" and the more meaningful "entrepreneurial competition." Kirzner suggests that "the *process* of price competition is as entrepreneurial and dynamic as that represented by the new commodity, new technique, or new type of

215

organization." See Kirzner, *Competition and Entrepreneurship* (Chicago: University of Chicago Press, 1973), 129.

10. Taken from Ralph C. Epstein, *The Automobile Industry* (Chicago, 1928), 164ff., and other sources cited in Donald A. Moore, "The Automobile Industry," in *The Structure of American Industry*, ed. Walter Adams, rev. 2d ed. (New York: Macmillan, 1954), 274ff.

11. Walter Adams, "The Military-Industrial Complex and The New Industrial State," *American Economic Review* 65 (May 1968), reprinted in *Superconcentration/ Supercorporation*, ed. Ralph Andreano (Andover, Mass.: Warner Modular Publications, 1973), R337-2-3.

12. Robert H. Wiebe, *Businessmen and Reform: A Study of the Progressive Movement* (Cambridge: Harvard University Press, 1962), 69ff.

13. Ibid., 82–84.

14. Ibid., 100.

15. Ibid., 221ff.

CHAPTER 1. MAKING THE WORLD SAFE FROM COMPETITION

1. William Leuchtenberg, *The Perils of Prosperity, 1914–1932* (Chicago: University of Chicago Press, 1958), 42–43.

2. Wiebe, *Search for Order*, 293.

3. For some excellent accounts of the War Industries Board, see: Cuff, *WIB*; Urofsky, *Big Steel*; Grosvenor Clarkson, *Industrial America in the World War* (Boston: Houghton Mifflin, 1923); Bernard Baruch, *American Industry in the War* (New York: Prentice-Hall, 1941); and Robert Himmelberg, "The War Industries Board and the Antitrust Question in November, 1918," *Journal of American History* 52 (June 1965): 59–74.

4. Arthur Schlesinger Jr., *The Crisis of the Old Order, 1919–1933* (Boston: Houghton Mifflin, 1957): 37.

5. Frederick Lewis Allen, *The Lords of Creation* (Chicago: Quadrangle Books, 1966), 206.

6. Baruch, *American Industry*, 21.

7. Clarkson, *Industrial America*, 154.

8. Cuff, *WIB*, 169ff.

9. Clarkson, *Industrial America*, 303.

10. Ibid., 299, 309.

11. Ibid., 308.

12. See Ferdinand Lundberg, *America's Sixty Families* (New York: Citadel Press, 1946), 144ff.; Cuff, *WIB*, 15ff.; Clarkson, *Industrial America*, 501ff.

13. Clarkson, *Industrial America*, 313.

14. Baruch, *American Industry*, 105.

15. Ibid.

16. *Addresses, Papers and Interviews by Walter S. Gifford: From April 13, 1913 to July 1, 1928* (New York: Information Dept. of American Telephone & Telegraph Company, 1928), 57.

17. *New York Times*, 21 September 1917, 7.

18. *Electrical Review* 74 (1919): 149–50.

19. Himmelberg, "The War Industries Board."

20. Ibid., 69; Urofsky, *Big Steel,* 295ff.
21. Baruch, *American Industry,* 7.
22. Ibid., 104.
23. Clarkson, *Industrial America,* 486.
24. Cuff, *WIB,* 149.
25. Gilbert, *Designing,* 16.
26. Weinstein, *Corporate Ideal,* xiii.
27. Quoted in Gilbert, *Designing,* 45.
28. The following example illustrates this point. Let us suppose that the federal government raises milk prices by ten cents per gallon. Let us further assume that a family of four would consume two gallons of milk per week. For this family, the price increase would amount to $10.40 per year, hardly enough to justify their hiring a lobbyist or a lawyer to represent them in their efforts to oppose the price hike. But for the dairy industry, the economic consequences are compelling. If there were fifty million of such families purchasing milk, this $10.40 figure would mean increased industry revenues of some $500 *million* per year, an amount that would afford the industry adequate incentives to seek such a policy.
29. John Kenneth Galbraith, *American Capitalism: The Concept of Counter-vailing Power* (Boston: Houghton Mifflin, 1952). Galbraith's thesis reflects another factor in the expansion of governmental power: the fear that a system of unrestrained competition will inevitably produce increased concentration (i.e., both fewer and larger firms) within most industries and that such a development could produce adverse social consequences that it would not be profitable for business firms to address. Such consequences include the failure of firms to internalize all the costs of their doing business (the "social costs" problem), which would include such practices as the disposal of industrial wastes into the atmosphere or waterways. The protection of employees, investors, and customers of such firms from the inconstancies of the business cycle (such as cyclical unemployment) and alleged "inequalities of bargaining power" are further rationales for expanded governmental authority. Another factor is the so-called public goods problem—that there are various services, such as national defense or police protection, for which nonpaying users cannot be excluded from enjoying the benefits. Within the context of this book, and as I shall explore more fully in chapter 2, the refusal of individual members of an industry to support higher prices by restricting production would qualify for such a "public goods" analysis. While it is not my purpose to address these various concerns herein, they do represent a significant source of popular support for government regulation. That many of these concerns represent the failure *not* of the *marketplace,* but of the *legal* system (consider the historic refusal of courts to enjoin industrial pollution as a trespass) or the attempt of various groups to elevate their social or political biases into the realm of accepted public policies should be considered. See Butler Shaffer, "The Social Responsibility of Business: A Dissent," *Business and Society* 17 (Spring 1977): 11–18; and idem, "The Social Responsibility of Business: A Flawed Dissent Response," *Business and Society* 18 (Spring 1978): 41–42. Neither is it my purpose, at this point, to assess the extent to which leading business interests were able to co-opt such policy concerns and employ them as additional rationales for a greater political enforcement of industry-desired restraints on competition.
30. The point being made here will be developed more fully later in this chapter and in chapter 3. At this point, suffice it to say that, to the extent any organization develops into a large and structured institution, it will have a *tendency* to lose its

resilient capacities and, in order to protect its interests, may endeavor to insulate itself from having to respond to the kinds of changes in its environment that are most threatening to it. In an unrestrained marketplace, such threats will come from other persons and firms, and if their self-seeking interests are to be repressed on behalf of such large institutions, a coercive agency (namely, the state) must be empowered to impose such restrictions.

31. William Letwin, *Law and Economic Policy in America: The Evolution of the Sherman Antitrust Act* (Westport, Conn.: Greenwood Press, 1980), 72–74.

32. Hans B. Thorelli, *The Federal Antitrust Policy* (Baltimore: Johns Hopkins University Press, 1955), 71.

33. Thomas K. McCraw, ed., *The Essential Alfred Chandler: Essays Toward a Historical Theory of Big Business* (Boston: Harvard Business School Press, 1988), 259.

34. Ibid., 69.

35. Ibid., 263.

36. Oliver E. Williamson, *Markets and Hierarchies: Analysis and Antitrust Implications* (New York: Free Press, 1975), 133.

37. Oliver E. Williamson, *Antitrust Economics: Mergers, Contracting, and Strategic Behavior* (Cambridge: Basil Blackwell, 1987), 138, 142.

38. Chandler, in McCraw, *Essential Chandler*, 69–70.

39. Ibid., 71.

40. Alfred D. Chandler Jr., *The Visible Hand: The Managerial Revolution in American Business* (Cambridge: Belknap Press of Harvard University Press, 1977), 6.

41. Ibid., 13.

42. Ibid., 7.

43. Ibid., 48–49.

44. Ibid., 95.

45. Ibid., 130–32, 188. Such voluntary efforts to regularize competition within the railroad industry have also been explored in Kolko's *Railroads and Regulation*.

46. Chandler, *Visible Hand*, 6, 12.

47. See, generally, Alfred D. Chandler Jr., *Strategy and Structure: Chapters in the History of the American Industrial Enterprise* (Cambridge: MIT Press, 1962).

48. Chandler, *Visible Hand*, 10.

49. Thorstein Veblen, *Absentee Ownership and Business Enterprise in Recent Times* (New York: B. W. Huebsch, 1923), 4; Thorstein Veblen, *The Instinct of Workmanship and the State of the Industrial Arts* (1914; reprint, New York: W. W. Norton, 1964), 232ff., 281–82, 344, 349.

50. Veblen, *Absentee Ownership*, 84, 208–9.

51. Ibid., 78 (emphasis added).

52. Ibid., 4, 76.

53. Thorstein Veblen, *The Theory of Business Enterprise* (1904; reprint, New York: Augustus M. Kelley, 1965), 66.

54. Ibid., 66–67.

55. Ibid., 293.

56. Ibid.

57. Thorelli, *Federal Antitrust*, 63ff.

58. Letwin, *Law and Economic Policy*, 75–76.

59. See Martin J. Sklar, *The Corporate Reconstruction of American Capitalism, 1890–1916* (Cambridge: Cambridge University Press, 1988), 187ff.

60. Thurman Arnold, *The Folklore of Capitalism* (New Haven: Yale University Press, 1937), 187. There is another explanation for the creation of the legal fiction of the corporation as a "person." In the common law, only "persons" could own property. This fiction became necessary in order to allow the corporation to own property in its own name, rather than in the name of its stockholder owners. The problems that have been associated with the legal manipulation of this sense of "personhood" need not concern us here. That the legal status of "slaves," "American Indians," "married women," "minors," the "mentally incompetent," and, more recently, "fetuses" has been inextricably tied up with the question of who is and who is not a "person" should afford some indication of how much philosophical, political, legal, and social conflict has been generated by this fiction.

61. Ibid., 211–21.

62. Ibid., 227.

63. John R. Munkirs, *The Transformation of American Capitalism: From Competitive Market Structures to Centralized Private Sector Planning* (Armonk, N.Y.: M. E. Sharpe, 1985), 18–21.

64. Schumpeter, *Capitalism,* 156.

65. Ibid., 134.

66. Adolf A. Berle Jr. and Gardiner C. Means, *The Modern Corporation and Private Property* (New York: Macmillan, 1932), 69.

67. Chandler, *Visible Hand,* 10.

68. See *The Structure of the American Economy: Part I, A Report Prepared Under the Direction of Gardiner C. Means, June, 1939* (New York: Augustus M. Kelley, 1966), 156ff.; see also Berle and Means, *Modern Corporation.*

69. Chandler, *Visible Hand,* 10.

70. Ibid.

71. Gifford, *Addresses,* 173–76.

72. Ilya Prigogine and Isabelle Stengers, *Order Out of Chaos: Man's New Dialogue with Nature* (New York: Bantam Books, 1984), 12.

73. Ibid., 177ff.

74. William Irwin Thompson, *Evil and World Order* (New York: Harper & Row, 1977), 83.

75. One sees this principle most vividly in living organisms. Unless living beings are able to consume energy from outside themselves in the form of food, water, and air, their orderly systems will begin to break down, and they will decay and die. The dynamical nature of life has been well stated by one observer: "As life expanded, Nature also instructed Life to continually invent new ways to grow." George T.L. Land, *Grow or Die: The Unifying Principle of Transformation* (New York: Random House, 1973), 73. "Life," in other words, "is the expression of a creative disequilibrium" (Thompson, *Evil and World Order,* 83) in which, as biologist Edmund Sinnott has expressed it, "[c]onstancy and conservatism are qualities of the lifeless, not the living." Edmund W. Sinnott, *The Biology of the Spirit* (New York: Viking, 1955), 61.

76. See, e.g., studies cited in note 3 of the introduction.

77. Prigogine and Stengers, *Order,* 188.

78. A. D. H. Kaplan study, cited in William Baldwin, *Market Power, Competition, and Antitrust Policy* (Homewood, Ill: Irwin, 1987), 161. At this point, one might wish to explore the extent to which *turnover* among firms (as opposed to *stability*) reflects the intensity of competition within a given industry. It has been

argued that a high degree of turnover reflects a vigorous competitive environment and that there is a positive correlation between industrial concentration and the stability of positions within a given industry. It has also been suggested, however, that instability can generate greater concentration within an industry. See, for example, Baldwin, *Market Power,* 161–63; F. M. Scherer and David Ross, *Industrial Market Structure and Economic Performance,* 3d ed. (Boston: Houghton Mifflin, 1990), 89–90; and William Lazonick, *Business Organization and the Myth of the Market Economy* (Cambridge: Cambridge University Press, 1991), 155ff.

79. Butler Shaffer, *Calculated Chaos: Institutional Threats to Peace and Human Survival* (San Francisco: Alchemy Books, 1985), 9. I am employing the word to refer to formal organizational entities, *not* to those more abstract belief systems (such as Judeo-Christian ethics) or social practices (such as marriage, the marketplace, or Western civilization) that we use to encompass a broad range of social customs. See Walter C. Neale, "Institutions," *Journal of Economic Issues* 21 (September 1987): 1177–206.

80. Anthony Downs, *Inside Bureaucracy* (Boston: Little, Brown, 1967), 20 (emphasis in original).

81. Ibid., 97, 99.

82. Ibid., 18.

83. Ibid., 18–19.

84. Ibid., 147, 196.

85. Ibid., 143 (emphasis in original).

86. Ibid., 197.

87. Carroll Quigley, *The Evolution of Civilizations* (Indianapolis, Ind.: Liberty Press, 1979).

88. Ibid., 101ff.

89. Arnold Toynbee, *A Study of History* (New York: Oxford University Press, 1958).

90. Will Durant and Ariel Durant, *The Lessons of History* (New York: Simon & Schuster, 1968).

91. Toynbee, *A Study,* 241.

92. Ibid., 245, 555.

93. Durant and Durant, *Lessons,* 91.

94. Ibid., 90, 92.

95. Lazonick, *Business Organization,* 155.

96. Quigley, *Evolution,* 127ff.

97. Arthur Dewing, *Corporate Promotions and Reorganizations* (Cambridge: Harvard University Press, 1930), 558.

98. Ibid., 546–47.

99. Ibid., 558.

100. Kolko, *Triumph,* 37.

101. Ibid., 46.

102. Ibid., 38. The very successes that many large businesses—such as U.S. Steel—had in becoming the predominant firms in their industries also attracted antitrust investigations and prosecutions. Indeed, U.S. Steel was undergoing a major antitrust prosecution during the time period covered by Kolko's study. Because aggressive competitive practices would have exacerbated its antitrust problems, this may have contributed to less-aggressive behavior that, in turn, could have led to a decline in market share. Such an explanation finds some support in the fact that U.S. Steel's

attitude toward independent producers had "never been characterized by any attempt at what is called 'destructive competition'" and, indeed, reflected "a certain far-sighted magnanimity toward competitors." See Louis Galambos, "The American Economy and the Reorganization of the Sources of Knowledge," in *The Organization of Knowledge in Modern America, 1860–1920,* ed. Alexandra Oleson and John Voss (Baltimore: Johns Hopkins University Press, 1979), 273; also, Abraham Berglund, "The United States Steel Corporation and Price Stabilization," *Quarterly Journal of Economics* 38 (November 1923): 1–30, at 29.)

103. Temporary National Economic Committee, *Competition and Monopoly in American Industry,* monograph no. 21 (Washington, D.C.: Government Printing Office, 1940), 311.

104. Ibid.

105. See Chandler's works, generally.

106. Leopold Kohr, *The Breakdown of Nations* (New York: E. P. Dutton, 1978), xviii.

107. Ibid., 26 (emphasis in original).

108. Ibid., 82.

109. Ibid., 84 (emphasis in original).

110. Holmes's comment was that "[t]he life of the law has not been logic: it has been experience." Oliver Wendell Holmes, *The Common Law* (Boston: Little, Brown, 1881), 1.

111. Wiebe, *Search for Order,* 294–97.

112. Allen, *Lords of Creation,* 195.

113. Gilbert, *Designing,* 16.

114. Ibid.

CHAPTER 2. TRADE ASSOCIATIONS AND CODES OF ETHICS

1. Robert Brady, *Business as a System of Power,* 6th ed. (New York: Columbia University Press, 1951), 195.

2. *Nation's Business,* 5 June 1924, 7–8; *Automotive Industries* 50 (1924): 1060; *Commercial and Financial Chronicle* 118 (17 May 1924): 2389–90 (emphasis added).

3. *Commercial and Financial Chronicle* 118 (17 May 1924): 2390.

4. Theodore Lowi, *The Politics of Disorder* (New York: Basic Books, 1971), 69.

5. Arthur Jerome Eddy, *The New Competition* (Chicago: A. C. McClurg & Co., 1916).

6. Ibid., 131.

7. Ibid., 150.

8. Ibid., 348.

9. Ibid., 353.

10. Ibid., 354–55.

11. Ibid., 356.

12. *United States v. Trans-Missouri Freight Association,* 166 U.S. 290 (1897).

13. *New York Times,* 15 January 1917, 13; 3 February 1919, 10; 5 April 1919, 19.

14. Himmelberg, *Origins,* 9ff.

15. *American Column & Lumber Company et al. v. United States,* 257 U.S. 377 (1921).

16. *United States v. American Linseed Oil Company et al.,* 262 U.S. 371 (1923).

17. 257 U.S. 377, 411 (1921).

18. 262 U.S. 371, 388 (1923).

19. *New York Times,* 17 November 1924, 1; *Commercial and Financial Chronicle* 118 (31 May 1924): 2664 at 2665.

20. *Maple Flooring Manufacturers Association et al. v. United States,* 268 U.S. 563 (1925).

21. *Cement Manufacturers Protective Association et al. v. United States,* 268 U.S. 588 (1925).

22. 268 U.S. 563, 583–84 (1925). The efforts of the lumber industry to stabilize conditions continued throughout the 1920s. The Western Pine Manufacturers' Association had once told its members that the condition of the market "rests entirely with the manufacturers," adding that a "[r]easonable restraint in production" would be beneficial, while "[a]ny disposition to greatly extend production" would be detrimental to industry interests. One manufacturer wrote another, "It is absolutely essential that there should be a general curtailment commensurate with the demand," while correspondence from other industry members alluded to various "cooperative" agreements between manufacturers to divide and allocate business, an approach that was found attractive as a means of keeping firms from "openly competing to force the market down." In addition, different lumber trade associations sent "barometers" of business activity out to their members, urging them to regulate their production therewith. Meanwhile, the National American Wholesale Lumber Association joined other industries, in 1925, in requesting a relaxation of federal laws in order to permit lumber manufacturers to enter into agreements to regulate production in order to prevent what the lumber industry felt was an "absolutely uncontrolled" condition leading to overproduction. See *Report of the Federal Trade Commission on Lumber Manufacturers' Trade Associations* (Washington, D.C.: Government Printing Office, 1922), 46ff., 116–17, 142; *New York Times,* 20 March 1925, 9.

23. Wilson Compton, cited in Lincoln Filene, *Unfair Trade Practices: How to Remove Them* (New York: Harper & Bros., 1934), 82.

24. Leverett Lyon and Victor Abramson, *The Economics of Open Price Systems* (Washington, D.C.: Brookings Institution, 1936), 19. The Federal Trade Commission did state, however, that as of 1929 there were about ninety open price associations in operation throughout the United States.

25. Charles Chapman, *The Development of American Business and Banking Thought, 1913–1936* (London: Longmans, Green and Co., 1936), 67–68; *Survey* 52 (1 June 1924): 313; *Nation's Business,* September 1924, 68 (emphasis in original).

26. *Nation's Business,* 5 June 1924, 16–18.

27. *Nation's Business,* 5 June 1928, 15ff.

28. F. M. Feiker, "The Profession of Commerce in the Making," *Annals of the American Academy of Political and Social Science* 101 (May 1922): 203 at 205. The suggestion that unrestricted competition led to "waste to the consumer" involves a strange twist of reasoning. Business objections to this so-called cutthroat competition were based principally upon the resulting lower prices. The implication that consumers were being victimized by lower prices and required the protection afforded by government regulation in order to end such "waste" taxes either one's credulity or sense of humor.

29. "Trade Associations and Business Combinations," *Proceedings of the Academy of Political Science* 11 (January 1926): 590–91.

30. *Nation's Business,* May 1927, 28.

31. *Iron Age* 119 (26 May 1927): 1524.

32. Brady, *Business as a System,* 204.

33. *Nation's Business,* July 1927, 32ff. The importance of intraindustrial control of trade practices was reinforced by Parker, who declared his support for the idea of voluntary agreements by members of an industry to abolish unfair competitive practices. Parker was of the opinion that government regulation of industry would not be necessary if business was successful in developing a strong sense of group consciousness and formulating its own trade practice standards. See *New York Times,* 18 October 1927, 31; *Wall Street Journal,* 18 October 1927, 19.

34. The Chamber resolution called for the "elimination of all wasteful practices and trade abuses" through joint trade relations committees within each trade working in cooperation with the Federal Trade Commission. See *Nation's Business,* 20 May 1927, 28.

35. Chapman, *Development,* 69–70. In a letter to President Coolidge, Pierson also praised the attitudes of the Federal Trade Commission, the Department of Justice, and the Department of Commerce in helping to elevate trade practice standards. See *New York Times,* 29 October 1927, 8.

36. Barnes maintained that the federal government should "in cooperation with business itself, preserve fair play between industries and individuals." See Julius Barnes, "Self-Government in Business," *Nation's Business,* 5 June 1926, 18.

37. *New York Times,* 29 January 1928, sec. 2, 17; 23 December 1928, sec. 2, 10.

38. Hugh Baker, "Trade Associations and Business Combinations," *Proceedings of the Academy of Political Science* 11 (1926): 634.

39. *Automotive Industries* 54 (1926): 843–45.

40. Albert Ritchie, "Business Can and Must Rule Itself," *Nation's Business,* 5 June 1926, 19–20.

41. Chapman, *Development,* 69.

42. Scoville Hamlin, *The Menace of Overproduction* (1930; reprint, Freeport, N.Y.: Books for Libraries Press, 1969), 178–80.

43. Ibid., 48–50.

44. Berglund, "United States Steel Corporation and Price Stabilization," 2–13; Kolko, *Triumph,* 30–56.

45. *New York Times,* 21 March 1926, sec. 9, 5.

46. *Outlook,* 1 September 1926, 6–7.

47. *New York Times,* 12 October 1924, sec. 11, 1.

48. *Nation's Business,* 20 May 1927, 15.

49. National Industrial Conference Board, *Trade Associations: Their Economic Significance and Legal Status* (New York: National Industrial Conference Board, 1925), 193, 304.

50. *New York Times,* 22 April 1923, sec. 2, 10. This same language was contained in a code of the American Specialty Manufacturers' Association, developed in 1922 in collaboration with the National Wholesale Grocers' Association, the American Wholesale Grocers' Association, and the National Association of Retail Grocers. See Edgar Heermance, *Codes of Ethics: A Handbook* (Burlington, Vt.: Free Press Printing Co., 1924), 209.

51. Code of the American Walnut Manufacturers' Association (1924), in Heermance, *Codes,* 308–9.

224   NOTES TO CHAPTER 2

52. Code of the American Face Brick Association (1913), in ibid., 60.
53. Code of the International Association of Electrotypers of America (1921), in ibid., 159.
54. Code of the National Food Brokers Association (1904), in ibid., 212.
55. The code of the American Face Brick Association, for example, urged its members to "[d]iscountenance the tendency to extravagant selling methods" and to "[a]void scrupulously all overstatements or misrepresentations of any kind in your own behalf." It went on to state that a member should "[h]old firmly the ideal . . . of co-operation with your competitors" (Heermance, Codes, 60). The International Association of Electrotypers of America beseeched its members "[t]o not degrade or demoralize our business. To remember that destructive competition is most injurious to those practicing it" (ibid., 159). The National Publishers Association pledged itself, in 1923, to the "[c]ourage to condemn every fraudulent, tricky or questionable practice" (ibid., 444), while the National Retail Hardware Association code embraced the sentiment of "avoiding any unfair or questionable act or practice," whether to gain the favor of a manufacturer, wholesaler, or the public (ibid., 225). The National Boot and Shoe Manufacturers code implored its members "[t]o always stand for fair dealing . . . avoiding and discouraging unfair competition" and "[t]o do our best to promote uniformity and certainty in the customs and usages of business, using every effort to reform any abuses now existing in our trade" (ibid., 475).
The attitude of conciliation that codes sought found expression in provisions such as that of the National Food Brokers Association, which urged its members to "respect the rights of competitors and never attempt by unfair means to interfere with their [i.e., competitors] business" (ibid., 212). The code of the Associated Office Furniture Manufacturers declared, "[O]ur mutual interest can be best conserved through co-operation with one another, and that through it is the life of trade rather than through competitive strife," adding that since "every man is entitled to a reward from his own efforts, it is our aim to . . . avoid any acts that may tend to injure them in their honest pursuit" (ibid., 188–89).
Some other representative code statements reflecting business attitudes toward "cooperation" were those of the National Association of Automotive Mutual Insurance Companies, urging members to "demonstrate a full measure of consideration toward our mutual competitors" (ibid., 253–54), or of the International Association of Garment Manufacturers, seeking to "establish and maintain intimate, cordial, friendly relations with other manufacturers," and to "practice clean and honorable competition" (ibid., 84, 86). The Western Retail Implement and Hardware Association code advised firms, "Be fair to your competitor, make him your friend. There is a sense of fairness in every man, which if unselfishly appealed to will be reciprocated" (ibid., 183).
The National Machine Tool Builder's Association adopted a specific prohibition against the "[f]ailure to maintain a friendly attitude toward competitors" (Iron Age 115 [May 1925]: 1359), while the Gas Products Association code declared, "Our mutual interests can be best served through co-operation with one another." It suggested that "[i]ntensive competition for business established by a competitor should be discouraged, as it has a tendency to tear down what another has built up, but competition in developing new business is to be commended and should be encouraged" (Heermance, Codes, 198–201).
Describing competition in the rubber industry as "vicious," J. C. Weston, retir-

ing president of the Rubber Association of America, urged a more reasonable approach to merchandising practices in the industry (*Rubber Age* 22 [1928]: 409). As a result of such sentiments, some of the leading rubber manufacturers formed, in 1928, the Rubber Institute with a purpose of establishing, in consultation with the FTC, a workable code of ethics. The institute's director declared that industry members were united on such objectives as eliminating "unfair discrimination between customers" and providing for a system of open pricing for rubber products. Hope was expressed that the formation of the institute would permit companies "to do business at a fair profit and on a basis of wholesome competition." Noting that members of the industry have had to endure "ignorant and often ruthless competition" that was "destructive of stability . . . and an opportunity to do business with an adequate financial return," the institute sought to take advantage of the "cooperation" that had made competition more "wholesome" in other industries. Announced prices would not be subject to any secret price concessions, a practice considered "wasteful, unbusinesslike and damaging to wholesome competition" (*Rubber Age* 23 [1928]: 253; *New York Times*, 24 May 1928, 31).

Members of the sugar-refining industry organized the Sugar Institute to reform trade practices, develop an effective code of business ethics, and serve as a clearing house for statistics and business practices. A member of the industry, W. S. Pardonner of the Savannah Sugar Refining Company, stated that the refining capacity in the industry was approximately 50 percent in excess of the annual consumption, which had "inevitably resulted in abnormally keen competition and the development and growth of harmful trade practices." Pardonner expressed hope that the Sugar Institute would prove effective in eliminating such conditions (*New York Times*, 12 January 1928, 46; 26 February 1928, sec. 2, 17).

56. *Eastern States Retail Lumber Dealers Association v. United States*, 234 U.S. 600 (1914).

57. Code adopted in 1923, in Heermance, *Codes*, 135.

58. Code of the American Walnut Manufacturers' Association (1924), in Heermance, *Codes*, 308–9; Code of the National Machine Tool Builders' Association, *Iron Age* 115 (May 1925): 1358–59; Code of the National Association of Ice Cream Manufacturers (1922), *System* 43 (March 1923): 342 at 376.

59. Code adopted in 1923, in Heermance, *Codes*, 58. A similar provision can be found in the codes of the Gas Products Association, the American PhotoEngravers Association, and the National Slate Association (198–201, 428–29, 480).

60. Code of the National Knitted Outerwear Association (1923), in ibid., 270.

61. Code of the American Warehousemen's Association (Cold Storage Division) (1924), in ibid., 95–96.

62. Codes of the International Association of Milk Dealers (1923) and the National Association of Ice Cream Manufacturers (1922), in ibid., 135, 246.

63. Code of the National Commercial Fixture Manufacturers' Association (1916), in ibid., 108.

64. Code of the American National Retail Jewelers Association (1922), in ibid., 255–56.

65. Code adopted in 1920, amended 1921, in ibid., 92. Similar provisions were contained in the codes of the National Association of Upholstered Furniture Manufacturers (1924), and the National Machine Tool Builders' Association (in ibid., 190; *Iron Age* 115 [May 1925]: 1358–59).

66. Code adopted in 1923, in Heermance, *Codes,* 215–17.

67. Codes of the Gas Products Association; the Plywood Manufacturers Association; the National Association of Retail Grocers; the International Association of Garment Manufacturers; the National Association of Oxy-Chloride Cement Manufacturers; and the National Machine Tool Builders' Association (in ibid., 198–201, 310, 215–17, 84–87, 73–74; and *Iron Age* 115 [May 1925]: 1358–59).

68. Roland Koller Jr., offers just such an explanation for the classic example of American Tobacco selling cigarettes, for a short period of time, below their actual cost. See Koller, "The Myth of Predatory Pricing: An Empirical Study," *Antitrust Law and Economics Review* 4 (1971): 105–23.

69. See, e.g., Richard A. Givens, *Antitrust: An Economic Approach* (New York: Law Journal Seminars-Press, 1995), 3–15.

70. Phillip Areeda and Donald F. Turner, "Predatory Pricing and Related Practices Under Section 2 of the Sherman Act," *Harvard Law Review* 88 (February 1975): 697 at 733.

71. A number of interesting studies and debates regarding predatory price cutting can be found, including ibid; John McGee, "Predatory Price Cutting: The Standard Oil (N.J.) Case," *Journal of Law and Economics* 1 (1958): 137–69; Wayne Leeman, "The Limitations of Local Price-Cutting as a Barrier to Entry," *Journal of Political Economy* 64 (1956): 329–34; Walter Adams and James W. Brock, *Antitrust Economics on Trial: A Dialogue on the New Laissez-Faire* (Princeton: Princeton University Press, 1991), 30–37; Kenneth G. Elzinga, "Collusive Predation: *Matsushita v. Zenith,*" in *The Antitrust Revolution,* ed. John E. Kwoka Jr. and Lawrence J. White (Glenview, Ill.: Scott, Foresman, 1989): 241–62; Kenneth G. Elzinga, "Unmasking Monopoly: Four Types of Economic Evidence," in *Economics and Antitrust Policy,* ed. Robert J. Larner and James W. Meehan Jr. (New York: Quorum Books, 1989), 11–38; Charles A. Holt and David T. Scheffman, "Strategic Business Behavior and Antitrust," in Larner and Meehan, *Economics and Antitrust Policy,* 39–82; Joseph F. Brodley and George A. Hay, "Predatory Pricing: Competing Economic Theories and the Evolution of Legal Standards," *Cornell Law Review* 66 (April 1981): 738–803; Wesley J. Liebeler, "Whither Predatory Pricing? From Areeda and Turner to Matsushita," *Notre Dame Law Review* 61 (1986): 1052–98; Paul L. Joskow and Alvin K. Klevorick, "A Framework for Analyzing Predatory Pricing Policy," *Yale Law Journal* 89 (December 1979): 213–70; Peter C. Carstensen, "Predatory Pricing in the Courts: Reflection on Two Decisions," *Notre Dame Law Review* 61 (1986): 928–71; Phillip Areeda, "Antitrust Law as Industrial Policy: Should Judges and Juries Make It?" in *Antitrust, Innovation, and Competitiveness,* ed. Thomas M. Jorde and David J. Teece (New York: Oxford University Press, 1992), 29–46; William J. Baumol and Janusz A. Ordover, "Antitrust: Source of Dynamic and Static Inefficiencies?" in Jorde and Teece, *Antitrust, Innovation, and Competitiveness,* 82–97; and Koller, "The Myth." It may well be that the fear of predatory price cutting has been fostered, in part, by the self-serving rhetoric directed against low prices and incorporated into public policy discussions.

72. Koller has identified ninety-five antitrust cases in which parties had been found to have engaged in predatory practices. Of these cases, only twenty-six generated a factual record from which one could determine an evidentiary basis for such allegations. Of these twenty-six cases, Koller concludes that there was *no* evidence of predation in sixteen, and inconclusive evidence for predation in three others. Of the remaining seven cases, Koller finds predation to have been attempted, but it was

successful in only five cases. Furthermore, in four of these seven cases in which predation was attempted, Koller finds the presence of governmental activity (such as tariff policies, licensing, and an excise tax) that contributed significantly to the pricing policies of the firms. As Koller concludes, "The major thrust of our findings, however, is not simply that predatory pricing does not occur very often but that, when it *does* occur, it produces little or no harm to competition" (Koller, "The Myth," 110–13, 121).

73. Code adopted in 1924, in Heermance, *Codes*, 320–21. A similar provision was contained in the code of the International Association of Garment Manufacturers (1924) (ibid., 85). A provision against lowering one's bid in order to be awarded a contract was also included in the code of the International Monumental Granite Producers' Association (National Industrial Conference Board, *Trade Associations*, 199).

74. Codes of the Western Retail Implement and Hardware Association (1924); the American Walnut Manufacturers' Association (1924); and the National Machine Tool Builders' Association, in Heermance, *Codes*, 183, 308–9; *Iron Age* 115 (May 1925): 1358–59.

75. *Printers' Ink Monthly*, September 1927, 87.

76. Code of the American Bottlers of Carbonated Beverages, in Heermance, *Codes*, 58.

77. Code of the International Association of Milk Dealers (ibid., 135–36). See also the code of the National Association of Ice-Cream Manufacturers (ibid., 246; *System* 43 [1923]: 342 at 376).

78. Codes of the National Basket and Fruit Package Manufacturers Association (1923), and the International Association of Garment Manufacturers, in Heermance, *Codes*, 53–54, 84–87.

79. Those who attack "discrimination" on the part of sellers have tended to ignore the discrimination practiced by buyers. Buyers are highly selective in deciding with whom to do business, seeking to purchase goods and services at the lowest possible prices. In the course of bargaining, buyers will discriminate among sellers, at times agreeing to pay one seller more for his product or service than he has already paid another. The suggestion that *buyers* should be prohibited from so discriminating would (properly) be met with outrage, yet it is popularly accepted that *sellers* should not have the same and equal right. Perhaps this seeming paradox is no more than a reflection of the fact that there are fewer manufacturers and distributors than there are buyers.

80. National Industrial Conference Board, *Public Regulation of Competitive Practices* (New York: National Industrial Conference Board, 1925), 67.

81. 38 Stat. 730 (Comp. St. §8835b) (1914).

82. *George Van Camp & Sons Company v. American Can Company et al.*, 278 U.S. 245 (1929).

83. See, e.g., *Mennen Company v. Federal Trade Commission*, 288 F. 774, cert. den. 262 U.S. 759 (1923); *National Biscuit Company v. Federal Trade Commission*, 299 F. 733, cert. den. 266 U.S. 613 (1924).

84. National Industrial Conference Board, *Public Regulation*, 144.

85. Williams Haynes, "Better Ethical Standards for Business," *Annals of the American Academy of Political and Social Science* 101 (May 1922): 221–23.

86. Codes of the National Commercial Fixture Manufacturers' Association; the American Photo-Engravers Association; the National Association of Oxy-Chloride

Cement Manufacturers; the Gas Products Association; the International Association of Garment Manufacturers; and the American Walnut Manufacturers' Association, in Heermance, *Codes*, at 109, 428–29, 73–74, 200, 86, 308–9.

87. See, e.g., the code of the National Association of Ice-Cream Manufacturers (1922), in ibid., 246; *System* 43 (1923): 342.

88. *New York Times*, 18 March 1927, 36.

89. Rexford Tugwell, *Industry's Coming of Age* (New York: Harcourt, Brace, 1927), 113.

90. Mergers, pools, and cartels have generally failed to provide the order and stability desired by members of an industry. This has been due, mainly, to the resiliency of market processes to resist their own subversion. The competitive self-interest motivations, coupled with an inability to enforce restrictive arrangements, have made such methods unsatisfactory for business purposes. See, e.g., Kolko, *Triumph*, 26ff.; Kolko, *Railroads*, generally; Ida Tarbell, *The Nationalizing of Business, 1878–1898* (New York: Macmillan, 1936), 62ff.; and Dewing, *Corporate Promotion*, 557ff. Although Alfred Chandler Jr. has identified the benefits associated with vertically integrated enterprises, he has acknowledged that mergers—which expressed "the strategy of horizontal combination"—were less effective. In his words, "horizontal combination rarely proved to be a viable long-term business strategy. The firms that first grew large by taking the merger route remained profitable only if after consolidating, they then adopted a strategy of vertical integration." See Chandler, *Visible Hand*, 315.

91. Edgar Heermance, *Can Business Govern Itself? A Study in Industrial Planning* (New York: Harper & Bros., 1933), 18–19. Some trade associations had experienced the problems of enforcing their policies even prior to this century. In the early 1870s, for example, local associations of food canners began to develop in an effort to stabilize prices. Later, the National Association of Canned Food Packers was founded, the stated purpose of which was "to reform abuses in trade; . . . to produce uniformity and certainty in the customs and usages of trade; . . . [and] to encourage legislation looking to the protection and fostering of the packing interests of the United States." In 1897, this association formed a committee to draft proposed legislation to regulate the canning and labeling of canned goods. The dissolution of the association the following year was due, in the opinion of one industry observer, to the fact that it "was powerless to enforce its rulings because the members of the industry had not progressed to a point in the conduct of their business where they could recognize the great benefit it might have been to them." See Edward Hampe Jr. and Merle Wittenberg, *The Lifeline of America: Development of the Food Industry* (New York: McGraw-Hill, 1964), 123–24.

92. Mancur Olson, *The Logic of Collective Action* (Cambridge: Harvard University Press, 1965).

93. Ibid., 9.

94. Ibid., 48.

95. Ibid., 9.

96. Ibid., 9–10.

97. Ibid., at 2, 36 (emphasis in original). An assessment consistent with Olson's declares:

The first problem of organization that presents itself to the trade association is the nonco-operator, the individualist, the entrepreneur, who, for any of widely differing reasons—low capital costs, higher efficiency, financial necessities, or mere ignorance—insists on playing the game his own way. Such competitors, even though a tiny minority, may nullify co-operative efforts toward market control. They raise the question of whether to give a majority group, by number or output, the right of imposing their standards on the obstreperous few or perhaps the right of making the minority become members of the majority association. (Avery Leiserson, *Administrative Regulation: A Study in Representation of Interests* [Chicago: University of Chicago Press, 1942], 23–24)

98. Robert Himmelberg, *Origins*, 116ff.
99. See, e.g., *Outlook*, 1 September 1926, 6–7.

CHAPTER 3. POLITICAL ALTERNATIVES

1. John T. Flynn, "Business and the Government," *Harpers* 156 (March 1928): 409 at 413–14. Flynn also stated:

If Congress and the legislatures do not enact more laws, however, it is not the fault of business. There are, to be sure, laws which regulate business and interfere with some of its plans. But most of the laws that control or hamper business have been passed—surprising as it may seem to those who clamor for "less government in business"—at the demand of business itself. . . . Innumerable bills are introduced into Congress and the legislatures every year to force business in some new direction or close up certain avenues to it altogether. But few of these proposals originate in the minds of legislators. They come from the legislative program committees of trade associations or from the special counsel of trade groups, and they come backed often by resolutions from trade conventions and chambers of commerce. (Ibid., 409)

Flynn, who described the trade association convention as "a perfect hothouse of proposals for government regulation," has provided a vivid account of a number of business-conceived legislative programs to resolve trade and employment problems, including the fatuous effort of one trade group to enact legislation requiring the posting of the "Lord's Prayer" in places of employment as an antidote to the menace of bolshevism among workers. Ibid., 411.
    Flynn's observations had support from Samuel O. Dunn, editor of the *Railway Age,* who stated that "practically every increase in taxes and in government interference with business is due more to our business men than to our politicians." Dunn went on to quote a Kansas farmer: "Paternalistic schemes of government are agitated, not at farmers' meetings, but in business men's organizations. I have heard more socialism preached at meetings of commercial bodies than in socialistic gatherings." *Nation's Business,* November 1928, 15.
2. Baruch, *American Industry,* 107.
3. Flynn, "Business and the Government," 413.
4. *New York Times,* 21 September 1925, 21.
5. *Nation's Business,* October 1927, 15.
6. National Industrial Conference Board, *Trade Associations,* 309, 315–16.

7. Ludwig von Mises, *Human Action* (New Haven: Yale University Press, 1963), 818.

8. *Nation's Business*, 5 June 1924, 10.

9. For an excellent investigation of American support for Mussolini's policies during this period, see John Diggins, *Mussolini and Fascism: The View From America* (Princeton: Princeton University Press, 1972); Herman Krooss, *Executive Opinion: What Business Leaders Said and Thought on Economic Issues, 1920s–1960s* (New York: Doubleday, 1970), 122–23; and Harvey O'Connor, *Mellon's Millions: The Life and Times of Andrew W. Mellon* (New York: John Day, 1933), 338.

10. *Nation's Business*, 5 June 1928, 15ff. One immediately notes, in Parker's proposal for a government agency to approve business codes, a similarity not only to the trade practice conference procedures but to the code procedures adopted under the National Industrial Recovery Act.

11. Francis H. Sisson, "The World-Wide Trend Toward Cooperation," *Annals of the American Academy of Political and Social Science* 82 (1919): 148.

12. *Business Week*, 7 May 1930, 14.

13. Chapman, *Development*, 70.

14. Ibid., 92–95. A new division was established within the FTC in 1926 to supervise trade practice conferences. The annual number of conferences rose from six in 1927 to fifteen in 1928, and to fifty in 1929. See Himmelberg, *Origins*, 62.

15. Quoted in Gerard Henderson, *The Federal Trade Commission* (1924; reprinted, New York: Agathon Press, 1968), 79.

16. Ibid., 80.

17. Act of 26 September 1914, c. 311, 38 Stat. 717, as amended.

18. From an address by Abram F. Myers, *National Petroleum News* 21 (16 January 1929), 29.

19. Watkins, *Public Regulation*, 244.

20. *National Petroleum News* 21 (16 January 1929): 29.

21. Heermance, *Codes*, 417–19.

22. Sumner Kittelle and Elmer Mostow, "A Review of the Trade Practice Conferences of the Federal Trade Commission," *George Washington Law Review* 8 (1939–40): 427, at 436–37.

23. Chapman, *Development*, 90–91.

24. Taeusch, *Policy and Ethics*, 326–27.

25. Kittelle and Mostow, "A Review," 436, 438.

26. Himmelberg, *Origins*, 63.

27. *Iron Age* 122 (1928): 1373.

28. *Nation's Business*, July 1927, 32ff.

29. *Nation's Business*, October 1927, 16–17. Cheney opposed the idea of allowing the government itself to initiate regulatory programs, preferring to "[l]et business deal honestly and fearlessly with its own offenses and offenders." At the same time, he advocated the use of the federal government to provide enforcement for self-regulatory efforts should they fail: "It is the duty of business to clean its own house and it has the right to expect the utmost in cooperation from the public and the Government. But it is the duty of the Government, when business fails in its duty, to devise sound economic measures for regulation and to enforce them without fear or favor." O. H. Cheney, "Facing the New Competition," *Nation's Business*, 5 June 1928, 28 at 65.

30. Filene, *Unfair Trade*, 38–39.

31. *New York Times,* 12 November 1924, 25.

32. Rush Butler, "The Sherman Anti-Trust Law and Readjustment," *Annals of the American Academy of Political and Social Science* 82 (1919): 226.

33. Quoted in Hugh Johnson, *The Blue Eagle From Egg to Earth* (New York: Doubleday, Doran, 1935), 156; *Business Week,* 14 May 1930, 22.

34. Quoted in Johnson, *Blue Eagle,* 156–57.

35. Joseph Appel, *The Business Biography of John Wanamaker, Founder and Builder* (New York: Macmillan, 1930), 198; *Business Week,* 12 March 1930, 5–6.

36. Tugwell, *Industry's Coming,* 224.

37. Ibid., 231.

38. Ibid., 233.

39. Statement of Oliver Sheldon, quoted by H. S. Person in "Management and Overproduction," in Hamlin, *Menace of Overproduction,* 143 at 151.

40. Ibid., 152–53.

41. Milton Friedman and Anna J. Schwartz, *A Monetary History of the United States, 1867–1960* (Princeton: Princeton University Press, 1963), 299ff.

42. Peter Temin, *Did Monetary Forces Cause the Great Depression?* (New York: W. W. Norton, 1976), 171.

43. Henry Simons, *Economic Policy for a Free Society* (Chicago: University of Chicago Press, 1948), 45–46, 54.

44. Charles P. Kindleberger, *Manias, Panics, and Crashes: A History of Financial Crises* (New York: Basic Books, 1989), 57ff., 149–51.

45. Herbert Hoover, *The Memoirs of Herbert Hoover,* vol. 3, *The Great Depression, 1929–1941* (New York: Macmillan, 1952), 2, 61–62.

46. John Kenneth Galbraith, *The Great Crash, 1929* (Boston: Houghton Mifflin, 1955), 173–93.

47. John J. B. Morgan, "Manic-Depressive Psychoses of Business," *Psychological Review* 42 (January 1935): 91–107; reprinted in Himmelberg, *Origins,* 8ff.

48. Rothbard, *Great Depression.*

49. A review of some of the principal theories as to the origins of the Great Depression can be found in Kindleberger, *Manias,* 77ff.

50. See, e.g., Rothbard, *Great Depression,* 182–90, 236–39.

51. Wallace Donham, "Business Ethics—A General Survey," *Harvard Business Review* 7 (July 1929): 385 at 390.

52. *Iron Age* 124 (24 October 1929): 1108.

53. *Iron Age* 124 (28 November 1929): 1443–45.

54. *Nation's Business,* April 1929, 123–26.

55. Henry Dennison, "Social Self-Control," *Annals of the American Academy of Political and Social Science* 149 (May 1930): 1–2.

56. Watkins, *Public Regulation,* 245–46.

57. Gerard Swope, *The Swope Plan,* ed. J. George Frederick (New York: Business Bourse, 1931), 25.

58. Ibid., 18 (emphasis added).

59. Ibid., 160–61.

60. Ibid., 165.

61. Krooss, *Executive,* 42; Swope, *Swope Plan,* 159. Swope was later to declare that legislation could be employed to deal with "recalcitrant minorities," again confirming his belief in the propriety of coercion to enforce industry-wide restraints on competition. See the *Wall Street Journal,* 24 May 1933, 5.

62. Swope, *Swope Plan*, 49–55, 62–69; Charles Beard and Mary Beard, *America in Midpassage*, 3 vols. (New York: Macmillan, 1939), 1:104.

63. Krooss, *Executive*, 152.

64. Swope, *Swope Plan*, 59–60.

65. Krooss, *Executive*, 165–66.

66. Swope, *Swope Plan*, 58.

67. Ibid., 60.

68. Ida Tarbell, *Owen D. Young: A New Type of Industrial Leader* (New York: Macmillan, 1932), 221.

69. Henry Dennison, *Ethics and Modern Business* (Boston: Houghton, Mifflin, 1932), 58–59.

70. *Annals of the American Academy of Political and Social Science* 165 (1933): 83; *Independent Petroleum Association of America Monthly* 3 (December 1932): 7; Beard and Beard, *America in Midpassage*, 107–8.

71. Quoted in James Magee, *Collapse and Recovery* (New York: Harper & Row, 1934), 21; Schlesinger, *Crisis*, 182; John Flynn, "Whose Child Is the NRA?" *Harpers Magazine* 169 (September 1934): 388.

72. Magee, *Collapse and Recovery*, 22–27.

73. See *Annals of the American Academy of Political and Social Science* 165 (1933): 83.

74. Francis Sisson, "The Growth of Industrial and Financial Units," in Hamlin, *Menace of Overproduction*, 115 at 127–28.

75. Ibid., 129.

76. Swope, *Swope Plan*, 73–74.

77. J. Harvey Williams, "How the Anti-Trust Laws Should Be Modified," *Annals of the American Academy of Political and Social Science* 165 (January 1933): 74–81.

78. W. A. Vincent, "Shall We Legislate Our Profits?" *Nation's Business*, April 1929, 126.

79. Schlesinger, *Crisis*, 182–83. The coercive implications in Harriman's remark are rather apparent. Other statements made by him, however, appear to propose only the legalization of voluntary stabilization agreements among industry members. Speaking to a meeting of the American Petroleum Institute in late 1932, Harriman suggested that agreements dealing with production, markets, and prices be permitted among producers. These agreements would be filed with an agency of the federal government and, if the attorney general did not bring an action before the agency within sixty days after it was filed, the agreement would take effect unless the attorney general or "some person showing interest" brought a formal complaint against it. At about the same time, however, Harriman's inclination for involuntary political solutions was reiterated in a speech to the annual convention of the Association of Life Insurance Presidents. Harriman again urged that business seek to regulate itself through trade associations, adding: "In sports, we have established rules that have taken much of the brutality out of the game. Will competition be less effective and business less profitable if rules are established, *binding upon all in a given trade or industry*, which insure a fair deal for the laborer, for the investor and for the members of the industry, be they large or small?" *New York Times*, 10 December 1932, 23, 29; *Independent Petroleum Association of America Monthly* 3 (December 1932): 7 (emphasis added).

80. See, e.g., Radosh and Rothbard, *A New History,* 111ff.; Rothbard, *Great Depression.*

81. See, e.g., Paul K. Conkin, *The New Deal,* 2d ed. (Arlington Heights, Ill.: A H M Publishing Corp., 1975), 75. Lundberg has listed some of the major contributors—including businessmen—to Roosevelt's campaigns in both 1932 and 1936. Lundberg, *Sixty Families,* 454–55, 480–81.

82. Otis Graham Jr., *Toward a Planned Society* (New York: Oxford University Press, 1976), 13ff.; Hoover, *Memoirs,* 3:334–35; *New York Times,* 18 May 1933, 1, 10.

83. Flynn, "Whose Child?," 388.

84. *Wall Street Journal,* 28 April 1933, 6.

85. *Wall Street Journal,* 20 May 1933, 1.

86. For a more detailed account, see Hawley, *New Deal,* 19ff.; Arthur Schlesinger Jr., *The Coming of the New Deal* (Boston: Houghton Mifflin, 1959), 87ff.; *Business Week,* 24 May 1933, 3–4.

87. *New York Times,* 14 May 1933, sec. 2, 15.

88. *Iron Age* 131 (4 May 1933): 716.

89. Quoted in Gerald Nash, *United States Oil Policy, 1890–1964* (Pittsburgh, Pa.: University of Pittsburgh Press, 1968), 134–35.

90. Schlesinger, *Coming of the New Deal,* 89–99; *New York Times,* 3 June 1933, 17; 8 June 1933, 4. In an attempt to secure a broader base of support for the bill, Henry Harriman declared that the immediate beneficiaries of its enactment would be labor, with at least ten million workers receiving wage increases within six months after the new law went into effect. Harriman had testified before a congressional committee that, in his opinion, the first codes to be set up would cover only wages and hours. He went on to declare that "the refinements of the codes can be developed later," with the "refinements" presumably consisting of such matters as "a fair price," "fair wages," and "a fair dividend," all of which Harriman considered to be the basic objectives of the bill. J. R. Tritle, vice-president of Westinghouse Electric, anticipated much the same provisions as Harriman, suggesting that industrial recovery might be promoted by fixing prices (to wholesalers, retailers, and consumers), by controlling production, and by the establishment of minimum wages. See Leverett Lyon et al., *The National Recovery Administration: An Analysis and Appraisal* (Washington, D.C.: Brookings Institution, 1935), 23–24; *New York Times,* 21 May 1933, 2; *Wall Street Journal,* 24 May 1933, 5.

91. *Business Week,* 10 May 1933, 32.

92. Schlesinger, *Coming of the New Deal,* 95.

93. *Wall Street Journal,* 23 May 1933, 3.

94. *Iron Age* 131 (25 May 1933): 832; *New York Times,* 14 June 1933, 1.

95. *New York Times,* 18 May 1933, 11; 29 May 1933, 27; 30 May 1933, 3; 31 May 1933, 11; 1 June 1933, 35; 4 June 1933, 2. ·

96. *Business Week,* 10 May 1933, 3–4.

97. *Wall Street Journal,* 6 May 1933, 5.

98. Krooss, *Executive,* 169.

99. Ibid., 153.

100. *New York Times,* 5 May 1933, 1–2.

101. *New York Times,* 6 May 1933, 1; *Wall Street Journal,* 6 May 1933, 1.

102. *Steel,* 8 May 1933, 20.

103. *New York Times,* 9 May 1933, 3, 6, 11.
104. *Wall Street Journal,* 5 May 1933, 2.

CHAPTER 4. UNDER THE BLUE EAGLE AND BEYOND

1. James Walker, *The Epic of American Industry* (New York: Harper & Bros., 1949), 405–6.
2. *Rotarian,* July 1936, 14. Johnson even managed to change the name of his agency. Originally denominated the NIRA, the *I* was removed from the abbreviation after a *Business Week* article referred to the NIRA as "Neera, My God, to Thee," a remark Johnson apparently considered too demeaning for so "holy" an agency.
3. *New York Times,* 20 May 1933, 1, 4; 8 June 1933, 29; *Business Week,* 15 July 1933, 3; Margaret Coit, *Mr. Baruch* (Boston: Houghton Mifflin, 1957), 441.
4. Marshall Dimock, *Business and Government* (New York: Henry Holt, 1949), 183.
5. Ibid.
6. Paul Conkin, *FDR and the Origins of the Welfare State* (New York: Thomas Y. Crowell, 1967), 35.
7. *Business Week,* 7 June 1933, 3.
8. *Steel,* 19 June 1933, 15.
9. *New York Times,* 28 April 1933, 14.
10. *New York Times,* 17 June 1933, 2. Harriman was to add, some five months after the NRA's enactment, that "it is inconceivable that [the NRA] should ever be entirely abandoned" (*Business Week,* 25 November 1933, 6).
11. David Loth, *Swope of G.E.* (New York: Simon & Schuster, 1958), 224.
12. *New York Times,* 23 May 1933, 16.
13. *New York Times,* 1 June 1933, 35.
14. *Wall Street Journal,* 6 June 1933, 14.
15. *Business Week,* 10 May 1933, 32.
16. William Rodgers, *Think: A Biography of the Watsons and IBM* (New York: Stein and Day, 1969), 110.
17. Krooss, *Executive,* 172.
18. *New York Times,* 15 June 1933, 33.
19. Lyon et al., *National Recovery,* 568–77; Filene, *Unfair Trade,* 133–34.
20. Dudley Cates, "A Current Appraisal of the National Recovery Administration," *Annals of the American Academy of Political and Social Science* 172 (March 1934): 133–34.
21. Alfred Lief, *The Firestone Story* (New York: McGraw-Hill, 1951), 198–203; *New York Times,* 8 June 1933, 29; *Wall Street Journal,* 9 June 1933, 13.
22. Rothbard, *Great Depression,* 26.
23. Ibid.
24. Lyon et al., *National Recovery,* 625.
25. Ibid., 629–31.
26. Ibid., 629–37.
27. *New York Times,* 15 November 1936, sec. 3, 9. A survey of some six thousand smaller manufacturers indicated that, while 34.2 percent of those responding favored a modification of the NRA and another 22.4 percent supported the NRA in its present form, 43.4 percent of the respondents favored total abolition of the agency.

Those favoring modification of the NRA largely desired a greater degree of flexibility in the matter of wages and hours, as well as a better administration of the codes themselves. In the words of John E. Edgerton, president of the Southern States Industrial Council, the smaller firms were unable "to protect themselves against majorities" and were especially disadvantaged by price fixing and control of production (*New York Times,* 29 December 1934, 3).

28. *New York Times,* 28 December 1934, 30; *Publishers Weekly,* 5 January 1935, 50. Likewise, a survey of small-, medium-, and large-sized business firms in New England resulted in the following demonstrations of support for the NRA codes in 1934 and 1935:

	1934	1935
In favor of the codes	76%	53%
Opposed to the codes	20	40
Not voting	4	7
	100%	100%

Business Week, 25 May 1935, 18.

29. *Literary Digest,* 3 February 1934, 8; George Sokolsky, "America Drifts Toward Fascism," *American Mercury* 32 (July 1934): 263.

30. *New York Times,* 13 March 1935, 5; 9 June 1935, 1, 28; *Business Week,* 25 May 1935, 18.

31. Quoted in Stanley Baron, *Brewed in America: A History of Beer and Ale in the United States* (Boston: Little, Brown, 1962), 325.

32. Ibid.

33. *New York Times,* 3 January 1933, 45.

34. William Saroyan, "Aspirin is a Member of the N.R.A.," *American Mercury* 32 (May 1934): 87–90. One might extend Saroyan's remarks by noting that the brewing industry, whose products have the capacity to dull the senses and distort reality, and the aspirin industry, whose product is often used as a remedy for the pains of overindulgence, were fitting NRA team members.

35. *New York Times,* 26 May 1935, sec. 4, 10.

36. *New York Times,* 7 December 1934, 1, 10.

37. *Publishers Weekly,* 25 May 1935, 1979. For further discussion of these measures see Hawley, *New Deal,* 111ff.

38. *New York Times,* 23 May 1935, 1.

39. *New York Times,* 18 January 1935, 4; 20 January 1935, sec. 2, 17; 14 March 1935, 1, 6; 15 March 1935, 40; 20 March 1935, 43; 21 March 1935, 41; 22 March 1935, 15; 26 March 1935, 37; 28 March 1935, 6, 39; 14 April 1935, sec. 2, 8; 18 April 1935, 33; 2 May 1935, 38; 4 May 1935, 26; 7 May 1935, 15, 41; 16 May 1935, 2, 42; 18 May 1935, 2; 24 May 1935, 40; 27 May 1935, 13; *Business Week,* 3 November 1934, 14; 25 May 1935, 18; *Publishers Weekly,* 25 May 1935, 1975–76, 1979.

40. *New York Times,* 16 June 1935, sec. 3, 9.

41. *New York Times,* 10 March 1935, sec. 2, 19.

42. *New York Times,* 1 May 1935, 2; 3 May 1935, 4.

43. Richard Hodgson, ed., *In Quiet Ways: George H. Mead—The Man and the Company* (Dayton, Ohio: Mead Corp., 1970), 266.

44. *A.L.A. Schechter Poultry Corp. et al. v. United States,* 295 U.S. 495 (1935).

It should be noted that the Supreme Court did not invalidate the concept of industrial self-regulation through enforceable "codes of fair competition." The unconstitutionality of the program related to the method by which the codes came into being and the scope of their application. Had the code-making process been channeled through Congress rather than the executive branch, had the Recovery Act provided more specific standards for determining the content of codes, and had the codes themselves been less pervasive and more confined to the regulation of practices with more direct national significance, a different conclusion might have been reached. The decision, in other words, can scarcely be interpreted as an attack upon economic interventionism. As the Court declared:

> The power of Congress extends not only to the regulation of transactions which are part of interstate commerce, but to the protection of that commerce from injury. It matters not that the injury may be due to the conduct of those engaged in intrastate operations. . . . Congress may protect the safety of those employed in interstate transportation "no matter what may be the source of the dangers which threaten it. . . ." (295 U.S. 495, 544)

45. *Panama Refining Company et al. v. Ryan et al.*, 293 U.S. 388 (1935).
46. Lowi, *Politics*, 75.
47. *New York Times*, 29 May 1935, 1, 11; 2 June 1935, sec. 4, 7.
48. *New York Times*, 5 June 1935, 11; 9 June 1935, sec. 3, 9.
49. *New York Times*, 29 May 1935, 10; 22 November 1936, 31. This proposition, coming after the *Schechter* case, also attempted to answer what was felt to be some of the Supreme Court's objections to federal control. Arguing that each state could act upon those subjects of particular interest to it and without imposing such regulations upon other states, the Chamber directors concluded that the courts would more likely apply a broad interpretation to such legislation as being an exercise of the reserved police powers of the states than they would for federal legislation, which must find its justification in express grants of constitutional authority. The alternative offered by the Chamber sought only to establish a regulatory system that would satisfy the Supreme Court. No objection was expressed by the Chamber officials to the *content* of the NRA system of regulation.
50. *New York Times*, 3 June 1935, 1–2.
51. *New York Times*, 29 May 1935, 14; 2 June 1935, 29; 4 June 1935, 1, 6; 5 June 1935, 11; 6 June 1935, 39; 7 June 1935, 39; 9 June 1935, 1, 28; *Business Week*, 8 June 1935, 3, 7; 15 June 1935, 11; *Publishers Weekly*, 1 June 1935, 2133–34.
52. *New York Times*, 29 May 1935, 1, 13, 15; 30 May 1935, 12; 2 June 1935, sec. 3, 1; 5 June 1935, 11; *Business Week*, 15 June 1935, 11.
53. *Wall Street Journal*, 1 June 1935, 5. This study has not focused on the investment banking industry; it prefers to leave the reader to Parrish's *Securities Regulation* and Vincent Carosso's *Investment Banking in America* (Cambridge: Harvard University Press, 1970). Beginning at least as early as the World War I era and continuing through the post-*Schechter* period, the Investment Bankers Association (IBA) and other securities trade leaders had advocated increased political supervision in order to promote industry objectives. Legislation proposed in March 1933 to allow the federal government to supervise securities transactions received the endorsement not only of FDR but of the *Wall Street Journal* and the *Financial Age* as well (Parrish, *Securities Regulation*, 47). While industry members generally rejected proposals re-

quiring the registration and disclosure of securities prior to issuance, they were active in promoting other political alternatives. Officials of the IBA, for example, advocated legislation that would punish those who engaged in fraudulent practices (see ibid., 53ff.). This is not to deny that other forces from outside the industry were actively pursuing legislative proposals hostile to industry interests, nor is it to suggest that Congress was only doing the bidding of Wall Street. It does, however, demonstrate a willingness on the part of members of the investment banking industry to employ political means when it suited their purposes to do so.

54. *Business Week,* 1 June 1935, 48.

55. *Business Week,* 8 June 1935, 40. Support for the continuation of NRA principles also came from less credible sources. The Council for Industrial Progress, a comic-opera concoction of the former labor leader Major George L. Berry, claimed to be representative of all segments of society, including business. It called for congressional enactment of a fair-competition law. The law would have been administered by a federal agency and called for the establishment of an industrial court to hear cases involving alleged violations. Owing to the nature of this organization, it would be unsafe to generalize its views as being representative of much more than Major Berry himself. See *New York Times,* 12 December 1936, 1, 11; Hawley, *New Deal,* 161–63.

56. *New York Times,* 14 January 1937, 46.

57. *New York Times,* 2 June 1935, sec. 3, 9; Kittelle and Mostow, "A Review," 431–33.

58. *New York Times,* 13 January 1926, 38.

59. For an excellent background on the sugar industry, see Richard Zerbe, "The American Sugar Refinery Company, 1887–1914: The Story of a Monopoly," *Journal of Law and Economics* 12 (October 1969): 339–75.

60. Hampe and Wittenberg, *Lifeline,* 132–34.

61. Leverett Lyon, Myron Watkins, and Victor Abramson, *Government and Economic Life,* 2 vols. (Washington, D.C.: Brookings Institution, 1939), 2:909–10.

62. Marver Bernstein, *Regulating Business by Independent Commission* (Princeton: Princeton University Press, 1955), 90–91; *New York Times,* 1 February 1935, 40; 21 February 1935, 31.

63. James Nelson, "The Motor Carrier Act of 1935," *Journal of Political Economy* 44 (August 1936): 464–65.

64. Nor was the ATA alone in its activity on behalf of such legislation. It was joined by the American Highway Freight Association, American Short Line Railroad Association, American Transit Association, Association of Railway Executives, National Highway Freight Association, Railway Business Association, Association of Regulated Lake Lines, and the Canal Carriers Association. The water carriers' attraction to federal regulation was well stated by one of its members, who envisioned the "stability of rates and all that goes along with it." Ibid., 470; *New York Times,* 22 February 1935, 43; 27 February 1935, 27; 3 May 1935, 1, 4.

65. The U.S. Chamber of Commerce, American Bankers Association, NAM, NICB, American Iron and Steel Institute, Institute of American Meat Packers, Grain and Feed Dealers National Association, Security Owners Association, and the National Association of Mutual Savings Banks joined the parade to Washington to support such an extension of regulation. *New York Times,* 27 February 1935, 27; 3 May 1935, 1, 4.

66. Bernard Schwartz, ed. *The Economic Regulation of Business and Industry:*

A Legislative History of U.S. Regulatory Agencies, 5 vols. (New York: Chelsea House, in association with R. R. Bowker Company, 1973), 4:3064–65; *New York Times,* 7 April 1938, 33.

67. Emmette Redford, *The Regulatory Process* (Austin: University of Texas Press, 1969), 28.

68. *Rotarian,* July 1936, 14.

69. Gardiner C. Means, *The Corporate Revolution in America* (New York: Crowell-Collier Press, 1962), 33–37.

70. Arnold, *Folklore,* 227.

71. See, e.g., Hawley, *New Deal,* 420ff.

72. Arnold, in a speech before the American Bar Association in San Francisco, in Brady, *Business,* 190.

CHAPTER 5. THE STEEL INDUSTRY

1. Chapman, *Development,* 69 (emphasis in original).

2. *Year Book of the American Iron and Steel Institute,* 1913, 18.

3. *Year Book of the American Iron and Steel Institute,* 1914, 284.

4. *New York Times,* 18 June 1922, sec. 2, 1.

5. *Iron Age* 108 (14 July 1921): 90; 109 (5 January 1922): 59ff.; 114 (28 August 1924): 523; 125 (2 January 1930): 125ff.

6. Kolko, *Triumph,* 37, 46. See also *United States v. United States Steel Corporation,* 251 U.S. 417 (1920); *United States v. International Harvester Corporation,* 274 U.S. 693 (1927).

7. See Richard Posner, *Economic Analysis of Law* (Boston: Little, Brown, 1972), 118 (n.11), citing an analysis of the *United States Steel Corporation* case by George Stigler.

8. *Year Book of the American Iron and Steel Institute,* 1914, 297; 1925, 220; *Iron Age* 119 (26 May 1927): 1513 at 1514.

9. *Year Book of the American Iron and Steel Institute,* 1925, 16–17.

10. *Year Book of the American Iron and Steel Institute,* 1914, 298.

11. *Year Book of the American Iron and Steel Institute,* 1925, 222–23.

12. *Iron Age* 113 (29 May 1924): 1558.

13. Ida Tarbell, *The Life of Elbert H. Gary: The Story of Steel* (New York: D. Appleton, 1925), 206 (emphasis in original). One of the initial purposes in the creation of U.S. Steel was the stabilization of prices in the industry by reducing sharp fluctuations. Indeed, it appears that a general moderation in prices took place in the industry during the years following the appearance of this corporation and up to the start of World War I. In spite of this fact, however, fluctuations in iron and steel production were greater in the years *after* 1901 (up into the early 1920s) than they were *before* U.S. Steel's creation. See Berglund, "United States Steel Corporation and Price Stabilization," 3ff.; also, Abraham Berglund, "The United States Steel Corporation and Industrial Stabilization," *Quarterly Journal of Economics* 38 (August 1924): 607–30.

14. *Iron Age* 116 (29 October 1925): 1196–97.

15. *Iron Age* 119 (26 May 1927): 1513 at 1514.

16. *Iron Age* 118 (28 October 1926): 1191.

17. *Iron Age* 111 (1 February 1923): 345.

18. *New York Times,* 29 October 1927, 3; *Iron Age* 120 (3 November 1927): 1230 (emphasis added).

19. *Year Book of the American Iron and Steel Institute,* 1928, 280.

20. Schwab and others had recommended that the antitrust laws be modified to permit firms in the steel industry to enter into agreements, possibly under government supervision, to eliminate uneconomic practices such as cross-hauling. For example, he thought that a manufacturer in Chicago who was going to ship to a buyer in Pittsburgh, and a manufacturer in Pittsburgh who was going to ship to a buyer in Chicago, should be able to work out an arrangement, perhaps through trading orders, to avoid unnecessary shipping costs. As a voluntary measure, such a proposal is entirely consistent with a system of free competition and would tend to greater efficiencies in the industry. See *New York Times,* 26 May 1928, 22; 27 October 1928, 1, 12; *Iron Age* 122 (1 November 1928): 1085–86; *Year Book of the American Iron and Steel Institute,* 1928, 276–77.

21. *Iron Age* 117 (27 May 1926): 1502; 120 (3 November 1927): 1230–31.

22. *Year Book of the American Iron and Steel Institute,* 1921, 236.

23. *Iron Age* 122 (1 November 1928): 1087.

24. Ibid., 635–36.

25. *Year Book of the American Iron and Steel Institute,* 1928, 283–84.

26. *Iron Age* 119 (27 January 1927): 287–88.

27. *Iron Age* 122 (29 November 1928): 1364.

28. *Iron Age* 124 (24 October 1929): 1107.

29. *Iron Age* 122 (29 November 1928): 1364–65.

30. Ibid., 1180–81.

31. Ibid.

32. Ibid.

33. *Iron Age* 123 (30 May 1929): 1484.

34. *Iron Age* 121 (26 April 1928): 1148.

35. *Iron Age* 117 (13 May 1926): 1347; 121 (10 May 1928): 1323.

36. *New York Times,* 23 March 1933, 6; 28 May 1933, sec. 4, 4.

37. George Perkins, "The Modern Corporation," reprinted in *The Currency Problem and the Present Financial Situation: A Series of Addresses Delivered at Columbia University, 1907–1908* (New York: Columbia University Press, 1908), 164; Chapman, *Development,* 111–12.

38. Watkins, *Public Regulation,* 38n.

39. John Garraty, *Right-Hand Man: The Life of George W. Perkins* (New York: Harper & Bros., 1957), 253.

40. Perkins, "The Modern Corporation," 166.

41. *New York Times,* 3 October 1919, 2.

42. Tarbell, *Elbert Gary,* 231–32.

43. *Iron Age* 107 (2 June 1921): 1457.

44. *Year Book of the American Iron and Steel Institute,* 1922, 21–22; *System,* January 1925, 28.

45. Julius Kahn, "A Plea for More Government Regulation," *Nation's Business,* February 1928, 20, 22.

46. *Scribner's Magazine* 66 (1919): 101.

47. *Iron Age* 107 (21 April 1921): 1043.

48. *Iron Age* 123 (7 February 1929): 426.

49. *Business Week,* 7 May 1930, 14.

50. Charles Abbott, "Balanced Prosperity," in Hamlin, *Menace of Overproduction*, 74, 77–78. It should be noted that, in a market economy, "value" is determined solely by exchange and fluctuates as the preferences of buyers and sellers and the supply of the product fluctuates. No commodity can, therefore, be said to have any "intrinsic value." The objection being offered by Abbott was that supply and/or demand factors had changed to such an extent that prices had fallen below a level minimally acceptable to many producers.

51. Swope, *Swope Plan*, 106.

52. Ibid., 104.

53. *New York Times*, 5 August 1932, 1, 3; 6 August 1932, 2.

54. *Wall Street Journal*, 26 May 1933, 10; *Steel*, 29 May 1933, 11.

55. *Steel*, 29 May 1933, 12.

56. *Wall Street Journal*, 26 May 1933, 10; *Iron Age* 131 (1 June 1933): 852.

57. *Iron Age* 131 (25 May 1933): 835. Copyright permission granted by Chilton Company, Capital Cities/ABC Inc.

58. *Steel*, 15 May 1933, 20.

59. *Steel*, 8 May 1933, 20.

60. *Steel*, 5 June 1933, 12.

61. *New York Times*, 16 May 1933, 23.

62. W. H. Daney, president of Canton Tin Plate Corp.; G. R. Hauks, president of Taylor-Wharton Iron & Steel Company; and A. M. Oppenheimer, president of Apollo Steel Company, in *Iron Age* 131 (1 June 1933): 872–73.

63. Ibid., 871.

64. Ibid.

65. *Wall Street Journal*, 26 May 1933, 10.

66. Remarks by G. H. Chisholm, F. J. Moore (president of E. Keeler Company), Roy C. McKenna (president of Vanadium-Alloys Steel Company), W. Nelson Mayhew (president of Montgomery Iron & Steel Company), and H. E. Hughes (president of Continental Bridge Company), in *Iron Age* 131 (1 June 1933): 871–75.

67. H. C. Thomas of Alan Wood Steel Company, in ibid., 871.

68. *Steel*, 19 June 1933, 10.

69. *Iron Age* 131 (23 March 1933): 484.

70. *Iron Age* 131 (8 June 1933): 907.

71. Remarks by George J. Meyer (president of George J. Meyer Manufacturing Company), Leroy Brooks Jr. (president of Tool Steel Gear & Pinion Company), E. S. Sawtelle (president of Sawbrook Steel Castings Company), E. Haupt (president of Strobel Construction Company), C. H. Henkel (receiver, Empire Steel Corporation), John T. Llewellyn (president of Chicago Malleable Castings Company; Allied Steel Castings Company), in ibid., 906–9. As we saw earlier, business leaders often defined selling "below cost" not just as subvariable cost pricing, but selling products at prices that did not return all fixed and variable costs plus a "reasonable profit." One steel company official defined selling "at a profit" to include "fair labor scale, full overhead, fair prices for raw materials plus a reasonable profit." H. A. Burkhardt, president of E. Burkhardt & Sons Steel and Iron Works, in ibid., 906. By use of such phrases as "fair" and "reasonable"—clearly subjective in nature—it is evident that pricing policies were being considered not on the basis of the actual costs experienced by a given producer, but on the basis of representative or average costs for the entire industry.

72. *Wall Street Journal,* 29 May 1933, 1, 2.
73. *Iron Age* 131 (29 June 1933): 1038-A; *Steel,* 22 May 1933, 10.
74. *Wall Street Journal,* 26 May 1933, 10.
75. Ibid.
76. *Wall Street Journal,* 19 May 1933, 6; *Steel,* 22 May 1933, 10.
77. *Steel,* 15 May 1933, 11; *Iron Age* 132 (20 July 1933): 26-H.
78. *Iron Age* 132 (10 August 1933): 30–31.
79. Eugene Grace, "Industry and the Recovery Act," *Scribner's Magazine* 95 (February 1934): 96–98.
80. Ibid., 97.
81. Ibid., 100.
82. *New York Times,* 28 May 1935, 21.
83. *New York Times,* 30 May 1935, 12.
84. *New York Times,* 28 May 1935, 21; 30 May 1935, 12; 4 June 1935, 1; 7 June 1935, 16; *Wall Street Journal,* 31 May 1935, 5; *Business Week,* 25 May 1935, 18; 15 June 1935, 11.

CHAPTER 6. THE NATURAL-RESOURCE INDUSTRIES

1. The railroads were active in promoting national parks, in order to promote tourism, while many eastern businessmen supported conservation in the Adirondacks as a way of helping to preserve inland waterways and, hence, prevent the railroads from monopolizing transportation. See, e.g., Frank Graham Jr., *Man's Dominion: The Story of Conservation in America* (New York: M. Evans and Co., 1971), 87, 159. Other industries made ample use of the conservation issue. One frequently runs across a statement by a manufacturer about the virtue of seeking to "conserve" such resources as capital and the value of labor from the "waste" of unrestrained competition. The steel industry's Charles F. Abbott, as has been noted, argued that "iron and steel products should command prices more in keeping with their intrinsic values" in order to insure the future development of remaining ore deposits. The rhetoric of "conservation" blended in very well with the purpose of preserving the positions of business firms from the risks associated with free competition. See Abbott, "Balanced Prosperity," 74, 77.

2. *New York Times,* 15 January 1917, 13.

3. The lumber industry was one of the earliest champions of conservation measures as a means of stabilizing trade conditions. An FTC report on lumber trade associations, issued in 1922, declared that members of the National Lumber Manufacturers' Association "have advocated for many years that they should be permitted to concertedly regulate the production of lumber for the expressed purpose of conserving the national resources." The Bureau of Corporations had previously announced that the lumber companies, in past years, had cooperated with one another in order to restrict lumber production whenever an oversupply threatened to decrease the price. The FTC then concluded, "[I]t appears to be the aim and purpose of the manufacturers not only to eliminate price competition within their respective associations but to eliminate, as far as possible, price competition among the competing kinds of lumber." See *Report of the Federal Trade Commission,* 2, 44–45.

4. The breakdown of figures on this graph is as follows (millions of barrels):

Year	Mid-Cont. Prod. (a)	U.S. Prod. (b)	Imports (b)	U.S. Prod. + Imports (b)	Demand (b)	Ave. Price Mid-Cont. Crude (c)
1920	250.1	442.9	106.2	549.1	531.2	$3.42
1921	258.5	472.2	125.4	597.6	529.7	1.65
1922	311.0	557.5	127.3	684.8	595.4	1.68
1923	348.5	732.4	82.0	814.4	733.5	1.56
1924	375.5	713.9	77.8	791.7	770.7	1.64
1925	425.1	763.7	61.8	825.5	842.2	1.87
1926	424.9	770.9	60.4	831.3	862.1	2.13
1927	547.6	901.1	58.4	959.5	894.9	1.38
1928	553.5	901.5	79.8	981.2	969.0	1.31
1929	584.3	1007.3	78.9	1086.3	1050.4	1.37

(a)   from Harold Williamson et al., *The American Petroleum Industry* (Evanston, Ill.: Northwestern University Press, 1963), 302.
(b)   from Nash, *United States Oil Policy*, 260.
(c)   from Ralph Cassady Jr., *Price Making and Price Behavior in the Petroleum Industry*, Petroleum Monograph Series, vol. 1 (New Haven: Yale University Press, 1954), 137.

5. From Williamson et al., *American Petroleum*, 302–3; J. Stanley Clark, *The Oil Century* (Norman: University of Oklahoma Press, 1958), 177–79; Erich Zimmermann, *Conservation in the Production of Petroleum: A Study in Industrial Control* (New Haven: Yale University Press, 1957), 115.
6. *Oil and Gas Journal* 26 (2 February 1928): 36. Copyright permission granted by Oil and Gas Journal.
7. Quoted in Nash, *United States Oil Policy*, 83.
8. Ibid., 84–85.
9. Henrietta Larson and Kenneth Porter, *History of Humble Oil & Refining Company* (New York: Arno Press, 1959), 254–55.
10. *New York Times*, 10 December 1926, 23; Zimmermann, *Conservation*, 126–29; Nash, *United States Oil Policy*, 86–91.
11. Among the more important discoveries in 1926 were the Seal Beach field (California); Bowlegs and Seminole fields (Oklahoma); and the Hendrick, Howard-Glasscock, McElroy, and Yates fields (West Texas). The 1927 finds included the Little River and St. Louis fields (Oklahoma). The 1928 discoveries included the Kettleman North Dome field (California); the Oklahoma City field (Oklahoma); and the Eunice-Monument and Hobbs fields (New Mexico). The year 1929 saw the discovery of the Van field (East Texas), while 1930 witnessed the discovery of the most prolific of all, the East Texas field. In 1931, the Conroe field (Texas Gulf Coast) was found. See John McLean and Robert Haigh, *The Growth of Integrated Oil Companies* (Boston: Division of Research, Graduate School of Business Administration, Harvard University, 1954), 87.
12. *New York Times*, 7 May 1927, 26; Williamson et al., *American Petroleum Industry*, 302–3; Clark, *Oil Century*, 177–79.
13. *New York Times*, 13 May 1927, 1, 7.
14. Zimmermann, *Conservation*, 116.

15. Henrietta Larson, Evelyn Knowlton, and Charles Popple, *History of Standard Oil Company (New Jersey): New Horizons, 1927–1950* (New York: Harper & Row, 1971), 63.

16. *New York Times,* 2 September 1926, 1; Larson, Knowlton, and Popple, *Standard Oil,* 87–88; Nash, *United States Oil Policy,* 86–91; Larson and Porter, *Humble Oil,* 313–14; *Oil and Gas Journal* 28 (3 October 1929): 100.

17. *New York Times,* 12 May 1927, 10.

18. Oklahoma Comp. Stat. 1921, secs. 7954–63.

19. W. P. Z. German, "Legal History of Oil and Gas in Oklahoma," in *Legal History of Conservation of Oil and Gas,* symposium by the Mineral Law Section of the American Bar Association (Chicago: Section of Mineral Law of the American Bar Association, 1938), 152.

20. *New York Times,* 13 May 1927, 1, 7; 25 May 1927, 32; 26 May 1927, 5; Clark, *Oil Century,* 178–81; Williamson et al., *American Petroleum Industry,* 322ff.

21. Clark, *Oil Century,* 177–78.

22. *New York Times,* 7 May 1927, 26; 12 May 1927, 10. See also William Farish, "A New Concept of the Oil Industry," *Lamp,* February 1934, 6.

23. *New York Times,* 22 May 1927, sec. 2, 17; 25 May 1927, 32.

24. *New York Times,* 25 May 1927, 32.

25. Nash, *United States Oil Policy,* 96.

26. *Wall Street Journal,* 20 October 1927, 16.

27. See, for example, D. T. Armentano, *The Myths of Antitrust* (New Rochelle, N.Y.: Arlington House, 1972); Harold Fleming, *Ten Thousand Commandments: A Story of the Antitrust Laws* (New York: Prentice-Hall, 1951); Lowell Mason, *The Language of Dissent* (New Canaan, Conn.: Long House, 1959); Isabel Paterson, *The God of the Machine* (New York: G. P. Putnam's Sons, 1943); Rothbard, *Power.*

28. Lester Uren, "What California's Gas Conservation Law Means to Our Industry," *National Petroleum News* 21 (26 June 1929): 55–56.

29. Ibid., 56–57.

30. O'Connor, *Mellon's,* 193–94.

31. From "Petroleum Investigation," *Hearings on H. Res. 441* (Washington, D.C.: Government Printing Office, 1934), pt. 1, 485, reported in William Kemnitzer, *Rebirth of Monopoly* (New York: Harper & Bros., 1938), 119.

32. "Petroleum Investigation," pt. 1, 493; Kemnitzer, *Rebirth,* 118.

33. See, e.g., references in note 3 of the introduction, supra.

34. Fritz Machlup, *The Political Economy of Monopoly* (Baltimore: Johns Hopkins University Press, 1952), 302–3.

35. An account of this argument is offered in Roger Miller, *The Economics of Energy: What Went Wrong* (New York: William Morrow, 1974), 17–18.

36. *National Petroleum News* 21 (25 September 1929): 139.

37. Larson and Porter, *Humble Oil,* 301.

38. Sir Henri Deterding, "Conservation of Oil National and International Problem," in Hamlin, *Menace of Overproduction,* 105–6. The board of directors of Standard Oil (N.J.) expressed similar sentiments, praising the FOCB, which, it said, "recognizes the need for cooperative effort not only among the units of the industry but between the industry and the government as well." Quoted in Kemnitzer, *Rebirth,* 212n.

39. *Oil and Gas Journal* 26 (12 April 1928): 36.

40. *Oil and Gas Journal* 26 (5 January 1928): 36.

41. E. P. Salisbury, "Overproduction in the Oil Industry," in Hamlin, *Menace of Overproduction*, 21.

42. Simon Whitney, *Antitrust Policies: American Experience in Twenty Industries*, 2 vols. (New York: Twentieth Century Fund, 1958), 1: 113.

43. *New York Times*, 5 December 1928, 18.

44. Quoted in Larson and Porter, *Humble Oil*, 319, 325.

45. *New York Times*, 5 December 1928, 18.

46. *New York Times*, 26 February 1928, sec. 2, 11.

47. *New York Times*, 5 April 1928, 40.

48. Deterding, "Conservation of Oil," 102 (emphasis added).

49. Ibid., 105 (emphasis added).

50. *Independent Petroleum Association of America Monthly* 1 (March 1931): 14.

51. Nash, *United States Oil Policy*, 94.

52. O'Connor, *Mellon's*, 313–14.

53. *Petroleum Age* 21 (1 June 1928): 20–21.

54. *National Petroleum News* 21 (24 July 1929): 19–21.

55. *National Petroleum News* 21 (13 March 1929): 83ff.

56. Nash, *United States Oil Policy*, 115ff.; Williamson et al., *American Petroleum Industry*, 540ff.; Whitney, *Antitrust*, 1:114–15.

57. *New York Times*, 19 May 1933, 4; Nash, *United States Oil Policy*, 115, 262.

58. Chapter 26, Vernon's Anno. Civ. Stat. (Texas), arts. 6008, 6014, 6029, 6032, 6036, 6049c.

59. *Champlin Refining Company v. Corporation Commission of Oklahoma et al.*, 286 U.S. 210 (1932).

60. Ibid., 233.

61. *R. S. Sterling et al. v. E. Constantin et al.*, 287 U.S. 378 (1932).

62. *New York Times*, 19 February 1932, 33; 18 May 1933, 27; *Wall Street Journal*, 1 April 1933, 9; 4 April 1933, 2, 10; Paul Giddens, *Standard Oil Company (Indiana)* (New York: Appleton-Century-Crofts, 1955), 460–61.

63. *New York Times*, 31 January 1932, sec. 2, 9, 16.

64. *New York Times*, 22 May 1932, sec. 2, 7, 10.

65. Quoted in Larson and Porter, *Humble Oil*, 467.

66. Hines H. Baker, quoted in ibid., 473.

67. *New York Times*, 3 April 1933, 26; 5 April 1933, 32; *Business Week*, 25 January 1933, 10; 19 April 1933, 7; 3 May 1933, 13–14.

68. Frederick Mills, *Prices in Recession and Recovery* (New York: National Bureau of Economic Research, 1936), 545.

69. *New York Times*, 15 May 1933, 3; 20 May 1933, 19; Clark, *Oil Century*, 194–95.

70. *Wall Street Journal*, 9 May 1933, 3.

71. *New York Times*, 18 May 1933, 27.

72. *New York Times*, 19 May 1933, 4; 21 May 1933, sec. 2, 7; 27 May 1933, 19; 9 June 1933, 25; *Wall Street Journal*, 20 May 1933, 1, 5; 22 May 1933, 1; 24 May 1933, 5.

73. *New York Times*, 7 May 1933, sec. 2, 7; *Wall Street Journal*, 20 May 1933, 5; 30 May 1933, 5.

74. *New York Times,* 5 April 1933, 32; 16 June 1933, 25; 18 June 1933, 9; *Business Week,* 22 July 1933, 6; Larson, Knowlton, and Popple, *Standard Oil,* 66–67.

75. Section 9(c).

76. *Business Week,* 31 May 1933, 5.

77. Quoted in Magee, *Collapse,* 52.

78. Ibid., 51.

79. Krooss, *Executive,* 173; Nash, *United States Oil Policy,* 135.

80. For an excellent account of the oil industry's experiences with the NRA, see Nash, *United States Oil Policy,* 128–56. See also Williamson et al., *American Petroleum Industry,* 548–51, 689–96.

81. Clark, *Oil Century,* 195; Lyon et al., *National Recovery,* 629ff.

82. Quoted in Larson and Porter, *Humble Oil,* 480.

83. Sokolsky, "America Drifts," 263.

84. See chapter 4, n. 45, supra.

85. *Business Week,* 15 June 1935, 11.

86. Machlup, *Political Economy,* 303.

87. Samuel Pettengill, *Hot Oil: The Problem of Petroleum* (New York: Economic Forum, 1936), 241–43.

88. Ibid., 243; Williamson et al., *American Petroleum Industry,* 550.

89. 49 Stat. 30, 15 USCA Sect. 715 *et seq.* (1940).

90. *New York Times,* 28 May 1935, 1, 21; *Wall Street Journal,* 29 May 1935, 1, 2; 5 June 1935, 1, 5.

91. *Bituminous Coal Data, 1963* (Washington, D.C.: National Coal Association), 110.

92. *Bituminous Coal Data, 1962* (Washington, D.C.: National Coal Association), 8–9.

93. J. Schmookler, "The Bituminous Coal Industry," in Adams, *Structure,* 76 at 82ff.

94. *Bituminous Coal Data, 1962,* 8.

95. Edward Devine, *Coal* (Bloomington, Ill.: American Review Service Press, 1925), 271.

96. Schmookler, "Bituminous," 85.

97. Schmookler also notes that "[w]hereas, in 1919, at the peak of unionization in the industry, about 72 per cent of all bituminous coal came from union mines, by 1925, the percentage was down to 40." Ibid., 87.

98. Ibid., 89 (emphasis added).

99. National Industrial Conference Board, *The Competitive Position of Coal in the United States* (New York: National Industrial Conference Board, 1931), 267.

100. *Bituminous Coal Data, 1962,* 8.

101. *Coal Age* 23 (28 June 1923): 1062–63.

102. *Coal Age* 33 (December 1928): 732.

103. Ibid., 733; *Coal Age* 29 (17 June 1926): 858, 862.

104. Machlup, *Political Economy,* 304.

105. C. E. Bockus, "The Cost of Overproduction in the Bituminous Mining Industry," in Hamlin, *Menace of Overproduction,* 1, at 14.

106. *Coal Age* 34 (November 1929): 667–68.

107. Bockus, "The Cost," 13–14.

108. *United States v. Trenton Potteries Company et al.,* 273 U.S. 392 (1927).

109. *Appalachian Coals, Inc., et al. v. United States,* 288 U.S. 344 (1933).
110. 288 U.S. 344, at 372, 374.
111. Glen Parker, *The Coal Industry: A Study in Social Control* (Washington, D.C.: American Council on Public Affairs, 1940), 109ff.
112. *New York Times,* 26 May 1935, sec. 4, 10; *Business Week,* 3 November 1934, 14; Parker, *Coal Industry,* 138.
113. *Carter v. Carter Coal Company et al.,* 298 U.S. 238 (1936); *Sunshine Anthracite Coal Company v. Adkins,* 310 U.S. 381 (1940). See also William Leuchtenberg, *Franklin D. Roosevelt and the New Deal, 1932–1940* (New York: Harper & Row, 1963), 161–62; Chapman, *Development,* 152–53; Machlup, *Political Economy,* 304; *Business Week,* 8 June 1935, 17.
114. The economic arguments against government conservation programs, demonstrating the superiority of the market in maximizing the efficient use of resources, have been developed elsewhere. See, e.g., Rothbard, *Power,* 63–70.
115. It is always assumed, without explanation, that future generations have a claim to the consumption of a given resource superior to that of the present generation, an assumption that has given rise to the humorous retort, "What has posterity done for *us?*" But if one considers the principal attraction for conservation measures to be the transfer of decision-making over resources from private to collective hands, the purpose for making this assumption becomes more clear.

CHAPTER 7. RETAILING AND TEXTILES

1. Chandler, in McCraw, *Essential,* 428.
2. Godfrey Lebhar, *Chain Stores in America,* 3d ed. (New York: Chain Store Publishing Corporation, 1963), 125. One cannot discuss the competition-restraining tendencies of many retailing interests without mentioning that local device known as the "Green River ordinance." Directed against retailers from outside the community who would go from door to door selling their products or services, the Green River ordinances ordinarily required itinerant salesmen to register with the local police and to have prior approval of a homeowner before soliciting a sale. Such restrictions, needless to say, tended to discourage the out-of-town competitors.
    An interesting anecdote: in a Wisconsin city a traveling photographer was prosecuted, at the urging of the resident photographers, for violating that city's Green River ordinance. The town's photographers came to court to witness the prosecution of this interloper, only to find themselves the target of the judge's ire. The judge told them: "Here is a man with ambition enough to go out and try to get business. You ask me to fine him for it. You want the law to protect you while you sit around waiting for business to come your way. If I had the power, I would fine every one of you instead." See *Business Week,* 11 December 1929, 33.
3. Lebhar, *Chain Stores,* 125ff.
4. Ibid., 162–65.
5. Taeusch, *Policy and Ethics,* 326–27, 364.
6. Edward Filene, "A Simple Code of Business Ethics," *Annals of the American Academy of Political and Social Science* 101 (1922): 224.
7. Edward Filene, *The Way Out* (New York: Doubleday, Page, 1924), 125.
8. *New York Times,* 9 November 1925, 21.

9. *New York Times,* 30 June 1926, 41.

10. Filene, *Unfair Trade,* 55–57.

11. Ibid., 68, 74–75.

12. A program with more teeth in it was begun by the Associated Fur Manufacturers, Inc. It provided for a binding contractual arrangement between the members to observe its provisions. Those who violated the contract could have future violations enjoined by a court of equity (or so it was contemplated) or, in the alternative, pay an agreed-upon rate as liquidated damages. The agreement sought to eliminate various "unethical" trade practices, such as the selling of any merchandise "on memorandum or consignment," as well as to require signatories to report all sales, including terms, and all payments received by them, and to adhere to a fixed schedule of discount rates. The enforceability of such a contract in a court of law was questionable, however, given the reluctance of courts to enforce agreements in restraint of trade or penalty provisions in contracts. See *New York Times,* 4 March 1928, sec. 2, 8.

13. Filene, *Unfair Trade,* 76.

14. *New York Times,* 25 February 1933, 28; 26 February 1933, sec. 2, 15; 26 March 1933, sec. 2, 15.

15. *Business Week,* 8 July 1933, 7–8.

16. *New York Times,* 8 June 1933, 3.

17. Krooss, *Executive,* 173.

18. *New York Times,* 1 June 1933, 37; 2 June 1933, 35; 3 June 1933, 5; 4 June 1933, sec. 2, 14.

19. *New York Times,* 18 June 1933, 10; *Business Week,* 1 June 1935, 8.

20. *Wall Street Journal,* 29 May 1933, 9; Herschel Deutsch, "The New Deal at the Drug Store Counter," *Advertising and Selling* 21 (3 August 1933): 15.

21. *Advertising and Selling* 21 (6 July 1933): 17ff.

22. Cates, "Current Appraisal," 135.

23. Edward Filene, "The New Relations Between Business and Government," *Annals of the American Academy of Political and Social Science* 172 (March 1934): 37–38.

24. Filene, *Unfair Trade,* 90.

25. Ibid., 90–96.

26. *New York Times,* 18 November 1934, 27; *Business Week,* 3 November 1934, 14.

27. *New York Times,* 28 May 1935, 18; 29 May 1935, 13, 15; 2 June 1935, 29; 3 June 1935, 1–2; 5 June 1935, 11; *Wall Street Journal,* 29 May 1935, 3.

28. *New York Times,* 28 May 1935, 14.

29. Ibid.

30. *Business Week,* 1 June 1935, 8.

31. *New York Times,* 29 May 1935, 15; 19 May 1936, 19; 2 December 1936, 9; *Business Week,* 15 June 1935, 11.

32. Murray Rothbard, *Man, Economy and State,* 2 vols. (Princeton, N.J.: D. Van Nostrand,1962) 2:493.

33. Lebhar, *Chain Stores,* 56, 74.

34. Robinson-Patman Act, 1936, 49 Stat., 1526, 15 U.S. Code 13.

35. *New York Times,* 2 March 1936, 29; 5 March 1936, 32; 13 March 1936, 32; 22 March 1936, sec. 3, 9; 26 May 1936, 39; 23 June 1936, 34; 4 August 1936, 37; 18 August 1936, 26; 25 January 1937, 5; 26 January 1937, 28.

248   NOTES TO CHAPTER 7

36. *New York Times,* 23 June 1936, 34.
37. *New York Times,* 27 February 1937, 30; B. S. Yamey, ed., *Resale Price Maintenance* (Chicago: Aldine, 1966), 68–69; Clair Wilcox, *Public Policies Toward Business,* 3d ed. (Homewood, Ill.: Richard D. Irwin, 1966), 706–7.
38. See Yamey, *Resale Price,* 69.
39. *New York Times,* 27 February 1937, 30; F. Marion Fletcher, *Market Restraints in the Retail Drug Industry* (Philadelphia: University of Pennsylvania Press, 1967), 54ff.; Lebhar, *Chain Stores,* 107ff.
40. *Old Dearborn Distributing Company v. Seagram-Distillers Corporation,* 299 U.S. 183 (1936).
41. Yamey, *Resale Price,* 73–75.
42. *New York Times,* 22 January 1937, 37; 15 June 1937, 32. The retailers' willingness to support minimum-wage laws was based largely upon the fact that legislation of that sort generally exempted members of the immediate family from coverage, an exemption conducive to the interests of the independent, family-owned retail establishments and detrimental to the interests of corporate-owned chain and discount stores.
43. Lebhar, *Chain Stores,* 113–14.
44. Adam Smith, *An Inquiry into the Nature and Causes of the Wealth of Nations* (1776; reprint, edited by Edwin Cannan, New York: Modern Library, 1937), 219–20.
45. This table is taken from appendix B, "Keep Market Street Open," a brief filed by chains opposing the Patman bill, and appears in the record of the hearing at page 652. It is reproduced in Lebhar, *Chain Stores,* 257.
46. Lewis Kimmel, *Federal Budget and Fiscal Policy, 1789–1958* (Washington, D.C.: Brookings Institution, 1959), 187.
47. Lebhar, *Chain Stores,* 272.
48. *Automotive Industries* 54 (20 May 1926): 843.
49. *Textile World* 73 (26 May 1928): 93–94.
50. Ibid., 96.
51. Louis Galambos, *Competition and Cooperation* (Baltimore: Johns Hopkins University Press, 1966), 89ff.
52. A. D. Whiteside in Hamlin, *Menace of Overproduction,* 27.
53. Galambos, *Competition,* 95–96.
54. *Textile World* 71 (21 May 1927): 147ff.
55. *Textile World* 73 (26 May 1928): 80.
56. Whitney, *Anti-Trust Policies,* 1:531ff.; 2:413ff.; C. T. Murchison, "Requisites of Stabilization in the Cotton Textile Industry," *American Economic Review* 23 (Supplement, 1933): 71–80; *Textile World* 71 (21 May 1927): 147ff.; 73 (26 May 1928): 96–97.
57. Archibald McIsaac, "The Cotton Textile Industry," in Adams, *Structure* (rev. ed. 1954), 47 at 48. See also Hawley, *New Deal,* 220–21.
58. U.S. Department of Commerce, *Commerce Yearbook, 1930* (Washington, D.C.: Government Printing Office, 1930), 468.
59. *New York Times,* 11 January 1928, 48; *Business Week,* 12 March 1930, 5–6; *Textile World* 71 (21 May 1927): 147ff.; 73 (26 May 1928): 80; Henry Kendall, "Factors in Restoring Equilibrium to the Cotton Textile Industry," in Hamlin, *Menace of Overproduction,* 22 at 24–25; Alexander Whiteside, "A Plan for Organizing Specific Industry," in Hamlin, *Menace of Overproduction,* 27 at 32; John Bassill,

"The Rayon Industry," in Hamlin, *Menace of Overproduction*, 40 at 49. Kendall was president of The Kendall Company, Whiteside was president of the Wool Institute, and Bassill was vice-president of the Tubize Chatillon Corporation.

    60. Statement of J. W. Cone, quoted in Krooss, *Executive*, 152; Hines quoted in Galambos, *Competition*, 179.

    61. *New York Times*, 14 January 1923, sec. 2, 13.

    62. *New York Times*, 22 April 1923, sec. 2, 10.

    63. John T. Flynn, "Business," 411.

    64. Quoted in Galambos, *Competition*, 177.

    65. *New York Times*, 11 May 1933, 7; *Textile World* 83 (May 1933): 901–2.

    66. Krooss, *Executive*, 171–72.

    67. *New York Times*, 10 June 1933, 24.

    68. *New York Times*, 19 May 1933, 4.

    69. Quoted in Galambos, *Competition*, 197.

    70. *Textile World* 83 (May 1933): 904–5.

    71. Ibid., 912–13.

    72. *Business Week*, 15 March 1933, 9.

    73. See Hawley, *New Deal*, 221; McIsaac, "Cotton Textile," 69–71.

    74. *New York Times*, 2 May 1935, 2.

    75. *New York Times*, 29 May 1935, 8; 31 May 1935, 9; 1 June 1935, 8; 2 June 1935, 29; 4 June 1935, 6; 5 June 1935, 11; 6 June 1935, 39; 7 June 1935, 39; 9 June 1935, 1; *Wall Street Journal*, 1 June 1935, 3.

    76. *New York Times*, 2 June 1935, sec. 3, 9.

    77. *New York Times*, 6 June 1935, 39.

    78. *Business Week*, 15 June 1935, 11.

    79. *Wall Street Journal*, 5 June 1935, 11.

    80. *New York Times*, 29 May 1935, 13.

    81. Edward Banfield, *The Unheavenly City Revisited* (Boston: Little, Brown, 1974), 108.

    82. That minimum-wage laws have served to increase unemployment—especially among the young and the poor—can no longer be denied. See, e.g., Yale Brozen, "The Effect of Statutory Minimum Wage Increases on Teen-Age Unemployment," *Journal of Law and Economics* 12 (1969): 109–22; M. C. Benewitz and R. E. Weintraub, "Employment Effects of a Local Minimum Wage," *Industrial and Labor Relations Review* 17 (January 1964): 276–88; Harry Douty, "Some Effects of the $1.00 Minimum Wage in the United States," *Economica*, n.s., 27 (May 1960): 137–47; John Peterson, "Employment Effects of State Minimum Wages for Women: Three Historical Cases Re-Examined," *Industrial and Labor Relations Review* 12 (April 1959): 406–22; *Industrial and Labor Relations Review* 13 (January 1960): 264–73; John Peterson, "Employment Effects of Minimum Wages, 1938–1950," *Journal of Political Economy* 65 (October 1957): 412–30; George Stigler, "The Economics of Minimum Wage Legislation," *American Economic Review* 36 (June 1946): 358–65.

CHAPTER 8. IN RETROSPECT

    1. Kolko, *Triumph*.

    2. Himmelberg, *Origins*, 219.

    3. Chandler, *Visible Hand*, 6ff.

4. A firm employing such a strategy might still face an antitrust conviction if its superior efficiencies were such that would-be competitors could not profitably compete at prevailing prices. In the *Alcoa* case, for example, the defendant was found to have violated the Sherman Act *even though* it had engaged in no abusive practices and enjoyed a virtual monopoly in the production of virgin aluminum ingot only by virtue of its acknowledged efficiencies and refusal to take advantage of its position by trying to charge monopolistic prices. In the words of the Court:

> It was not inevitable that it [Alcoa] should always anticipate increases in the demand for ingot and be prepared to supply them. Nothing compelled it to keep doubling and redoubling its capacity before others entered the field. It insists that it never excluded competitors; but we can think of no more effective exclusion than progressively to embrace each new opportunity as it opened, and to face every newcomer with new capacity already geared into a great organization, having the advantage of experience, trade connections and the elite of personnel. (*United States v. Aluminum Company of America*, 148 F2d 416, at 431 [1945])

5. See, e.g., the work of Niles Eldredge and Stephen Jay Gould, "Punctuated Equilibria: An Alternative to Phyletic Gradualism," in *Models in Paleobiology*, ed. T. J. M. Schopf (San Francisco: Freeman, Cooper and Company, 1972), 82–115.
6. Adams, "Military-Industrial," R-337-2.
7. Robert Dahl and Charles Lindblom, *Politics, Economics, and Welfare* (New York: Harper & Row, 1953), 200.
8. Smith, *Wealth of Nations*, 137 (emphasis added).

Bibliography

Abbott, Charles F. "Selling Code Is Prime Need." *The Iron Age* 122 (29 November 1928): 1350–52.

Adams, Henry. "The Relation of the State to Industrial Action." *Publications of the American Economic Association* 1 (1886): 471–549.

Adams, Walter. "The Military-Industrial Complex and the New Industrial State." *American Economic Review* 58 (May 1968): 652–65.

———. *The Structure of American Industry.* 1st ed. New York: Macmillan, 1950. Rev. 2d ed., 1954. 3d ed., 1961. 4th ed., 1971. 5th ed., 1977.

Adams, Walter, and James W. Brock. *Antitrust Economics on Trial: A Dialogue on the New Laissez-Faire.* Princeton: Princeton University Press, 1991.

Alderson, Bernard. *Andrew Carnegie: The Man and His Work.* New York: Doubleday, Page, 1905.

Alexander, George J. *Honesty and Competition: False Advertising Law and Policy Under FTC Administration.* Syracuse, N.Y.: Syracuse University Press, 1967.

Allen, Frederick Lewis. *The Lords of Creation.* Chicago: Quadrangle Books, 1966.

Allen, Hugh. *The House of Goodyear: Fifty Years of Men and Industry.* Cleveland: Corday and Gross, 1949.

Anderson, James E. *The Emergence of the Modern Regulatory State: A Study of American Ideas on the Regulation of Economic Enterprise, 1885–1917.* Washington, D.C.: Public Affairs Press, 1962.

Andreano, Ralph L., ed. *Superconcentration/Supercorporation.* Andover, Mass.: Warner Modular Publications, 1973.

Appel, Joseph. *The Business Biography of John Wanamaker, Founder and Builder.* New York: Macmillan, 1930.

Areeda, Phillip. "Antitrust Law as Industrial Policy: Should Judges and Juries Make It?" In *Antitrust, Innovation, and Competitiveness,* edited by Thomas M. Jorde and David J. Teece, 29–46. New York: Oxford University Press, 1992.

Areeda, Phillip, and Donald F. Turner. "Predatory Pricing and Related Practices Under Section 2 of the Sherman Act." *Harvard Law Review* 88 (February 1975): 697–733.

Armentano, Dominick T. *Antitrust and Monopoly.* 2d ed. New York: Holmes & Meier, 1990.

———. *The Myths of Antitrust.* New Rochelle, N.Y.: Arlington House, 1972.

Arnold, Thurman W. *The Folklore of Capitalism.* New Haven: Yale University Press, 1937.

Ayres, Leonard P. *The Economics of Recovery.* New York: Macmillan, 1934.

Babcock, Glenn D. *History of the United States Rubber Co.* Bloomington, Ind.: Indiana University Press, 1966.

Baker, Charles W. *Government Control and Operation of Industry in Great Britain and the United States during the World War.* New York: Oxford University Press, 1921.

———. *Pathways Back to Prosperity.* New York: Funk and Wagnalls, 1932.

Baker, Hugh. "Practical Problems of Trade Associations." *Proceedings of the Academy of Political Science* 11 (January 1926): 629–43.

Baldwin, William. *Market Power, Competition, and Antitrust Policy.* Homewood, Ill.: Irwin, 1987.

Ballinger, Willis J. "Big Business Begs for Socialism." *The Forum* 87 (February 1932): 97–100.

Banfield, Edward. *The Unheavenly City Revisited.* Boston: Little, Brown, 1974.

Barnes, Julius H. "Self-Government in Business." *The Nation's Business* 14 (5 June 1926): 16–18.

Baron, Stanley. *Brewed in America: A History of Beer and Ale in the United States.* Boston: Little, Brown, 1962.

Baruch, Bernard M. *American Industry in the War: A Report of the War Industries Board (March, 1921).* New York: Prentice-Hall, 1941.

———. *My Own Story.* New York: Henry Holt, 1957.

Baumhart, Raymond. *An Honest Profit.* New York: Holt, Rinehart & Winston, 1939.

Baumol, William J., and Janusz A. Ordover. "Antitrust: Source of Dynamic *and* Static Inefficiencies?" In *Antitrust, Innovation, and Competitiveness,* edited by Thomas M. Jorde and David J. Teece, 82–97. New York: Oxford University Press, 1992.

Beard, Charles A. *The Future Comes.* New York: Macmillan, 1933.

Beard, Charles A., and Mary R. Beard. *America in Midpassage.* 3 vols. New York: Macmillan, 1939.

Beckman, Theodore N., and Herman C. Nolen. *The Chain Store Problem.* New York: McGraw-Hill, 1938.

Benet, Christie. "Dealing With Trade Disputes." *The Nation's Business* 16 (5 June 1928): 30–31.

Benewitz, M.C. and R.E. Weintraub. "Employment Effects of a Local Minimum Wage." *Industrial and Labor Relations Review* 17. (January 1964): 276–88.

Berglund, Abraham. "The United States Steel Corporation and Industrial Stabilization." *The Quarterly Journal of Economics* 38 (August 1924): 607–30.

———. "The United States Steel Corporation and Price Stabilization." *The Quarterly Journal of Economics* 38 (November 1923): 1–30.

Berle, Adolf A. *The American Economic Republic.* New York: Harcourt, Brace & World, 1963.

Berle, Adolf A., and Gardiner Means. *The Modern Corporation and Private Property.* New York: Macmillan, 1932.

Bernstein, Marver H. *Regulating Business by Independent Commission.* Princeton: Princeton University Press, 1955.

Blaisdell, Thomas C., Jr. *The Federal Trade Commission.* New York: Columbia University Press, 1932.

Bloesch, Ed. "Enforcement of Existing Gas Waste Laws Would Prevent Overproduction." *National Petroleum News* 21 (25 September 1929): 139, 142.

Borth, Christy. *True Steel: The Story of George Matthew Verity and His Associates.* New York: Bobbs-Merrill, 1941.

Boulding, Kenneth. *The Organizational Revolution: A Study in the Ethics of Economic Organization.* New York: Harper, 1953.

Boyd, T. A. *Professional Amateur: The Biography of Charles Franklin Kettering.* New York: E. P. Dutton, 1957.

Brady, Robert A. *Business as a System of Power.* 6th ed. New York: Columbia University Press, 1951.

Brodley, Joseph F., and George A. Hay. "Predatory Pricing: Competing Economic Theories and the Evolution of Legal Standards." *Cornell Law Review* 66 (April 1981): 738–803.

The Brookings Institution. *The Recovery Problem in the United States.* Washington, D.C.: The Brookings Institution, 1936.

Brooks, David B., ed. *Resource Economics: Selected Works of Orris C. Herfindahl.* Baltimore: Resources for the Future, 1974.

Brown, Douglas, Edward Chamberlin, Seymour Harris, Wassily Leontief, Edward Mason, Joseph Schumpeter, and Overton Taylor. *The Economics of the Recovery Program.* New York: McGraw-Hill, 1934.

Brozen, Yale. "The Effect of Statutory Minimum Wage Increases on Teen-Age Employment." *The Journal of Law and Economics* 12 (1969): 109–122.

Burn, Bruno, in collaboration with S. Flink. *Codes, Cartels, National Planning: The Road to Economic Stability.* New York: McGraw-Hill, 1934.

Burns, Arthur R. "The First Phase of the National Industrial Recovery Act." *Political Science Quarterly* 49 (June 1934): 161–94.

Butler, Joseph B., Jr. *Fifty Years of Iron and Steel.* Cleveland: The Penton Press, 1918.

Butler, Rush. "The Sherman Anti-Trust Law and Readjustment." *The Annals of the American Academy of Political and Social Science* 82 (March 1919): 215–30.

Cabot, Richard C. "Ethics and Business." *The Survey* 56 (1 April 1926): 18–20.

Carnegie, Andrew. *Autobiography of Andrew Carnegie.* Boston: Houghton Mifflin, 1920.

Carosso, Vincent. *Investment Banking in America.* Cambridge: Harvard University Press, 1970.

Carr, Charles C. *Alcoa: An American Enterprise.* New York: Rinehart & Co., 1952.

Carstensen, Peter C. "Predatory Pricing in the Courts: Reflection on Two Decisions." *Notre Dame Law Review* 61 (1986): 928–71.

Carver, Thomas N. *The Present Economic Revolution in the United States.* Boston: Little, Brown, 1925.

Cassady, Ralph, Jr. *Price Making and Price Behavior in the Petroleum Industry.* New Haven: Yale University Press, 1954.

Cates, Dudley. "A Current Appraisal of the National Recovery Administration." *The Annals of the American Academy of Political and Social Science* 172 (March 1934): 130–38.

Caves, Richard. *Air Transport and Its Regulators.* Cambridge: Harvard University Press, 1962.

Chandler, Alfred D., Jr. *The Essential Alfred Chandler.* Edited, with an introduction, by Thomas K. McCraw. Boston: Harvard Business School Press, 1988.

——. *Giant Enterprise.* New York: Harcourt, Brace, & World, 1964.

——. *Strategy and Structure: Chapters in the History of the Individual Enterprise.* Cambridge: The MIT Press, 1962.

——. *The Visible Hand: The Managerial Revolution in American Business.* Cambridge: The Belknap Press of Harvard University Press, 1977.

Chandler, Lester V. *America's Greatest Depression, 1929–1941.* New York: Harper & Row, 1970.

Chapman, Charles C. *The Development of American Business and Banking Thought, 1913–1936.* New York: Longmans, Green, 1936.

Chapman, Dudley H. *Molting Time for Antitrust.* New York: Praeger, 1991.

Chase, Stuart. *The Economy of Abundance.* New York: Macmillan, 1934.

——. *Government in Business.* New York: Macmillan, 1935.

——. *The New Deal.* New York: Macmillan, 1932.

——. *Prosperity—Fact or Myth?* New York: Albert and Charles Boni, 1930.

Cheney, O. H. "The Answer to the New Competition." *The Nation's Business* 14 (October 1927): 15–17, 80–81.

——. "Facing the New Competition." *The Nation's Business* 16 (5 June 1928): 28–29, 65.

——. "The New Competition." *The Nation's Business* 14 (June 1926): 13–15.

Chrysler, Walter P., in collaboration with Boyden Sparkes. *Life of an American Workman.* New York: Dodd, Mead, 1950.

Clark, John M. *Social Control of Business.* New York: McGraw-Hill, 1939.

Clark, Joseph S. *The Oil Century.* Norman: University of Oklahoma Press, 1958.

Clarkson, Grosvenor B. *Industrial America in the World War.* Boston: Houghton Mifflin, 1923.

Clarkson, Jesse, and Thomas Cochran, eds. *War as a Social Institution.* New York: Columbia University Press, 1941.

Cochran, C. Thomas, and William Miller. *The Age of Enterprise.* New York: Macmillan, 1942.

Coit, Margaret L. *Mr. Baruch.* Boston: Houghton Mifflin, 1957.

Compton, Wilson. "How Competition Can Be Improved Through Association." *Proceedings of the Academy of Political Science* 11 (January 1926): 584–91.

Conkin, Paul K. *FDR and the Origins of the Welfare State.* New York: Thomas Y. Crowell, 1967.

——. *The New Deal.* 2d ed. Arlington Heights, Ill.: A H M Publishing Corp., 1975.

Cotter, Cornelius P. *Government and Private Enterprise.* New York: Holt, Rinehart, & Winston, 1960.

Crawford, Kenneth. *The Pressure Boys.* New York: J. Messiner, 1939.

Creed, Wiggington E. *Safeguarding the Future of Private Business.* Boston: Houghton Mifflin, 1923.

Crissey, Forrest. *Alexander Legge.* Chicago: Alexander Legge Memorial Committee, 1936.

Crowell, Benedict, and Robert Wilson. *How America Went to War: An Account From Official Sources of the Nation's War Activities, 1917–1920.* New Haven: Yale University Press, 1921.

Crowther, Samuel. *John H. Patterson.* Garden City, N.Y.: Garden City Publishing Co., 1926.

Cuff, Robert D. *The War Industries Board: Business-Government Relations during World War I.* Baltimore: The Johns Hopkins University Press, 1973.

The Currency Problem and the Present Financial Situation: A Series of Addresses Delivered at Columbia University, 1907–1908. New York: Columbia University Press, 1908.

Cushman, Robert E. *The Independent Regulatory Commissions.* New York: Oxford University Press, 1941.

Dahl, Robert, and Charles E. Lindblom. *Politics, Economics, and Welfare.* New York: Harper & Row, 1953.

Dameron, Kenneth. "The Retail Department Store and the NRA." *Harvard Business Review* 13 (April 1935): 261–70.

Dearing, Charles, Paul Homan, Lewis Lorwin, and Leverett Lyon. *The ABC of the NRA.* Washington, D.C.: The Brookings Institution, 1934.

Degler, Carl N., ed. *The New Deal.* Chicago: Quadrangle Books, 1970.

deJouvenal, Bertrand. *On Power.* Boston: Beacon Press, 1962.

Dennison, Henry S. *Ethics and Modern Business.* Boston: Houghton Mifflin, 1932.

———. "Social Self-Control." *The Annals of the American Academy of Political and Social Science* 149 (May 1930): 1–2.

Dennison, J. S., and John K. Galbraith. *Modern Competition and Business Policy.* New York: Oxford University Press, 1938.

Deutsch, Herschel. "The New Deal at the Drug Store Counter." *Advertising and Selling* 21 (3 August 1933): 15ff.

Devine, Edward. *Coal: Economic Problems of the Mining, Marketing and Consumption of Anthracite and Soft Coal in the United States.* Bloomington, Ill.: American Review Service Press, 1925.

Dewing, Arthur S. *Corporate Promotions and Reorganizations.* Cambridge: Harvard University Press, 1930.

———. *Financial Policy of Corporations.* 2 vols. New York: The Ronald Press Co., 1941.

Diggins, John P. *Mussolini and Fascism: The View from America.* Princeton: Princeton University Press, 1972.

Dimock, Marshall E. *Business and Government.* New York: Henry Holt, 1949.

Domhoff, G. William. *The Higher Circles*. New York: Random House, 1970.

———. *Who Rules America?* Englewood Cliffs, N.J.: Prentice-Hall, 1967.

Donald, William John Alexander. *Trade Associations*. New York: McGraw-Hill, 1933.

Donham, Wallace B. "Business Ethics—A General Survey." *Harvard Business Review* 7 (July 1929): 385–94.

Douglas, Paul H. *Controlling Depressions*. New York: W. W. Norton, 1935.

Douty, Harry M. "Some Effects of the $1.00 Minimum Wage in the United States." *Economica*, n.s., 27 (May 1960): 137–47.

Downs, Anthony. *Inside Bureaucracy*. Boston: Little, Brown, 1967.

Dubrul, Ernest F. *The Machine Tool Industry's Code of Business Principles*. New York: American Management Association, 1928.

Dunn, Samuel O. "The 'Practical' Socialist." *The Nation's Business* 16 (November 1928): 15–17, 178–180.

duPont, Bessie G. *E. I. duPont de Nemours and Company, A History 1802–1902*. Boston: Houghton Mifflin, 1920.

Durant, Will, and Ariel Durant. *The Lessons of History*. New York: Simon & Schuster, 1968.

Dutton, William S. *DuPont: One Hundred and Forty Years*. New York: Charles Scribner's Sons, 1942.

Eddy, Arthur Jerome. *The New Competition*. New York: Appleton & Co., 1912. Reprinted, New York: A. C. McClurg & Co., 1916, 1939.

Eichner, Alfred S. *The Emergence of Oligopoly*. Baltimore: The Johns Hopkins University Press, 1969.

Ekirch, Arthur. *The Decline of American Liberalism*. New York: Longmans, Green, 1955.

Elchibegoff, Ivan. *United States International Timber Trade in the Pacific Area*. Stanford, Calif.: Stanford University Press, 1949.

Elzinga, Kenneth G. "Collusive Predation: *Matsushita v. Zenith*." In *The Antitrust Revolution*, edited by John E. Kwoka Jr. and Lawrence J. White, 241–62. Glenview, Ill.: Scott, Foresman and Company, 1989.

———. "Unmasking Monopoly: Four Types of Economic Evidence." In *Economics and Antitrust Policy*, edited by Robert J. Larner and James W. Meehan Jr., 11–38. New York: Quorum Books, 1989.

Epstein, Ralph C. *The Automobile Industry: Its Economic and Commercial Development*. Chicago: A. W. Shaw Co., 1928.

Erickson, Don V. *Armstrong's Fight for FM Broadcasting: One Man Versus Big Business and Bureaucracy*. University: The University of Alabama Press, 1973.

Farish, William. "A New Concept of the Oil Industry." *The Lamp*, February 1934, 6.

Faulkner, Harold V. *The Decline of Laissez-Faire, 1897–1917*. Vol. 7 of *The Economic History of the United States*. New York: Rinehart and Company, 1951.

Federal Trade Commission. *Report of the Federal Trade Commission on Lumber Manufacturers' Trade Associations*. Washington, D.C.: Government Printing Office, 1922.

Feiker, F. M. "The Profession of Commerce in the Making." *The Annals of the American Academy of Political and Social Science* 101 (May 1922): 203–7.

Filene, Edward A. "A Simple Code of Business Ethics." *The Annals of the American Academy of Political and Social Science* 101 (May 1922): 223–28.

———. "The New Relations Between Business and Government." *The Annals of the American Academy of Political and Social Science* 172 (March 1934): 37–44.

———. *The Way Out.* New York: Doubleday, Page, 1924.

Filene, Lincoln. *Unfair Trade Practices: How to Remove Them.* New York: Harper & Bros., 1934.

Fine, Sidney. *The Automobile under the Blue Eagle.* Ann Arbor: The University of Michigan Press, 1963.

———. *Laissez-Faire and the General-Welfare State.* Ann Arbor: The University of Michigan Press, 1967.

Fitts, Charles N. "Trade Association Is a Necessity." *The Iron Age* 124 (24 October 1929): 1107–8.

Fleming, Harold. *Ten Thousand Commandments: A Story of the Antitrust Laws.* New York: Prentice-Hall, 1951.

Fletcher, F. Marion. *Market Restraints in the Retail Drug Industry.* Philadelphia: The University of Pennsylvania Press, 1967.

Flynn, John T. "Business and the Government." *Harpers* 156 (March 1928): 409–15.

———. *God's Gold.* New York: Harcourt, Brace, 1932.

———. "Whose Child Is the NRA?" *Harpers* 169 (September 1934): 385–94.

Foster, Thomas J. "What Industry Thinks of Industrial Control." *The Iron Age* 132 (10 August 1933): 30–31.

Foth, Joseph H. *Trade Associations.* New York: The Ronald Press, 1930.

Fox, Eleanor M., and James T. Halverson, eds. *Antitrust Policy in Transition: The Convergence of Law and Economics.* Chicago: Section of Antitrust Law of the American Bar Association, 1984.

Frederick, Duke, William Howenstine, and June Sochen. *Destroy to Create: Interaction with the Natural Environment in the Building of America.* Hinsdale, Ill.: The Dryden Press, 1972.

Friedman, Milton, and Anna J. Schwartz. *A Monetary History of the United States, 1867–1960.* Princeton: Princeton University Press, 1963.

Galambos, Louis. "The American Economy and the Reorganization of the Sources of Knowledge." In *The Organization of Knowledge in Modern America, 1860–1920,* edited by Alexandra Oleson and John Voss. Baltimore: The Johns Hopkins University Press, 1979.

———. *Competition and Cooperation: The Emergence of a National Trade Association.* Baltimore: The Johns Hopkins University Press, 1966.

Galbraith, John K. *The Great Crash, 1929.* Boston: Houghton Mifflin, 1955.

———. *American Capitalism: The Concept of Countervailing Power.* Boston: Houghton Mifflin, 1952.

Garraty, John A. *Right-Hand Man: The Life of George W. Perkins.* New York: Harper & Bros., 1960.

258 BIBLIOGRAPHY

Gaskill, Nelson B. "Public Interest Versus Private Interest in the Federal Trade Commission Act." *Proceedings of the Academy of Political Science* 11 (January 1926): 673–83.

Gates, William B., Jr. *Michigan Copper and Boston Dollars.* Cambridge: Harvard University Press, 1951.

Giddens, Paul H. *Standard Oil Company (Indiana).* New York: Appleton-Century-Crofts, 1955.

Gifford, Walter S. *Addresses, Papers and Interviews: From April 13, 1913 to July 1, 1928.* New York: Information Department of American Telephone & Telegraph Co., 1928.

Gilbert, James. *Designing the Industrial State: The Intellectual Pursuit of Collectivism in America, 1880–1940.* Chicago: Quadrangle Books, 1972.

Givens, Richard A. *Antitrust: An Economic Approach.* New York: Law Journal Seminars-Press, 1995.

Goldschmid, Harvey J., H. Michael Mann, and J. Fred Weston, eds. *Industrial Concentration: The New Learning.* Boston: Little, Brown, 1974.

Grace, Eugene G. *Charles M. Schwab.* New York: American Iron & Steel Institute, 1947.

———. "Industry and the Recovery Act." *Scribner's Magazine* 95 (February 1934): 96–100.

Graham, Frank, Jr. *Man's Dominion: The Story of Conservation in America.* New York: M. Evans & Company, 1971.

Graham, Otis L., Jr. *An Encore for Reform: The Old Progressives and the New Deal.* New York: Oxford University Press, 1967.

———. *Toward a Planned Society.* New York: Oxford University Press, 1976.

Greenleaf, William, ed. *American Economic Development Since 1860.* Columbia: University of South Carolina Press, 1968.

Grimes, Warren S. "The Seven Myths of Vertical Price Fixing: The Politics and Economics of a Century-Long Debate." *Southwestern University Law Review* 21 (1992): 1285–1316.

Haines, Henry S. *Restrictive Railway Legislation.* New York: Macmillan, 1905.

Hamilton, Daniel C. *Competition in Oil: The Gulf Coast Refinery Market, 1925–1950.* Cambridge: Harvard University Press, 1958.

Hamlin, Scoville, ed. *The Menace of Overproduction.* New York: John Wiley & Sons, 1930; Freeport, N.Y.: Books for Libraries, 1969.

Hampe, Edward C., Jr., and Merle Wittenberg. *The Lifeline of America: Development of the Food Industry.* New York: McGraw-Hill, 1964.

Handler, Milton. "Unfair Competition and the Federal Trade Commission." *The George Washington Law Review* 8 (1939–40): 399–426.

Hardwicke, Robert E. *Antitrust Laws, et al. v. Unit Operation of Oil or Gas Pools.* New York: American Institute of Mining and Metallurgical Engineers, 1948.

Hartz, Louis. *Economic Policy and Democratic Thought: Pennsylvania, 1776–1860.* Cambridge: Harvard University Press, 1948; Chicago: Quadrangle Books, 1968.

Hawley, Ellis. *The New Deal and the Problem of Monopoly.* Princeton: Princeton University Press, 1966.

Haynes, Williams. "Better Ethical Standards for Business." *The Annals of the American Academy of Political and Social Science* 101 (May 1922): 221–23.

Hazlitt, Henry. "The Fallacies of the N.R.A." *The American Mercury* 30 (December 1933): 415–23.

Heermance, Edgar L. *Can Business Govern Itself? A Study in Industrial Planning.* New York: Harper & Bros., 1933.

———. *Codes of Ethics: A Handbook.* Burlington, Vt.: Free Press Printing Co., 1924.

Heilbroner, Robert L. *The Making of Economic Society.* Englewood Cliffs, N.J.: Prentice-Hall, 1962.

Heinz, Howard J. "Business Is Building Confidence in Itself." *The Nation's Business* 16 (July 1928): 17–18, 102.

Heller, Lawrence J. "Practice Before the Federal Trade Commission." *Commercial Law League Journal* 35 (May 1930): 225–29.

Henderson, Gerard C. *The Federal Trade Commission: A Study in Administrative Law and Procedure.* New Haven: Yale University Press, 1924; New York: Agathon Press, 1968.

Hendrick, Burton. *The Life of Andrew Carnegie.* London: William Heinemann, 1933.

Herring, E. Pendleton. "Politics and Radio Regulation." *Harvard Business Review* 13 (January 1935): 167–78.

Hidy, Ralph W., Frank E. Hill, and Allan Nevins. *Timber and Men: The Weyerhaeuser Story.* New York: Macmillan, 1963.

Himmelberg, Robert F. *The Great Depression and American Capitalism.* Boston: D. C. Heath, 1968.

———. *The Origins of the National Recovery Administration.* New York: Fordham University Press, 1976.

———. "The War Industries Board and the Antitrust Question in November, 1918." *Journal of American History* 52 (June 1965): 59–74.

Hitchcock, Curtice N. "The War Industries Board: Its Development, Organization, and Functions." *The Journal of Political Economy* 26 (June 1918): 545–66.

Hodgson, Richard, ed. *In Quiet Ways: George H. Mead: The Man and the Company.* Dayton, Ohio: The Mead Corporation, 1970.

Hofstadter, Richard. *The Age of Reform.* New York: Knopf, 1955.

Holmes, Oliver W. *The Common Law.* Boston: Little, Brown, 1881.

Holt, Charles A., and David T. Scheffman. "Strategic Business Behavior and Antitrust." In *Economics and Antitrust Policy,* edited by Robert J. Larner and James W. Meehan Jr., 39–82. New York: Quorum Books, 1989.

Hood, E. W. *Introduction to Study of Business Ethics.* Buffalo, N.Y.: R. W. Bryant, 1930.

Hook, James W. "What Industry Thinks of Industrial Control." *The Iron Age* 132 (20 July 1933): 26-H–26-I.

Hoover, Herbert. *The Memoirs of Herbert Hoover.* Vol. 2, *The Cabinet and the Presidency, 1920–1933.* New York: Macmillan, 1952.

———. *The Memoirs of Herbert Hoover.* Vol. 3, *The Great Depression, 1929–1941.* New York: Macmillan, 1952.

———. "We Can Cooperate and Yet Compete." *The Nation's Business* 14 (5 June 1926): 11–14.

Horner, W. S. "Associations Remedy Trade Ills." *The Iron Age* 119 (27 January 1927): 287–88

Hungerford, Edward. *Daniel Willard Rides the Line.* New York: G. P. Putnam's Sons, 1938.

Hunt, E. E., F. G. Tryon, and J. H. Willits. *What the Coal Commission Found.* With a foreword by J. H. Hammond. Baltimore: The Williams & Wilkins Co., 1925.

Irons, Peter H. *The New Deal Lawyers.* Princeton: Princeton University Press, 1982.

Ise, John. *The United States Forest Policy.* New Haven: Yale University Press, 1920.

Javits, Benjamin A. "The Anti-Trust Laws." *The Annals of the American Academy of Political and Social Science* 149 (May 1930): 128–31.

———. "The Javits Plan for Trade Associations Organization." *Commercial Law Journal* 35 (August 1930): 410–16.

Jemison, Robert. "Self-Government Must Be Deserved." *The Nation's Business* 14 (5 June 1926): 21–22.

Jenks, Jeremiah W. *The Trust Problem.* New York: Doubleday, Page, 1909.

Johnsen, Julia. *Government Regulation of the Coal Industry.* New York: The H. W. Wilson Company, 1926.

Johnson, Hugh S. *The Blue Eagle from Egg to Earth.* New York: Doubleday, Doran, 1935.

Jones, Franklin D. "Historical Development of the Law of Business Competition." *Yale Law Journal* 36 (1926–27): 351–83.

———. *Trade Association Activities and the Law.* New York: McGraw-Hill, 1922.

———. "The Trade Association as a Factor in Reconstruction." *The Annals of the American Academy of Political and Social Science* 82 (March 1919): 159–69.

Jones, Stiles P. "State Versus Local Regulation." *The Annals of the American Academy of Political and Social Science* 53 (May 1914): 94–107.

Jordan, Virgil. "Self-Rule of Industry a Delusion." *The Iron Age* 122 (29 November 1928): 1350–52.

Jorde, Thomas M., and David J. Teece, eds. *Antitrust, Innovation, and Competitiveness.* New York: Oxford University Press, 1992.

Josephson, Matthew. *The Robber Barons.* New York: Harcourt, Brace & World, 1962.

Josko, Paul L., and Alvin K. Klevorick. "A Framework for Analyzing Predatory Pricing Policy." *The Yale Law Journal* 89 (December 1979): 213–70.

Kahn, Julius. "A Plea for More Government Regulation." *The Nation's Business* 16 (February 1928): 20–22.

Kahn, Otto. *Reflections of a Financier: A Study of Economic and Other Problems.* London: Hodder & Stoughton, 1921.

Kemnitzer, William S. *Rebirth of Monopoly.* New York: Harper & Bros., 1938.

Kile, Orville M. *The Farm Bureau Through Three Decades.* Baltimore: The Waverly Press, 1948.

Kimmel, Lewis H. *Federal Budget and Fiscal Policy, 1789–1958.* Washington, D.C.: The Brookings Institution, 1959.

Kindleberger, Charles P. *Manias, Panics, and Crashes: A History of Financial Crises.* New York: Basic Books, 1989.

Kirkland, Edward C. *Dream and Thought in the Business Community, 1860–1900.* Chicago: Quadrangle Books, 1964.

Kirzner, Israel. *Competition and Entrepreneurship.* Chicago: The University of Chicago Press, 1973.

Kittelle, Sumner S., and Elmer Mostow. "A Review of the Trade Practice Conferences of the Federal Trade Commission." *The George Washington Law Review* 8 (1939–40): 427–51.

Knight, Frank H. *The Ethics of Competition.* New York: Harper & Bros., 1935.

Kohr, Leopold. *The Breakdown of Nations.* New York: E. P. Dutton, 1978.

Kolko, Gabriel. *Railroads and Regulation, 1877–1916.* Princeton: Princeton University Press, 1965.

———. *The Triumph of Conservatism.* Glencoe, Ill.: The Free Press, 1963.

Koller, Roland H., Jr. "The Myth of Predatory Pricing: An Empirical Study." *Antitrust Law and Economics Review* 4 (Summer 1971): 105–23.

Kreps, Theodore J. *Business and Government under the National Recovery Administration.* New York: Institute of Pacific Relations, 1936.

Krooss, Herman E. *Executive Opinion: What Business Leaders Said and Thought on Economic Issues, 1920s–1960s.* Garden City, N.Y.: Doubleday, 1970.

Kwoka, John E., Jr., and Lawrence J. White, eds. *The Antitrust Revolution.* Glenview, Ill.: Scott, Foresman and Company, 1989.

Lamb, George P., and Sumner S. Kittelle. *Trade Association Law and Practice.* Boston: Little, Brown, 1956.

Land, George T. L. *Grow or Die: The Unifying Principle of Transformation.* New York: Random House, 1973.

Larner, Robert J., and James W. Meehan Jr., eds. *Economics and Antitrust Policy.* New York: Quorum Books, 1989.

Larson, Henrietta M., and Kenneth Porter. *History of Humble Oil & Refining Company.* New York: Arno Press, 1959.

Larson, Henrietta M., Evelyn H. Knowlton, and Charles S. Popple. *History of Standard Oil Company (New Jersey): New Horizons, 1927–1950.* New York: Harper & Row, 1971.

Lawrence, Mark. *Relation of Government to Industry.* New York: Macmillan, 1925.

Lazonick, William. *Business Organization and the Myth of the Market Economy.* Cambridge: Cambridge University Press, 1991.

Lebhar, Godfrey M. *Chain Stores in America, 1859–1962.* 3d ed. New York: Chain Store Publishing Corp. 1963.

Leeman, Wayne. "The Limitations of Local Price-Cutting as a Barrier to Entry." *Journal of Political Economy* 64 (1956): 329–34.

Leiserson, Avery. *Administrative Regulation: A Study in Representation of Interests.* Chicago: The University of Chicago Press, 1942.

Letwin, William. *Law and Economic Policy in America: The Evolution of the Sherman Antitrust Act.* Westport, Conn.: Greenwood Press, 1980.

Leuchtenberg, William E. *Franklin D. Roosevelt and the New Deal, 1932–1940.* New York: Harper & Row, 1963.

———. *The Perils of Prosperity, 1914–1932.* Chicago: The University of Chicago Press, 1958.

Liebeler, Wesley J. "Whither Predatory Pricing? From Areeda and Turner to Matsushita." *Notre Dame Law Review* 61 (1986): 1052–98.

Lief, Alfred. *The Firestone Story.* New York: McGraw-Hill, 1951.

Link, Arthur S. *Woodrow Wilson and the Progressive Era, 1910–1917.* New York: Harper & Bros., 1954.

Loth, David. *Swope of G.E.* New York: Simon & Schuster, 1958.

Lowi, Theodore. *The Politics of Disorder.* New York: Basic Books, 1971.

Lundberg, Ferdinand. *America's Sixty Families.* New York: The Vanguard Press, 1937; New York: The Citadel Press, 1946.

Lyon, Leverett, and Victor Abramson. *The Economics of Open Price Systems.* Washington, D.C.: The Brookings Institution, 1936.

Lyon, Leverett, Myron Watkins, and Victor Abramson. *Government and Economic Life.* 2 vols. Washington, D.C.: The Brookings Institution, 1939.

Lyon, Leverett, Paul Homan, Lewis Lorwin, George Terborgh, Charles Dearing, and Leon Marshall. *The National Recovery Administration: An Analysis and Appraisal.* Washington, D.C.: The Brookings Institution, 1935.

MacDonald, William. *The Menace of Recovery.* New York: Macmillan, 1934.

Machlup, Fritz. *The Political Economy of Monopoly.* Baltimore: The Johns Hopkins University Press, 1952.

Magee, James D. *Collapse and Recovery.* New York: Harper & Bros., 1934.

Magee, James D., Willard Atkins, and Emanuel Stein. *The National Recovery Program.* Rev. ed. New York: F. S. Crofts & Co., 1934.

Marcosson, Isaac F. *Wherever Men Trade: The Romance of the Cash Register.* New York: Dodd, Mead, 1945.

Marcus, Sumner. *Competition and the Law.* Belmont, Calif.: Wadsworth, 1967.

Mason, David T. *The Lumber Code.* Lumber Industries Series, no. 11. New Haven: Yale University Press, 1935.

Mason, Lowell. *The Language of Dissent.* New Canaan, Conn.: The Long House, 1959.

Mayers, Lewis, ed. *A Handbook of NRA.* 2d ed. New York: Federal Codes, 1934.

McAdam, Dunlap J. *Coal: Government Ownership or Control.* New York: Authors and Publishers Corp., 1921.

McCune, Wesley. *Who's Behind Our Farm Policy.* New York: Frederick A. Praeger, 1956.

McGee, John. "Predatory Price-Cutting: The Standard Oil (N.J.) Case." *The Journal of Law and Economics* 1 (1958): 137–69.

BIBLIOGRAPHY 263

McHenry, Robert, ed. *A Documentary History of Conservation in America.* New York: Praeger, 1972.

McLean, John, and Robert Haigh. *The Growth of Integrated Oil Companies.* Boston: Division of Research, Graduate School of Business Administration, Harvard University, 1954.

Means, Gardiner C. *The Corporate Revolution in America.* New York: The Crowell-Collier Press, 1962.

———. *The Structure of the American Economy: Part I. A Report Prepared under the Direction of Gardiner C. Means, June, 1939.* New York: Augustus M. Kelley, 1966.

Miller, Roger. *The Economics of Energy: What Went Wrong.* New York: William Morrow, 1974.

Mills, C. Wright. *The Power Elite.* New York: Oxford University Press, 1956.

Mills, F. C. *Economic Tendencies in the United States.* New York: J. J. Little and Ives Co., 1932.

Mills, Frederick. *Prices in Recession and Recovery.* New York: The National Bureau of Economic Research, 1936.

Mineral Law Section of the American Bar Association. *Legal History of Conservation of Oil and Gas.* Chicago: American Bar Association, 1939.

Mises, Ludwig von. *The Anti-Capitalistic Mentality.* Princeton, N.J.: D. Van Nostrand, 1956.

———. *Human Action.* New Haven: Yale University Press, 1963.

Moley, Raymond. *The First New Deal.* New York: Harcourt, Brace & World, 1966.

Moos, Malcolm, ed. *H. L. Mencken on Politics.* New York: Vintage Books, 1960.

Morgan, John J.B. "Manic-Depressive Psychoses of Business." *Psychological Review* 42 (1935).

Mund, Vernon. *Government and Business.* 3d ed. New York: Harper & Bros., 1960.

Munkirs, John R. *The Transformation of American Capitalism: From Competitive Market Structures to Centralized Private Sector Planning.* Armonk, N.Y.: M. E. Sharpe, 1985.

Murchison, C. T. "Requisites of Stabilization in the Cotton Textile Industry." *The American Economic Review* 23 (Supplement, 1933): 71–80.

Nash, Arthur. *The Golden Rule in Business.* New York: Fleming H. Revell Company, 1923.

Nash, Gerald D. *United States Oil Policy, 1890–1964.* Pittsburgh, Pa.: University of Pittsburgh Press, 1968.

National Industrial Conference Board. *The Competitive Position of Coal in the United States.* New York: National Industrial Conference Board, 1931.

———. *Public Regulation of Competitive Practices.* New York: National Industrial Conference Board, 1925.

———. *Trade Associations: Their Economic Significance and Legal Status.* New York: National Industrial Conference Board, 1925.

Neale, Walter C. "Institutions." *Journal of Economic Issues* 21 (September 1987): 1177–1206.

Nelson, James C. "The Motor Carrier Act of 1935." *Journal of Political Economy* 44 (August 1936): 464–504.

Nelson, Milton. *Open Price Associations.* Urbana: University of Illinois Press, 1923.

Nelson, Saul. "Trade Practice Conference Rules and the Consumer." *The George Washington Law Review* 8 (1939–40): 452–68.

Nevins, Allan. *Study in Power: John D. Rockefeller, Industrialist and Philanthropist.* Vol. 2. New York: Charles Scribner's Sons, 1953.

Nock, Albert Jay. *Our Enemy the State.* Caldwell, Idaho: Caxton Printers, 1959.

O'Connor, Harvey. *Mellon's Millions: The Life and Times of Andrew W. Mellon.* New York: The John Day Co., 1933.

Oleson, Alexandra, and John Voss, eds. *The Organization of Knowledge in Modern America, 1860–1920.* Baltimore: The Johns Hopkins University Press, 1979.

Olson, Mancur. *The Logic of Collective Action.* Cambridge: Harvard University Press, 1965.

Paine, Albert B. *In One Man's Life.* New York: Harper, 1921.

———. *Theodore N. Vail, A Biography.* New York: Harper & Bros., 1929.

Parker, Edwin B. "The Elimination of Trade Abuses." *The Nation's Business* 15 (July 1927): 32, 80, 82.

Parker, Glen L. *The Coal Industry: A Study in Social Control.* Washington, D.C.: American Council on Public Affairs, 1940.

Parrish, Michael. *Securities Regulation and the New Deal.* New Haven: Yale University Press, 1970.

Paterson, Isabel. *The God of the Machine.* New York: G. P. Putnam's Sons, 1943.

Peek, George N., in collaboration with Samuel Crowther. *Why Quit Our Own.* New York: D. Van Nostrand, 1936.

Perkins, Dexter. *The New Age of Franklin Roosevelt, 1932–1945.* Chicago: The University of Chicago Press, 1957.

Perkins, George. "The Modern Corporation." Reprinted in *The Currency Problem and the Present Financial Situation: A Series of Addresses Delivered at Columbia University, 1907–1908.* New York: Columbia University Press, 1908.

Peterson, John M. "Employment Effects of State Minimum Wages for Women: Three Historical Cases Re-Examined." *Industrial and Labor Relations Review* 12 (April 1959): 406–22. Peterson's reply to a criticism of this article is given in *Industrial and Labor Relations Review* 13 (January 1960): 264–73.

———. "Employment Effects of Minimum Wages, 1938–1950." *Journal of Political Economy* 65 (October 1957): 412–30.

Peterson, Shorey. "Motor Carrier Regulation and Its Economic Bases." *Quarterly Journal of Economics* 43 (August 1929): 604–47.

Pettengill, Samuel B. *Hot Oil: The Problem of Petroleum.* New York: Economic Forum Co., 1936.

Posner, Richard. *Economic Analysis of Law.* Boston: Little, Brown, 1972.

Powell, G. Harold. "Regulation of the Perishable Food Industries After the War." *The Annals of the American Academy of Political and Social Science* 82 (1919): 183–88.

Powell, Horace B. *The Original Has This Signature—W. K. Kellogg.* Englewood Cliffs, N.J.: Prentice-Hall, 1956.

Prigogine, Ilya, and Isabelle Stengers. *Order Out of Chaos: Man's New Dialogue with Nature.* New York: Bantam Books, 1984.

Prothro, James W. *The Dollar Decade: Business Ideas in the 1920s.* Baton Rouge: Louisiana State University Press, 1954.

Quigley, Carroll. *The Evolution of Civilizations.* Indianapolis, Ind.: Liberty Press, 1979.

Radin, Max. *The Lawful Pursuit of Gain.* Boston: Houghton Mifflin, 1931.

Radosh, Ronald, and Murray Rothbard, eds. *A New History of Leviathan.* New York: E. P. Dutton, 1972.

Rae, John B. *American Automobile Manufacturers: The First Forty Years.* Philadelphia: Chilton, 1959.

Redford, Emmette S. *The Regulatory Process.* Austin: University of Texas Press, 1969.

Riley, John J. *A History of the American Soft Drink Industry—Bottled Carbonated Beverages,1807–1957.* Washington, D.C.: American Bottlers of Carbonated Beverages, 1958.

Ripley, William Z. *Main Street and Wall Street.* Boston: Little, Brown, 1927.

Ritchie, Albert C. "Business Can and Must Rule Itself." *The Nation's Business* 14 (5 June 1926): 19–20.

Rockefeller, John D. *Random Reminiscences of Men and Events.* New York: Doubleday, Page, 1908.

Rodgers, William. *Think: A Biography of the Watsons and IBM.* New York: Stein and Day, 1969; New York: New American Library, 1969.

Romasco, Albert U. *The Poverty of Abundance: Hoover, the Nation, the Depression.* London: Oxford University Press, 1965.

Roos, Charles Frederick. *NRA Economic Planning.* Bloomington, Ind.: The Principia Press, 1937.

Rothbard, Murray N. *America's Great Depression.* Princeton, N.J.: D. Van Nostrand, 1963.

———. *Man, Economy and State.* 2 vols. Princeton, N.J.: D. Van Nostrand, 1962.

———. *Power and Market: Government and the Economy.* Menlo Park, Calif.: Institute for Humane Studies, 1970.

Saroyan, William. "Aspirin Is a Member of the N.R.A." *The American Mercury* 32 (May 1934): 87–90.

Sayre, F. B. *The Way Forward.* New York: Macmillan, 1939.

Schapsmeier, Edward L., and Frederick H. Schapsmeier. *Henry A. Wallace of Iowa.* Ames: Iowa State University Press, 1968.

Scherer, F. M., and David Ross. *Industrial Market Structure and Economic Performance.* 3d ed. Boston: Houghton Mifflin, 1990.

Schlesinger, Arthur M., Jr. *The Coming of the New Deal.* Vol. 2 of *The Age of Roosevelt.* Boston: Houghton Mifflin, 1959.

———. *The Crisis of the Old Order, 1919–1933.* Vol. 1 of *The Age of Roosevelt.* Boston: Houghton Mifflin, 1956.

Schumpeter, Joseph A. *Business Cycles*. New York: McGraw-Hill, 1939.

————. *Capitalism, Socialism, and Democracy*. 3d ed. New York: Harper & Bros., 1950.

Schuyler, Montgomery. "Some Difficulties of the Trade Practice Rule." *The Magazine of Business* 55 (February 1929): 186–88.

Schwartz, Bernard, ed. *The Economic Regulation of Business and Industry: A Legislative History of U.S. Regulatory Agencies*. 5 vols. New York: Chelsea House, in association with R. R. Bowker Company, 1973.

Scoville, John, and Noel Sargent. *Fact and Fancy in the T.N.E.C. Monographs*. New York: National Association of Manufacturers, 1942; New York: Arno Press, 1972.

Shaffer, Butler D. *Calculated Chaos: Institutional Threats to Peace and Human Survival*. San Francisco: Alchemy Books, 1985.

————. "In Restraint of Trade: Trade Associations and the Emergence of 'Self-Regulation'." *Southwestern University Law Review* 20 (1991): 289–347.

————. "Responses to Competition in the Steel Industry, 1918–1935." *Southwestern University Law Review* 10 (1978): 835–83.

————. "Violence as a Product of Imposed Order." *University of Miami Law Review* 29 (1975): 732–63.

Shannon, David A., ed. *The Great Depression*. Englewood Cliffs, N.J.: Prentice-Hall, 1960.

Sharfman, I.L. "The Trade Association Movement." *American Economic Review* 16 (Supplement, 1926): 203–18.

Simonds, William A. *Henry Ford*. Garden City, N.Y.: Doubleday, Doran, 1929.

Simons, Henry. *Economic Policy for a Free Society*. Chicago: The University of Chicago Press, 1948.

Sinnott, Edmund W. *The Biology of the Spirit*. New York: Viking, 1955.

Sisson, Francis H. "The World-Wide Trend Toward Cooperation." *The Annals of the American Academy of Political and Social Science* 82 (March 1919): 143–49.

Sklar, Martin J. *The Corporate Reconstruction of American Capitalism, 1890–1916*. Cambridge: Cambridge University Press, 1988.

Smith, Adam. *An Inquiry into the Nature and Causes of the Wealth of Nations*. 1776. Reprint, edited by Edwin Cannan, New York: The Modern Library, 1937.

Sobel, Robert. *The Age of Giant Corporations*. Westport, Conn.: Greenwood Press, 1972.

Sokolsky, George. "America Drifts Toward Fascism." *The American Mercury* 32 (July 1934): 257–64.

Soule, George. *Prosperity Decade, From War to Depression, 1917–1929*. Vol. 8 of *The Economic History of the United States*. New York: Rinehart and Company, 1947.

Stevens, William H. S. *Unfair Competition*. Chicago: The University of Chicago Press, 1917.

————. "What Has the Federal Trade Commission Accomplished?" *The American Economic Review* 15 (December 1925): 625–51.

Stickells, Austin T. *Legal Control of Business Practice*. Mt. Kisco, N.Y.: Baker, Voorlis, 1965.

Stigler, George. "The Economics of Minimum Wage Legislation." *American Economic Review* 36 (June 1946): 358–65.

Swenson, Rinehart J. "The Chamber of Commerce and the New Deal." *The Annals of the American Academy of Political and Social Science* 179 (May 1935): 136–43.

Swope, Gerard. *The Swope Plan.* Edited by J. George Frederick. New York: The Business Bourse, 1931.

Taeusch, Carl F. *Policy and Ethics in Business.* New York: McGraw-Hill, 1931; New York: Arno Press, 1973.

Tarbell, Ida. *The Life of Elbert H. Gary: The Story of Steel.* New York: D. Appleton & Co., 1925.

———. *The Nationalizing of Business, 1878–1898.* Vol. 9 of *A History of American Life.* New York: Macmillan, 1936.

———. *Owen D. Young: A New Type of Industrial Leader.* New York: Macmillan, 1932.

Taylor, Emmett Hay. *Trade Associations: Their Organization and Management.* New York: The Ronald Press Co., 1921.

Taylor, Michael. *Anarchy and Cooperation.* London: John Wiley & Sons, 1976.

Temin, Peter. *Did Monetary Forces Cause the Great Depression?* New York: W. W. Norton, 1976.

Temporary National Economic Committee. *Competition and Monopoly in American Industry.* Monograph no. 21. Washington, D.C.: Government Printing Office, 1940.

Terborgh, George. *Price Control Devices in NRA Codes.* Washington, D.C.: The Brookings Institution, 1934.

Thompson, William I. *Evil and World Order.* New York: Harper & Row, 1977.

Thorelli, Hans B. *The Federal Antitrust Policy.* Baltimore: The Johns Hopkins University Press, 1955.

Thornton, Harrison J. *The History of the Quaker Oats Company.* Chicago: The University of Chicago Press, 1933.

Tosdal, H. R. "Open Price Associations." *American Economic Review* 7 (June 1917): 331–52.

Toulmin, Harry A., Jr. *Trade Agreements and the Anti-Trust Laws.* Cincinnati, Ohio: W. H. Anderson Co., 1937.

Toynbee, Arnold J. *A Study of History.* New York: Oxford University Press, 1958.

Truman, David. *The Governmental Process.* New York: Knopf, 1951.

Tugwell, Rexford G. *Industry's Coming of Age.* New York: Harcourt, Brace, 1927.

Tugwell, Rexford G., and Howard C. Hill. *Our Economic Society and Its Problems.* New York: Harcourt, 1934.

Uren, Lester. "What California's Gas Conservation Law Means to Our Industry." *National Petroleum News* 21 (26 June 1929): 55–58.

Urofsky, Melvin I. *Big Steel and the Wilson Administration: A Study in Business-Government Relations.* Columbus: Ohio State University Press, 1969.

U.S. Department of Commerce. *Commerce Yearbook, 1930.* Washington, D.C.: Government Printing Office, 1930.

————. *The Lumber Industry*. Washington, D.C.: Government Printing Office, 1936.

Valenstein, L., and E. Weiss. *Business Under the Recovery Act*. New York: McGraw-Hill, 1933.

Van Cise, Jerrold G. *Understanding the Antitrust Laws*. New York: Practising Law Institute, 1966.

Vanderblue, Homer B., and William L. Crum. *The Iron Industry in Prosperity and Depression*. Chicago: A.W. Shaw Company, 1927.

Van Vlissingen, Arthur, Jr. "Unfair Buying—and Weak-Kneed Selling." *The Magazine of Business* 55 (April 1929): 380–81, 439.

Veblen, Thorstein. *Absentee Ownership and Business Enterprise in Recent Times*. New York: B. W. Huebsch, 1923.

————. *The Instinct of Workmanship and the State of the Industrial Arts*. New York: Macmillan, 1914; New York: W. W. Norton, 1964.

————. *The Theory of Business Enterprise*. 1904. New York: Augustus M. Kelley, 1965.

————. *The Theory of the Leisure Class: An Economic Study of Institutions*. New York: Macmillan, 1899; New York: The New American Library, 1953.

Villard, Henry. *Memoirs of Henry Villard, Journalist and Financier, 1835–1900*. Westminster, U.K.: Archibald Constable & Co., 1904.

Vincent, W.A. "Shall We Legislate Our Profits?" *The Nation's Business* 17 (April 1929): 123–26.

Wagoner, Harless D. *The U.S. Machine Tool Industry from 1900 to 1950*. Cambridge: The MIT Press, 1968.

Walker, James B. *The Epic of American Industry*. New York: Harper & Bros., 1949.

Walker, Q. Forrest. "A Retail Attitude Toward Resale Price Fixing." *The Journal of Marketing* 1 (April 1937): 334–43.

Watkins, Myron W. "The Federal Trade Commission: A Critical Survey." *Quarterly Journal of Economics* 40 (August 1926): 561–85.

————. "Price Stabilization Through Trade Organization and Statistical Cooperation." *The Annals of the American Academy of Political and Social Science* 139 (September 1928): 44–50.

————. *Public Regulation of Competitive Practices in Business Enterprise*. 3d ed. New York: National Industrial Conference Board, 1940.

Weidenbaum, Murray L. *Government-Mandated Price Increases: A Neglected Aspect of Inflation*. Washington, D.C.: American Enterprise Institute for Public Policy Research, 1975.

Weinstein, James. *The Corporate Ideal in the Liberal State, 1900–1918*. Boston: Beacon Press, 1968.

————. *The Decline of Socialism in America, 1912–1925*. New York: Vintage Books, 1969.

Whitney, Simon N. *Anti-Trust Policies: American Experience in Twenty Industries*. 2 vols. New York: The Twentieth Century Fund, 1958.

————. *Trade Associations and Industrial Control*. New York: Central Book Co., 1934.

Wiebe, Robert H. *Businessmen and Reform: A Study of the Progressive Movement.* Cambridge: Harvard University Press, 1962.

————. *The Search for Order, 1877–1920.* New York: Hill and Wang, 1967.

Wilcox, Clair. *Public Policies Toward Business.* 3d ed. Homewood, Ill.: Richard D. Irwin, 1966; 4th ed., Homewood, Ill.: Richard D. Irwin, 1971.

Williams, J. Harvey. "How the Anti-Trust Laws Should Be Modified." *The Annals of the American Academy of Political and Social Science* 165 (January 1933): 72–84.

————. "The Practical Politics of the Sherman Act." *The Magazine of Business* 55 (February 1929): 155–57.

Williamson, Harold, Ralph Andreano, Arnold Daum, and Gilbert Klose. *The American Petroleum Industry: The Age of Energy, 1899–1959.* Evanston, Ill.: Northwestern University Press, 1963.

Williamson, Oliver E. *Antitrust Economics: Mergers, Contracting, and Strategic Behavior.* Cambridge: Basil Blackwell, 1987.

————. *Markets and Hierarchies: Analysis and Antitrust Implications.* New York: The Free Press, 1975.

Willoughby, William F. *Government Organization in War Time and After.* New York: D. Appleton and Company, 1919.

Winkler, John K. *Morgan the Magnificent: The Life of J. Pierpont Morgan, 1837–1913.* Garden City, N.Y.: Garden City Publishing Company, 1930.

Yamey, B. S., ed. *Resale Price Maintenance.* Chicago: Aldine, 1966.

Yoder, Dale. *Depression and Recovery.* New York: McGraw-Hill, 1934.

Zerbe, Richard. "The American Sugar Refinery Company, 1887–1914: The Story of a Monopoly." *The Journal of Law and Economics* 12 (1969): 339–75.

Zimmermann, Erich W. *Conservation in the Production of Petroleum: A Study in Industrial Control.* New Haven: Yale University Press, 1957.

Index

Holmes, Oliver W., 47–48
Holmes, R. C., 165
Hood, Ernest, 202–3
Hook, James W., 141
Hoover, Herbert, 91, 99, 159; responses to depression, 91; trade association movement, 52, 54–55
Horner, W. S., 131
"Hot oil." *See* Petroleum industry
Hudson Motor Car Co., 24
Hughes, H. E., 240n. 66
Humble Oil Co., 148, 150, 165, 169
Hurley, Edward N., 159

Illinois Manufacturers Assn., 114, 159
Independent Petroleum Assn. of America (IPA), 160, 167, 169–70
Individualism, 19, 29, 34–35, 50, 51, 52, 61, 79, 80, 92, 97, 104, 110, 111, 131–33, 136, 137, 139, 164, 176, 185, 203, 207, 228–29n. 97
Industrial self-regulation, 19, 26, 28, 49, 59, 75, 77–78, 81, 86, 89–90, 94, 99, 104, 120–22, 157, 177, 184, 202, 208, 235–36n. 44. *See also* Competition: "cooperative"
Industry and Business Committee for NRA Extension, 205
Industry "dictators," 137, 140, 151, 159
Institute of American Meat Packers, 237n. 65
Institute of Carpet Manufacturers of America, 118
Institutionalization, 41–45, 95, 108, 122
International Assn. of Electrotypers of America, 224nn. 53 and 55
International Assn. of Garment Manufacturers, 118, 199, 224n. 55, 226n. 67, 227nn. 73 and 78, 227–28n. 86
International Assn. of Milk Dealers, 64–65, 225n. 62, 227n. 77
International Business Machines (IBM), 104, 110
International Harvester Co., 24, 45, 123, 125
International Monumental Granite Producers' Assn., 227n. 73

Interstate Commerce Commission (ICC), 53, 118, 119
Interstate compacts, 117, 148, 164, 170
Interstate Compact to Conserve Oil and Gas, 170
Investment Bankers Assn., 118, 236–37n. 53
Iron Age, 128, 136, 138

Johnson, Alba B. 25–26
Johnson, Hugh, 25, 100, 106, 111, 120, 178, 234n. 2
Joint Trade Relations Committee, 186
Jones & Laughlin Steel Corp., 130, 143
Jordan, Virgil, 100–101
Jouett, E. S., 104

Kahn, Julius, 135
Kahn, Otto, 80
Keeler (E.) Co., 240n. 66
Kelly, Cornelius, 95
Kendall, Henry, 202, 248–49n. 59
Kindleberger, Charles, 91
King, Willis L., 130
Kirzner, Israel, 215–16n. 9
Kittelle, Sumner, 85
Knox Consolidated Coal Co., 176
Kohr, Leopold, 46–47
Kolko, Gabriel, 15, 45–47, 209, 210, 215n. 3, 218n. 45
Koller, Roland, Jr., 226n. 68, 226–27n. 72
Kuhn, Loeb and Co., 80

Labor policies, 94, 99, 116, 117, 121, 134, 138, 140, 141–42, 166, 175, 176, 178–79, 188, 195, 198, 199, 202–3, 205, 208–9; collective bargaining, 101, 102; employment and wages, 89, 112, 116, 117, 138, 140, 141–42, 166, 176, 178–79, 189, 195, 199, 202–3, 205, 208–9, 233n. 90, 234n. 27; minimum wages, 99, 101, 116, 176, 188, 195, 203, 205, 208–9, 233n. 90, 248n. 42; unemployment compensation, 94, 97; working hours, 97, 99, 101, 116, 117, 166, 179, 188, 195, 198, 202–3, 205, 233n. 90;

National Assn. of Ice Cream Manufacturers, 225 nn. 58 and 62, 227 n. 77, 228 n. 87
National Assn. of Independent Oil Producers, 152
National Assn. of Manufacturers (NAM), 51, 80, 95, 97, 100, 102, 109, 110, 115, 117, 237 n. 65
National Assn. of Mutual Savings Banks, 237 n. 65
National Assn. of Oxy-Chloride Cement Manufacturers, 226 n. 67, 227–28 n. 86
National Association of Retail Druggists (NARD), 191, 193, 197. See also Pharmaceuticals industry
National Assn. of Retail Grocers (NARG), 66, 118, 183–84, 188, 193, 197, 223 n. 50, 226 nn. 66 and 67. See also National Retail Grocers Association
National Assn. of Sheet and Tin Plate Manufacturers, 131
National Assn. of Upholstered Furniture Manufacturers, 225 n. 65
National Assn. of Wool Manufacturers, 118
National Automobile Dealers Assn., 118, 191
National Basket and Fruit Package Manufacturers Assn., 227 n. 78
National Bituminous Coal Commission, 179
National Boot and Shoe Manufacturers, 224 n. 55
National Bridge Works, 130
National City Bank of New York, 197.
National Coal Association (NCA), 176, 177
National Commercial Fixture Manufacturers' Assn., 225 n. 63, 227 n. 86
National Conference of Bituminous Coal Producers, 179
National Distribution Conference, 185
National Electrical Manufacturers Assn., 93, 118
National Federation of Textiles, 205
National Fertilizer Assn., 109

National Flat Rolled Steel Products Assn., 133
National Food Brokers Assn., 193, 224 nn. 54 and 55
National Founders Assn., 131
National Hardware Assn., 133
National Highway Freight Assn., 237 n. 64
National Industrial Conference Board (NICB), 58–59, 61–62, 79, 93, 100, 237 n. 65
National Industrial Recovery Act, 14, 19, 54, 81, 82, 90, 103, 105, 137–38, 166, 205; drafting of, 99–104, 166–68; renewal efforts, 115–16, 118, 190–91, 205
National Knitted Outerwear Assn., 225 n. 60
National Labor Relations Act, 14
National Lumber Manufacturers' Assn., 58, 241 n. 3
National Machine Tool Builders' Assn., 224 n. 55, 225 nn. 58 and 65, 226 n. 67, 227 n. 74
National Petroleum Marketers Assn., 84
National Publishers Assn., 224 n. 55
National Recovery Administration (NRA), 15, 86, 93, 103, 105–22, 141–44, 178–79, 188–91, 194–95, 202–6, 213, 235–36 n. 44; business attitudes toward, 106–18, 120–22, 137–44, 165–70, 178–79, 188–91, 194–95, 202–5, 234 n. 10, 234–35 n. 27, 235 n. 28; coal industry, 178–79; code authorities, 107–8; 178; code-drafting procedures, 106–8; codes of fair competition, 101, 105–13, 121, 137, 168–69, 178–79, 185, 188–91, 203–5; Industrial Advisory Board, 116; inventory controls, 112, 169; labor policies, 99, 100–102, 111, 112, 116, 121, 141, 143, 169, 178, 203, 234 n. 27; petroleum industry, 168–69; poultry industry, 117 (see also Schechter case); productive capacities, 105, 112; regulation of